Also by Teresa Carpenter

MISSING BEAUTY

TERESA CARPENTER

MOB GIRL

A WOMAN'S LIFE IN THE UNDERWORLD

SIMON & SCHUSTER

NEW YORK LONDON TORONTO SYDNEY TOKYO SINGAPORE

SIMON & SCHUSTER
Simon & Schuster Building
Rockefeller Center
1230 Avenue of the Americas
New York, New York 10020

Designed by Laurie Jewell
Manufactured in the United States of America

10   9   8   7   6   5   4   3   2   1

Library of Congress Cataloging-in-Publication Data

Carpenter, Teresa.
Mob girl : a woman's life in the underworld / Teresa Carpenter.
p.   cm.
Includes bibliographical references
1. Brickman, Arlyne.   2. Informers—New York (N.Y.)—Biography.
3. Mafia—New York (N.Y.)   I. Title.
HV6248.B724C37   1992
364.1′06′092—dc20
[B]   91-43256   CIP

ISBN: 0-671-68345-4

ACKNOWLEDGMENTS

I would like to thank the following for their cooperation and encouragement: Nick Pileggi, Victor Kovner, Laura Handman, Emily Remes, Sterling Lord, Flip Brophy, David Kanter, Mervyn Keizer, George Diehl, Joe Spina, Mike Minto, Bill Vormittag, Philly Buckles, Greg Hendrickson, Jeff Dossett, Tom Roche, Diane Giacalone, Grady O'Malley, Eddie Lindberg, Bill Noonan, Paul Scudiere, Aaron Marcu, Bruce Repetto, Jon Liebman, Rich Tofani, Mary Ellen Luthy, Joseph Smith, Steve Markardt and Loren Feldman. Special appreciation goes to Ken Brown and Oliver and Molly Halle as well as Esther Newberg, to whom I owe a continuing debt of gratitude. I would also like to thank my vigilant editor, Alice Mayhew, and my reassuring husband, Steven Levy.

For Leslie

AUTHOR'S NOTE

The people and events in this story are real. Conversations have been taken from surveillance transcripts or reconstructed by eyewitnesses to the events. Only the following names have been changed: Cousin Solly, Paulie Messina, Walter Perlmutter, Matthew Burton, Nathan Pincus, Tilly Palladino, "Beatrice," "Jilly," "Yvette," "Nino" and members of the families Silverstein, Lamattina and Paterno. The name of Tommy Luca has been changed at the request of Arlyne Brickman because of her stated concern for her safety.

CONTENTS

INTRODUCTION

When I arrived at Arlyne Brickman's apartment one early afternoon, her drapes were drawn against the bright tropical sun, leaving the living room in a kind of perpetual twilight. Everything was perfect, as spotless and orderly as a nun's chambers. The only evidence of habitation was a glass bookshelf on which rested three volumes: *Wiseguy, Donnie Brasco* and *Mob Star*. The kitchen was similarly austere except for an arrangement of purple chrysanthemums. I touched one and remarked, "They are beautiful!"

"Teresa," Arlyne replied. "Don't you know that old whores always have fresh flowers? It makes them feel clean."

She was grinning.

When my buxom, red-headed hostess describes herself as a "whore," she means it quite literally. For a time she worked as a call girl under the tutelage of a Manhattan madame. But on the occasion of our first meeting—July of 1988—I discerned that she also defines that self-inflicted barb in a more universal sense, meaning that she has lived a life oblivious to the tyranny of reputation. In the best and worst sense of the term, Arlyne Brickman is an outlaw.

The notorious Mrs. Brickman came to my attention earlier that summer when I began hearing tales of her adventures in the New York underworld. Not only was she a "Mafia princess," being the daughter of a well-connected Jewish racketeer from the Lower East Side. Not only was she "married to the mob" by virtue of her carnal association with a string of wiseguys. Arlyne was racketeer in her own right, insinuating herself into the implacably male underworld, first as a courier of messages and then as the proprietor of a thriving bookmaking operation. Later, for reasons of fear, revenge and power, she turned informant. For over a decade she wore wires for New York and New Jersey police as well as federal agencies, including the FBI. Her surveillance of the Colombo Family led to the 1986 conviction of one of Carmine Persico's top lieutenants.

Two years later, at the age of fifty-four, Arlyne decided it was time to immortalize her exploits in a book. Happily, she was not wed to the idea of a first-person account rendered through a ghostwriter. What she had in mind was an independent author who would be given a free hand to write a book *about* her. Arlyne, it turned out, had surprisingly sophisticated instincts about publishing, and realized that such an account would be more credible.

She first approached my husband, an investigative reporter and author who, after talking with her by phone, concluded her story was fascinating. "But," he added turning to me, "this really seems more up your alley." What he meant was that during my ten years as a crime reporter for the *Village Voice,* I made a career of studying bad girls. Specifically the kind who come from "good" homes and with middle-class expectations and somehow get rerouted into crime, prostitution and perversity. I'm sure there is an element of "there-but-for-the-grace of-God" in my interest. But that is not the whole story. I found myself admiring my own disreputable subjects. For the most part, they are women of considerable energy and enterprise. For all her apparent docility, Dorothy Stratten, the Playboy Playmate of the Year whose short life and tragic death I chronicled for the *Voice* in 1980, seemed impelled to make something of her life. The same thing could be said of Robin Benedict, the antiheroine of my previous book, *Missing Beauty.* Benedict strayed into the orbit of a pimp who perceived not only her beauty but also her energetic drive and turned her into a successful call girl. (Her enterprise had deadly consequences; Benedict was murdered by one of her johns, an eminent research biologist.) For a woman, however, the underworld often offers opportunities that the straight world does not.

Nowhere was that more apparent than in the case of Arlyne Brickman.

From the time she was twelve, Arlyne was driven by an almost fanatic ambition to become a mob girl. Although it is difficult, perhaps, to imagine how a child deliberately sets her sights on becoming a moll, it becomes easier if one understands the time and place in which the young Arlyne Weiss passed her formative years. The Lower East Side during the early part of the century was a precinct of a little over one square mile that was home to thousands of immigrants from Southern and Eastern Europe. For many young men from this teeming quarter, the pursuit of the American dream took the form of bookmaking, bootlegging and black-marketeering. The East Side, therefore, became a sanctuary for hoodlums and, ultimately, the birthplace of the mob—both Italian and Jewish. Arlyne's father made his own fortune in the rackets during the thirties and forties, yet he craved respectability for his two daughters. The younger opted for the straight life. As the older, Arlyne had the opportunity to do the same, but she declined, preferring to follow the example of her maternal grandmother, the proprietress of an East Side funeral parlor. A woman of considerable charm and influence, the grandmother was also benefactress to a crew of racketeers who hung out in her cellar. She reveled openly in the "East Side Life," tacitly encouraging her granddaughter to do the same.

Arlyne's imagination was further piqued by the highly publicized exploits of Virginia Hill, the flamboyant red-headed girlfriend of Bugsy Siegel. During her heyday, Virginia refined and elevated the status of a gangster's moll to that of national celebrity. One newspaper called her "the most successful woman in America." It is small wonder that young Arlyne Weiss could imagine no calling more exalted than that of mob girl.

The job description was vague. A mob girl had to be good-looking, since a lot of her time was spent serving as a "showpiece" on a gangster's arm. She had to be trustworthy, since she was often called upon to run errands and deliver messages. This was particularly important during an era when federal investigators were aggressively developing expertise at wiretaps and the phones were becoming unsafe. She served as lover and confidante, a mistress *cum* geisha, whose tough-minded company provided relief from the demands of a hoodlum's often staunchly traditional homelife. In exchange for these services, she received gifts, status and—as far as young Arlyne Weiss could discern from the exploits of her grandmother and the gossip column accounts of her idol, Virginia Hill—respect.

From the time she was about fourteen, Arlyne was an active seductress of the underworld and by the time she was twenty, she had slept with upward of fifty hoods from the Lower East Side. Some of these were Jewish racketeers from her tribal circle. During most of her adult life, however, she showed a marked preference for Italian men, who were technically off-limits, hence infinitely more desirable. Forever status conscious, she amassed a slate of conquests that included the notorious Bonanno hit man Tony Mirra and, briefly, Joe Colombo. But as Arlyne would learn in her more than thirty years in the underworld, living the mob girl ideal was a considerably tawdrier proposition than imagining it.

Far from the romanticized characters of story and film, wiseguys—as revealed through the eyes of Arlyne Brickman—are callous, shallow, vain, often homicidal narcissists who would rather spend time with one another than with a woman. On several occasions, Arlyne vowed to give up her promiscuous ways. In 1957, at the age of twenty-three, she married a furrier named Brickman. That union, however, was done in by his philandering and ultimate conviction for grand larceny. Left with a baby daughter and a restless spirit, Arlyne resumed her destructive pursuit of glamour and influence only to be raped and beaten by wiseguys she thought were her friends.

The rape marked in Arlyne's career the advent of a new ruthlessness, born simultaneously of a desire for revenge and the need for protection. She spent the next thirteen years of her life in a tortured and often violent relationship with a Genovese wiseguy named Tommy Luca. During this period she also became a "businesswoman," engaging in bookmaking, then drug dealing, in an obsessive pursuit of money. It was this cynical worldview that allowed her to progress rather naturally into a career as an informant. The nominal reason for her defection was clear enough. A crew of loansharks were threatening to harm her daughter and she turned to the police for help. Once she had broken the taboo against ratting, however, she discovered that she enjoyed it.

It has been my feeling since first meeting Arlyne that turning informant (she bridles at this term, preferring to be called a "cooperating individual") was her way of avenging herself for all the indignities and abuse suffered at the hands of the mob. This explanation, I'm sure, is too simple. Arlyne not only turned in her enemies when she went on the federal payroll but began supplying information about old friends as well. Informing gave her things that had been missing: power over Tommy Luca, power to protect herself and—not least—a sense of purpose. There is no evidence that she was ever won over to the side of justice. Arlyne always evinced a curiously amoral attitude toward working for the government. What she felt, rather, seems to have been a mercenary's pride in her own prowess. She found deception and betrayal on both sides of the law and was exhilarated by it. Informing gave her a thrill that she likened to a chemical high. "Some people drink," she once told me. "Some people take drugs. I work. It's just something that satisfies."

Having recognized in Arlyne this love of intrigue, I often found myself wary of her. For her, as for most informants, manipulation is a way of life. It became clear to me in our initial encounters that she was a keen observer of humans and had a tendency to tailor her responses to please the listener. After one glance at my 110-pound frame and Louise Brooks haircut, she concluded I was a "classy broad" who might be offended by the brash, and often obscene, tough-girl act she pulls on federal agents. As a result, she donned another of her masks, that of the doting Jewish mother. I did not resist this, since I recognized that this guise, as indeed all her others, represented a legitimate aspect of her personality. In time, she was to reveal them all—the tough broad, the yenta and even demure "little Arlyne."

A more challenging problem during the course of my research was getting to the bottom of her elusive motives. If the first half of her life was unconventional, it at least unfolded according to the dictates of human emotion. When her husband cheats on her, she seeks revenge. When she is raped, she feels outrage. By contrast, the behavior of her mature years often seemed to defy analysis. She professes great affection for her "uncle" Paulie Messina, a hoodlum who seems to have shown her genuine kindness, yet she rats him out to drug agents without a qualm. She develops what appears to be a friendship with those same agents, yet deals drugs behind their backs with Tommy Luca. In fact, Arlyne seems to feel no loyalty to anyone, an observation that, at times, caused me to suspect she might be a sociopath, cruising through life like a shark, simulating human emotion whenever it suited her purposes. A closer look at her history, however, led me to conclude that Arlyne does feel loyalty, however fleeting, to whomever happens to be stroking her ego. When Luca is the source of affection and excitement, she is loyal to Luca; when the feds offer her money and attention, she is loyal to the feds. It is a primitive response, but one that makes perfect sense in light of her impulsive nature.

Over the many months I spent interviewing Arlyne Brickman—watching her spoonfeed her lapdog, Lucky, while spinning tales of intrigue—I also concluded that her apparent duplicity was made possible by an extraordinary ability to compartmentalize. It was literally possible for her to be fond of someone while, at the same time, conducting a surveillance on him. The fondness comes from a side of her nature that deals with "personal" things; the surveillance is business. She does not allow one to interfere with the other. This occasionally produces tragic results. During the years she was dealing drugs with Tommy Luca, her daughter, who had fallen in with fast company, was on her way to becoming a heroin addict. As much as she claimed to love her child, Arlyne would not quit the drug business. Throughout our many conversations, drugs remained the one subject Arlyne was not anxious to discuss. Beyond the fact that her involvement in the narcotics trade placed her own daughter in peril, Arlyne maintained a personal conviction that drugs were shameful. She had, therefore, devised an elaborate scheme of rationalizations to avoid taking blame: She did not actually *do* drugs. She was not actually a *dealer,* just someone who lent a hand and, in return, got "house money." Although interviews with law enforcement officials and documents obtained through a Freedom of Information request indicate that Arlyne was involved with drugs without the government's knowledge, her own position seemed to be that because she worked intermittently for the DEA and FBI, any contacts she made—for whatever reason—were with those agencies' tacit approval. She steadfastly refuses to admit to double-dealing.

As for her general rendering of the facts, however, Arlyne Brickman was impressively scrupulous. As an informant, she took professional pride in delivering quality information, and she applied the same standard to this enterprise. Whenever I asked her something she couldn't recall, her response was invariably, "I don't remember . . . and I'm not going to make anything up." (Only once did she deliberately mislead me, by suggesting that she was Meyer Lansky's "niece." This, in fact, was a myth she had spun and refined over the years to improve her standing among wiseguys. As such, I considered it a lie more of vanity than deceit.) Over a period of two years, we went over her stories many times and her telling of them was remarkably consistent. I took pains to corroborate her accounts with family members, police, attorneys and federal agents. In certain instances there were discrepancies, which I have noted herein. When these occur, a reporter has to decide whom she will believe. In most instances, I have found myself believing Arlyne. For all her masks and poses, she wanted this book to count for something. In telling her story she has spared herself nothing—revealing the ugly along with the flattering—so that it might stand as an accurate testament to her exploits: the life and times of a mob girl.

How do you describe a mob girl? There are all types of mob girls. There's a mob girl who sleeps with one guy and she's connected to a mob . . . there's a mob girl who sleeps around with a lot of different guys, gets loads of presents and favors. There was Virginia Hill . . . a broad that really made it good.

And there was me. I considered myself a mob girl.

—ARLYNE BRICKMAN

PART
ONE

PART
ONE

HOUSE OF MIRRORS

Every Friday night as long as Arlyne could remember, the Weiss family had paid a visit to The Grandmother. It was a sacred obligation, which could not be breached under any circumstances. As a small child, Arlyne had looked forward to those outings with innocent enthusiasm, accepting and uncomprehending. Around the year 1944 when she was eleven—an age at which her curiosity was piqued by a growing awareness of the mysteries that lay beneath ordinary events— these visits assumed a new importance.

At three o'clock, when Arlyne and her younger sister, Barbara, arrived home from school, they would bathe and put on fresh dresses, which the maid had laid out on the bed. Then they presented themselves to their mother, seated—as was her custom at that hour—on a bench before her vanity dresser. Billie Weiss would appraise her daughters with a critical squint, then position the younger before her. As she braided the long honey-blond hair, the child's head bobbed compliantly. This peaceful idyll ended, however, the moment her older daughter stepped to the mirror. As Billie jerked the strands tighter, the girl stiffened for combat. It was a domestic battle played out every Friday afternoon like clockwork; a battle that Arlyne Weiss fought valiantly and one that Billie Weiss invariably won.

At dusk, mother and daughters strolled out of the large iron gates of Knickerbocker Village, a twelve-story apartment complex, which sat near the East River just north of the Brooklyn Bridge. Knickerbocker was a model development erected ten years earlier on the site of what had been New York City's most appalling slum. "Lung Block," it had been called, because many of the three thousand tenants who had been crammed into tenements there suffered from tuberculosis. The razing of those rookeries had been part of a continuing effort to clean up the Lower East Side, an unruly quarter, teeming with prostitutes and pickpockets who gave it an unsavory reputation. It is no wonder then that for second-generation Jews like Arlyne's parents it was the source of considerable pride to give a Knickerbocker Village address. It was a sign that one had risen above the rabble.

If one walked north from the Knickerbocker along the Bowery, one found oneself in the Italian quarter. This was something the Weisses rarely did, since decades of antagonism between Italians and Jews did not promise safe passage. Instead, they would head east on Monroe Street, stopping at the K&K Candy Store where Mrs. Weiss bought cigarettes. Billie prided herself on being a modern woman. Then, if The Grandmother had requested it, the little party would detour onto Hester Street to purchase pickles and peppers from peddlers whose enormous wooden tubs stood exposed to the open air. Arlyne could smell them a block away and she was perpetually horrified to see the vendors wiping vinegar on their aprons. For a child, she was unusually particular about cleanliness. And since the streets were crowded with milling, unwashed bodies, she was always quite anxious by the time the Weiss entourage arrived at 202 East Broadway. There, sitting like a blessed sanctuary, was the Blum and Oxman Funeral Parlor.

The chapel's dark stone façade was devoid of the grime that covered the surrounding buildings, the result of a weekly scrubbing. The brass railings that extended up the front steps were buffed to a high gloss by a rather simple Irish girl named Lily Higgins. She also swept the sidewalk and street for several yards around the stair. In this clearing, a gaggle of females consisting of blood relatives and honorary relations known as "Aunts" congregated, sitting on folding chairs or wooden boxes normally used for sitting *shiva,* the vigil for the dead. Billie promptly joined them, brushing off compliments on her Lartiga hat or little voile collar. Barbara went looking for the cousins, who all then scampered through the embalming room—blithely ignoring the marble slab upon which lay a corpse newly processed for burial on Sunday— into the tiny backyard to play at the duck pond. Arlyne, who only a year earlier had been content to join the others, now held back until she was sure she was alone, then engaged in a ritual of her own devising.

Ascending the white tile steps to the living compartment above the funeral parlor, she avoided the kitchen, from which emanated sporadic laughter and the clatter of cooking. Instead, she turned right into the deserted living room. There, illuminated by the glow of an enormous French fireplace, was a feast for the senses. Pink satin love seats. White brocaded sofas with feet carved like a lion's paws. Oriental rugs and an upright piano. Arlyne would sit for a while, not on the sofa, for Grandmother was always fussy about soiling the upholstery, but on the floor, basking in the splendor. When she had had her fill, she moved on to the bedroom, which lay at the rear of the apartment overlooking the duck pond. It was small, less lavishly appointed than the other rooms, yet clearly the sanctum of a woman accustomed to luxury. The closet was filled with furs, meticulously arranged. The top of the dresser was covered with bottles of expensive foreign perfumes. More intriguing to Arlyne, however, was the top drawer, which held her grandmother's jewelry. There was something about gazing upon that jumble of emerald bracelets and diamond brooches that excited her. Running her fingers over the facets of the gems, Arlyne was habitually tempted to slip one of the pieces into her pocket. But cowed by reverence for The Grandmother, she left them untouched.

In the center of the room stood a double bed with a headboard of dark wood carved as expansive, curving arms. Unlike the other beds in the house, it was never covered by a quilt, only a blanket. Arlyne found this strangely out of character with her grandmother's taste. When she'd satisfied herself that there was no one outside the door, she would lift a corner of the mattress and from one of the coils withdraw a large white handkerchief knotted in the middle. Untying it, she released a small fortune in bills, between two thousand and five thousand dollars. Grandmother's pin money.

For as long as she dared, Arlyne sat at the foot of the bed, fingering the bills, creasing them, rolling them, counting them, delirious. It was the beginning of her lifelong love affair with money, from which, she perceived at eleven, all things desirable flowed. Money bought the glow of an antique fireplace and emerald bracelets. Money bought cleanliness and safety. It bought power and position, assuring that one would never be mistaken for one of the poor Jews of Hester Street smelling of sweat and pickles. It was money that sustained the rich and highly unorthodox lifestyle of Grandmother Ida Blum.

From the kitchen came the seductive sound of laughter. Arlyne would put the bills back in their hiding place and join the revelers. Entering the open door she encountered a long table laden with a tureen of mushroom and barley soup and covered dishes of pot roast and carrots. Family wandered in and out filling their plates as they pleased. At the far end of the table, bent over the stove, Ida stood resplendent in a sheer blouse and tight skirt. Her platinum hair was twisted into an immaculate bun. On her left hand was a large diamond and ruby ring. On her right, an Eastern Star Ring. Her fingers were covered with matzoh meal.

Spotting her granddaughter, Ida wiped her hands, revealing a set of long and perfect vermilion nails. Then she raised them in a welcoming gesture. Arlyne ran to hug her grandmother around the waist. Ida would not return the hug. (She was not a cuddly *bubba*.) But the way she said "Dahhhhhling!" left her granddaughter limp with delight. It signified that at that moment she merited the great woman's entire attention. As Ida turned back to her cooking, Arlyne watched with admiration. She was not a beautiful woman in the conventional sense. Her nose was too broad and her lips too narrow. Throughout most of her life she carried too much weight in her hips. But she transformed the initial impression of awkwardness by force of will. Her posture was always perfect, her diction flawless. Yet underlying that composure was a frank earthiness that men found appealing. The Grandmother, Arlyne observed, was always surrounded by men, most considerably younger than herself.

Among those *tummlers* who hung around Ida's kitchen on a Friday night were the chauffeurs, Jimmy and Jake, who drove the hearses in the funeral processions. Both young men were clearly fond of their bene-factress. Jake, a ladies' man, would engage Ida in good-natured teasing and go on his way. The other, however, was more seriously smitten. Jimmy the Gentile, as he was called, was a timid soul who could never seem to find a girlfriend. Ida had taken pity on him and had offered to teach him to dance. Later, when her duties as cook were complete, she would take him by the hand and lead him to the living room where she would put a record on a phonograph. Then, to the delight of onlookers, she would initiate Jimmy into the erotic delights of the tango. Their bodies did not mesh perfectly; Ida overwhelmed her slender partner. But Jimmy was an avid pupil and Arlyne found it exciting to watch their silhouettes against the fire.

Jimmy waited on Ida in mute adoration. Every Saturday night, he drove her to the Roseland Ballroom where she competed in dance contests. Summers and holidays, he drove her to the Concord Hotel, a Jewish resort in the Catskills where she flirted with the dance instructors. He waited and waited. His vigil came to nothing. Ida already had a boyfriend who had staked a firmer claim upon her affections.

Uncle Frankie Oxman had been around as long as anyone could remember. He was a short, rotund man with a jovial disposition. On Friday nights Frankie circulated throughout the funeral parlor dispensing goodwill. The children were fond of him because he had a habit of handing out dollar bills, a princely sum in those days. He was indulgent, buying each of the cousins a duck for the pond. Frankie himself kept pigeons in the tiny backyard and he had an Irish setter upon whom he doted. Every afternoon he and Ida, she decked out in diamonds and an ermine stole, would strut down East Broadway walking the dog. They seemed improbable lovers and their affair was one that Billie and The Aunts were reluctant to acknowledge. Even years later when Frankie died one afternoon of a heart attack in Ida's bed, The Aunts told themselves he had gone there for a "nap." This delicacy was due in part to the fact that Ida's husband, Jacob Blum, was still alive and living in exile somewhere in Brooklyn.

Arlyne remembered her grandfather as a sober, white-haired little man who always wore a black morning coat. Over the years she was to learn very little about his departure. Indeed, the facts of Jacob and Ida's entire marital history were obscure and Arlyne could never discern whether this was a product of her family's faulty collective memory or a deliberate amnesia in deference to Frankie Oxman's position in the household.

Ida's maiden name, Arlyne knew, was Lasker, and she had come to America as a child with her parents from a region in Poland then under the control of Austria. The family went into the grocery business and became moderately prosperous. Ida was betrothed at the age of sixteen to Jake Blum, who, it was assumed, had a good head for business and could take over the store. Jake, however, had ideas of his own and it was to the general consternation of the Laskers that he abandoned the family enterprise to become an undertaker. He reasoned, quite soundly, that the grocery business was subject to the vagaries of seasons and suppliers, while death produced an enduring clientele. No one was more distressed by Jake Blum's defection than his young wife, who was revolted by the prospect of sharing a house with corpses. Ida loved life and funerals depressed her. Still, she tried to be a good helpmate. Even if she had no acquaintance with the deceased, she could be found weeping copiously at graveside. Her ostentatious displays of compassion won Jake the business of over a hundred of the funeral societies that had sprung up around the turn of the century to assure that immigrants would be buried, if not with pomp, then at least with a measure of dignity.

The Blums had three children. It was Ida's destiny to bury two of them. Emmanuel died at the age of thirteen of a burst appendix. Harriet succumbed in early adulthood to pneumonia. Each time, Ida sank into depression. And, as having to endure her grief in the funeral home was intolerable to her, she would pack her bags and move to the Concord. After several months of dancing and merrymaking, she returned to East Broadway, her equilibrium restored.

On her remaining daughter, Ida lavished her undivided attention. Sylvia, a slender, dark girl with rather hawkish features, inherited her mother's zest for living. Having taken dancing lessons from the time she was a toddler, she aimed for a career on the stage. At the age of fourteen, she secured a place in the chorus line of a troupe called the Manhattan Steppers, who were about to embark on a national tour. Jake Blum objected, his sense of propriety offended by the prospect of his daughter showing her ankles in dance halls around the country. Ida, however, overrode her husband's objections, saying, "Let her have her fun." Sylvia spent over six months traveling with the troupe under the stage name of "Billie Young." She was known forever after as Billie.

In later years, Arlyne read her mother's letters from the road— sweet, chaste letters that were no doubt intended to put Jake Blum's worries to rest. She had them pegged as not-so-artful deception. She was sure that her mother had enjoyed what might then have been termed a "fling." Even as a child, Arlyne was the skeptical sort who had limited tolerance for the little lies that families tell to save face. But, at the age of eleven, she found herself increasingly perturbed by the story of her grandfather's disappearance.

If you listened to The Aunts—and Arlyne did a good deal of eavesdropping from various vantage points throughout the funeral parlor—Grandfather Blum had met another woman, also an undertaker, at a society meeting and had run off with her. Arlyne, who considered her grandmother the most desirable of all women, found this scenario wholly incredible. The truth, she suspected, was that The Grandfather had been cast out. Jacob Blum was a decent man with few enemies and it was difficult to imagine who might have engineered his downfall. Arlyne's youthful suspicion, however, fell upon Frankie Oxman.

As good as Frankie was in many respects, Arlyne never fully trusted him. There was something too eager, too opportunistic in his effusive goodwill. He had originally come to work for the Blums as a chauffeur but had seized upon every opportunity to run errands for Ida, collecting corpses from the Kings' County Mortuary and the "crazy house" out at Pilgrim State, thereby making himself indispensable to her.

Uncle Frankie was always into something shady, which enhanced his stature around the funeral home. No matter what it was you needed, Frankie could get it for you. Pots and pans, bolts of cloth, appliances.

When the miraculous phenomenon of television was scarcely rumored in households on the Lower East Side, Frankie got his hands on one of the first models, an RCA with a tiny round screen in an enormous console. Ida was so thrilled with this acquisition that she invited a throng of family and friends into the living room, where she allowed her visitors the rare privilege of sitting on the brocade couches.

But Uncle Frankie's talents did not end at procuring desirable and presumably purloined commodities. He was also a bookmaker. Long before Jacob Blum went into exile, the chauffeur was taking bets from the neighborhood boys. He kept his money, it was rumored, in one of the caskets. (Arlyne would have happily canvassed those crypts one by one looking for Frankie's fabled stash, but the lids were heavy and resisted prying.)

After Grandfather Blum's unexplained departure, Frankie abandoned discretion and brought his bookmaking operation out into the open, headquartering it in a small basement compartment next to the funeral parlor. Throughout most of the morning and early afternoon, a stream of men dressed in suits and fedoras entered and exited by a shallow cement stair from the street. The Clinton Street Boys, as they were known, were small-time racketeers who belonged to a social club a couple of doors down from Blums'. The Boys were a shiftless, fun-loving lot who spent the days playing pool, cards and baseball. Ida courted their goodwill by sponsoring the team, even providing uniforms. They were all avid gamblers and Frankie took their bets.

Sometimes, Arlyne visited her grandmother on Saturday afternoons, preferable to other days because there were no funerals in progress and she could play on the stairs. On those occasions, she would descend a back stairway that led to the basement compartment next door and pay a visit to Uncle Frankie and his friends. She would find them lounging on a pair of old sofas, reading the racing form and listening to an old floor-standing radio for race results. They didn't seem to mind a child in their midst. Frankie or one of the others might slip her a quarter and pat her cheek. Indeed, for as long as she could remember these men had been "The Uncles." There was Uncle Milty Tillinger, the shylock. Once when one of Milty's relatives was on the run from the law, Ida had hidden him in the casket room until the heat was off, incurring the Tillinger family's loyalty for life. There was Izzy Smith, proprietor of Zion Memorial down the block. Like Frankie a purveyor of hot merchandise, he customarily left his own establishment at midday to place a bet.

The Clinton Street Boys also counted among their number a

substantial number of union officials. Now and then one of these men would take Frankie aside and whisper something in his ear. Giving a nod, Frankie would lead the petitioner up the stair to his private office, which was located next to the chapel behind a high brass door. High on the door was a tiny square window with a curtain hung from the inside. When that curtain was pulled, it meant that secret business was being discussed. Arlyne often climbed the stair and, under the guise of playing in the hallway, furtively studied the door. It was taller than any other she had seen. Except for a large, rounded copper knob, it was perfectly plain. The surface was polished daily by the industrious Lily Higgins and it shone like an amber mirror. Arlyne would stare at it, hoping to see through it. But all that came back was her own dark, frustrated face.

The imposing portal with its impenetrable curtain was an affront, since every other door in the funeral parlor was left open, a reflection of Ida Blum's free, abundant nature. And Arlyne, whose talents for prying were already admirably developed, was galled by the existence of the one enclave to which she was denied access. She was always alert to those few seconds when the door was open admitting Frankie's visitors. If she was quick, she could catch a peek at the interior of the forbidden compartment.

What she saw was a disappointingly ordinary pair of rooms. In front was a small office with desk and telephone. Behind it was an antechamber with several wooden file cabinets and a large cast-iron safe. One afternoon the opportunity arose to inspect these rooms more closely when Frankie hurried out of his office, inadvertently leaving the door ajar. Arlyne, who had been playing in the chapel, looked down the hall and could not believe her good fortune. Fearful that this lapse signified Frankie's momentary return, she ambled idly down the hall until she arrived at the office door. Several minutes passed. Frankie was nowhere in sight. Emboldened, Arlyne pushed the door wider and slipped inside. From the front room, she could see that the safe had also been left open. As she moved closer to it she saw that it contained a stack of bound books. The temptation to touch them was irresistible. She knelt by the opening and picking up one of the volumes opened it to a page at random. It contained columns of figures whose significance she could not understand. She studied them fiercely but they remained as impenetrable as the polished surface of the brass door. Then she heard Frankie Oxman's voice in the vestibule and his heavy tread on the stair. She snapped the book shut, careful to return it to the place she had found it, then scampered out the doorway into the safety of the chapel.

The mystery surrounding Uncle Frankie's business dealings, and more particularly his presumed role in the departure of Jake Blum, was to nag Arlyne Weiss throughout her remaining childhood years. The answer to this riddle did not come in any sudden revelation, but rather with the slowly evolving awareness of who tugged the strings of the players at Blum's chapel. From the time Arlyne was about eight, she had noticed among the visitors to Frankie's office a very tall man with heavy bags under his eyes, his face in a perpetual scowl. "Uncle Red," as she was instructed to call him, never stopped to joke with her or give her money like the other uncles. He would make a brief weekly visit to Frankie, pay his respects to Ida, then leave. Arlyne could tell from the way Frankie fluttered and fawned in Red's presence that he was a dangerous man, the term "dangerous" connoting then, as it would for the remainder of her life, the ability to command respect, and more generally to get things done.

Red Levine, she learned as time went on, was a close friend of Meyer Lansky, a soft-spoken Polish immigrant who was already a legend on the Lower East Side. Shortly after his arrival in America in 1911, at the age of nine, he embarked upon a career as a street gambler, and in the years to come he succeeded in forging a criminal empire of gambling, rum running and protection. Castigated as a pariah by Orthodox religious leaders, he was, nonetheless, regarded with admiration, even awe, throughout the Jewish quarter, where he was considered a local-boy-made-good. "Meyer," as he was called familiarly, enjoyed the status of statesman by virtue of having forged an alliance with the East Side Italian gangs, headed by Charles Lucania—later "Lucky" Luciano.

Luciano and Lansky were later joined by an irascible Jewish hood named Louis Buchalter, also know as "Lepke," and they came to be referred to collectively as Lucky, Lansky and Lepke. While Luciano and Lepke mingled with showgirls and even socialites, Lansky—the reputed brains of the operation—remained in the background reading books on management. Throughout his fifty-year career he displayed an uncanny instinct for predicting which aspects of American life might be ripe for exploitation. During Prohibition, he brought his gang full-tilt into rum running. Even before the repeal of the Volstead Act in 1933 restored the flow of legal booze, Lansky had his eye on the next field of opportunity: the unions.

The early days of the labor movement were chaotic and violent, particularly in the "rag trade," whose workers, largely poor immigrants, were crammed into sweatshops and forced to work under deplorable conditions on the Lower East Side. Even after the Garment District moved north into more hospitable accommodations on Seventh Avenue, dissatisfaction grew. Management threatened violence to workers disposed to organize: The unions threatened violence to those who were not. Both sides hired thugs, often professional hoodlums, to enforce their threats. In some cases, the hood was simply a hired gun who would work for whichever side paid most, sometimes working for both. (Others, like Dopey Benny Fein, felt the tug of principle and would break legs only under the union banner.) At first the racketeers merely demanded extortionary rates for their services, which included burning or bombing shops that refused to toe the union line. Soon, however, they moved into more sophisticated applications of terror, demanding and receiving leadership positions. Organizations like the ILGWU were so disrupted by strikes and infighting that "Little Augie" Orgen, a gunman originally hired to protect workers, simply walked in and took over, ushering in the era of the union racketeer.

Recognizing that the unions were fertile territory, Lansky went into business with his old friend Lepke who, as a former protégé of Little Augie, had managed to gain control of trucking in the Garment District. This he did with the help of a squad of thugs commanded by a muscleman named Jake "Gurrah" Shapiro. Lepke and Gurrah, who came to be known as "L&G" or simply "The Boys," called the shots on Seventh Avenue, where literally no business could be conducted without their approval. Many a legitimate businessman was convinced to make "L&G" silent partners in exchange for assurances that his cargo would be delivered on time. Those who declined were threatened with sabotage and often death. Lansky and The Boys conducted their criminal enterprises virtually unmolested until 1933, when they found themselves drawn into a riptide of politics.

President Franklin Delano Roosevelt, who emerged victorious from the 1932 Democratic National Convention with support from political bosses under Lansky's control, promptly turned on his old allies, launching an all-out war on organized crime. That move proved so popular that local politicians all over the country took up the standard. The governor of New York, Herbert Lehman, appointed a young and politically ambitious special prosecutor named Thomas Dewey to bring the racketeers to justice. Dewey swung into action with fervor, targeting hoodlums across the spectrum of suspect industries. The brunt of his prosecutorial fury, however, fell upon Lepke and Gurrah, whom he called "the two greatest racketeers in the country." Realizing the indictments were imminent, The Boys went into hiding for nearly a year, all the while the subjects of an intensive national manhunt. At length, hoping for clemency, they gave themselves up. For Gurrah, the gamble paid off. He was convicted of extortion and got a three-year prison term. Lepke was not so lucky. Federal and state prosecutors both went after him and when they were through he was sentenced to life at Leavenworth.

Lepke's problems grew worse. In the months after he turned himself in, New York police arrested Abe Reles, a Lansky gunman whom they suspected of several murders. Threatened with the prospect of electrocution, Reles turned state's evidence and reeled off a string of crimes committed by the Lansky crew over two decades. Among these was the murder of a trucker who had been cooperating with the Dewey investigation. Reles had killed the man, he said, at Lepke's command. Reles's confession set in motion a new round of prosecution, which eventually sent Lepke to the electric chair.

The damage of which Reles was capable did not stop there. Reles had knowledge that also threatened to convict Lansky's lieutenant, Bugsy Siegel. Then, one night as he was being held in protective custody at the Half Moon Hotel in Coney Island, Abe Reles went flying out the window to his death. The question of exactly how a man might be murdered under the watchful eye of six New York City policemen gave rise to a number of theories. Perhaps he hadn't been murdered at all. Perhaps Reles had repented of his confession, or more likely, realized his life wasn't worth a plugged nickel, and took an honorable leap. Perhaps someone paid the cops to turn a blind eye, giving safe passage to an assassin. The mystery lingered long after his death.

Arlyne had been only three years old when Abie, as he was known to the Clinton Street Boys, went sailing out the window. As her impression of death was rather imperfectly formed, she never imagined him spreadeagled on the pavement, but rather lying in a coffin, rouged and serene like the other corpses at the funeral home. She had only the most general notion of what his sin might have been. But even a child could see that telling tales on your friends could have dangerous consequences. For each rat, there was an avenging demon. And the identity of Abie Reles's personal demon was widely debated among The Uncles in Ida Blum's basement parlor. One candidate was Bugsy Siegel's right-hand man, Frank Costello, who was rumored to have bribed the police. But those intimately acquainted with the players—and Clinton Street Boys prided themselves on those connections—insisted that the killer was none other than Red Levine.

Arlyne Weiss had no reason to doubt that what The Uncles said was true. The lowering figure who made weekly visits to Frankie Oxman struck her as a menacing presence. It was only after several years of eavesdropping from the stairwell that Arlyne understood what business had originally brought him to Blum's. During the early forties, there had been a movement afoot on the Lower East Side to unionize the chauffeurs and hearse drivers at funeral parlors. Grandfather Jacob Blum had wanted no part of it, insisting he paid his drivers a fair wage. Jake didn't want to go into the union out of respect for the old man and Jimmy would go along with whatever Jake did. In the face of this intransigence, the chauffeur's union had dispatched Red Levine to the Blum funeral parlor hoping he could make Jacob Blum see reason. In short, Uncle Red had threatened to bomb the place, and Jacob Blum, who did not have the stomach for this kind of fight, had given in to the union. With that, all of the other funeral parlors on the Lower East Side followed suit.

The showdown with Red Levine broke Jake Blum's spirit. After that, he did not manage his business or personal affairs with the rigor that he had used to. Into the vacuum stepped Frankie Oxman, the only one of the Blum chauffeurs who had welcomed the union. He became Red's boy on the scene, taking over more of the day-to-day running of the business. Gradually he usurped more and more of Jacob Blum's domain, including his wife. For years Frankie had courted Ida through obsequious errands but now that his star was on the rise, he became bolder. Just when her grandmother and Frankie Oxman became lovers, Arlyne never knew. It had to have occurred, she figured, when she was between the ages of eight (the year Red Levine appeared) and ten (the year Grandfather Blum disappeared). And it had to have occurred under the nose of her mother and the others as they appeared without fail for their Friday night get-togethers. Finally, Jake Blum had packed his bags and walked out the door. It was Arlyne's conviction that Ida, weary of Jake Blum's lugubrious presence, flattered by the attention of Frankie Oxman and the seductive prospect of becoming patroness to a crew of racketeers, had thrown her husband out. In time, Ida took Frankie in as a partner. She hauled down the old canopy and hoisted a new one, which read, "Blum and Oxman," thus announcing to the world that she had decided to live the East Side Life.

Notably absent from these affairs was Arlyne's father, Irving Weiss. The Aunts and more particularly The Uncles would make deferential inquiries about his health, knowing full well that Irving had forgone an evening at Blum and Oxman's to play gin with his cronies. Curiously, that absence was not regarded as a cause for scandal. It was, rather, accepted as a fact of life. Irving Weiss harbored an ill-concealed contempt for Frankie Oxman, whom he considered a small-time operator. Frankie's fawning irked Irving, who was generally acknowledged as a much classier sort of racketeer.

The Weiss brothers—Henry, Irving, Eddy, Joe and Natie—did not belong to the Clinton Street Boys but to a different crew whose territory extended from Houston Street through Attorney Street and as far east as the Williamsburg section of Brooklyn. Sons of Hungarian emigrants, the Weiss boys had grown up on Kosciuszko Street, where their parents owned a grocery store and milk route. That thriving enterprise was to have fallen to the sons, providing them with the means to make their fortune, their parents hoped, within the confines of traditional American values. But the Weiss boys had no taste for work. They were a handsome, indolent bunch who slept late and preened before a mirror until noon. They were fond of white suits, wingtips and shirts from an expensive haberdasher on Clinton and Grand. They liked fancy cars and good restaurants, and since honest work would not support their tastes, they fell quite naturally into racketeering.

Until the day he died, Arlyne was never quite sure what her father did. She knew that before she was born he and his brothers had left the grocery business and started a funeral parlor on Houston Street. The upright Jacob Blum was not taken in by this facade of respectability. To him, Irving was simply a racketeer. But if the Weiss brothers' effrontery offended Jacob Blum, it intrigued his daughter.

Billie admired all of the Weisses. But it was Irving—dark, quiet and handsome as a movie star—who appealed to her most. From the moment she became aware of his presence on the Lower East Side, she would seize any excuse to walk down Houston Street. If she were lucky, she would find one or more of the boys lounging on the steps. They were always polite, mindful of her father's place in the community, and would tip their hats and murmur "Miss Blum." This formality, while at first gratifying, began to wear on Miss Blum's patience. Constrained by convention, she could not initiate contact without a suitable pretext. Happily, one presented itself.

One of the funeral societies was holding a raffle and each of the East Side undertakers received a handful of tickets to sell. Ida Blum, who usually managed these matters, called her daughter to see if she might be interested in approaching the Weiss brothers. At her mother's opportune suggestion, Billie marched to Houston Street with ten raffle tickets as a pretext. Irving was eager to buy all ten, but was stopped by Henry, who thought five were quite enough. That confirmed Billie's assessment of Irving as the more generous—and the better catch. Billie had, in fact, left nothing to chance. Before coming, she had surreptitiously lifted the red seals on the tickets to make sure she sold the Weiss brothers a winner, thus assuring her of a future visit. When the drawing was held a week later, Irving had won a wool car blanket. Billie ran over to Houston Street to tell him, suggesting they might want to drive to Brooklyn together to pick it up. That excursion ended with dinner at an Italian restaurant, and six months later, Billie Blum was married to Irving Weiss, six years her senior.

Jacob Blum objected to the match on familiar grounds, that Irving was a hoodlum. This did not particularly bother Ida, who was more concerned that her daughter, like her, would be entombed for life in a funeral parlor. She made peace with her new son-in-law when, a few months after marriage, he and his brothers abandoned the funeral business and began running excursions by touring car to the Catskills. Their clientele were largely Jewish mobsters and their destination was an establishment called The Dodge Inn on Lake Louise Marie. The inn had an unsavory reputation as a gangster hangout and a haven for cheating lovers. (There was a standing joke that you had to "dodge in and dodge out.") Ida approved of Irving's new venture, finding it a much gayer occupation than undertaking. Often the entire family, with the exception of the taciturn Jacob Blum, would take to the country, Irving at the wheel, Billie by his side and Ida in the back seat flanked by young chauffeurs.

Ida's delight increased a year after her daughter's marriage with the arrival of her first grandchild, a baby girl. Arlyne—Billie found this unusual spelling elegant—was a roly-poly baby. She was not exactly beautiful but from the moment of her birth her tiny features were animated with vitality. Ida paraded the child proudly down Broadway, where she was known as "Little Arlyne" or "Princess Arlyne." By the time she was four years old, the child had already been inculcated with the conviction that the most important thing in life was dressing well. Her grandmother never bought off the rack. Neither did her mother, whose wardrobe, right down to her bathrobes, was custom made. Following in that grand tradition, Little Arlyne was taken as a toddler to Madame Webber, a petite blond seamstress, who outfitted her with little velvet coats and muffs with matching pillbox hats. Arlyne also accompanied her mother to Madame Berger's Beauty Salon, which lay at the top of several flights of stairs on Clinton Street. Madame Berger, a short woman with wavy reddish curls pressed close to her scalp, wielded a vigorous pair of shears and would chop and chop away, twirling the strands and securing them under a helmet of bobby pins. When she had finished, Arlyne's mop was a tight, shiny mass of sculpted curls.

Twice a week, Billie visited Madame Berger to have her own hair hennaed and styled in a pompadour supported by large tortoiseshell combs. Those visits were not only a fashion ritual, but a reconnaissance mission to discover who was aligned, or more particularly sleeping, with whom on the Lower East Side. Madame Berger's little shop catered to the wives and girlfriends of racketeers, most of whom showed up early on Friday afternoons to keep an eye on one another. A hair appointment at Madame Berger's offered a most civilized way of spying on your enemies. According to the prescribed rules of warfare, most of the antagonists maintained a pretense of civility. Every now and again, one would overestimate the power of her position and make a tactical blunder. One such incident, which etched itself irradicably into the mythology of the Lower East Side, occurred when Gurrah Shapiro's mistress, dripping with jewelry from her famous conquest, had the temerity to introduce herself to the wife. The latter drew herself up and announced with withering hauteur, "I am still *Mrs.* Shapiro."

Billie Weiss, who was fairly wise in the ways of the world, maintained a studied naivete in regard to the criminal element. The term "racketeer" offended her. Gurrah Shapiro, Milty Tillinger and Red Levine were all "nice men." And since it was possible to relate to them on an entirely social level, one did not need to acknowledge what they did for a living. Billie, for instance, had struck up a friendship with Red's wife, May, who also had her hair done at Madame Berger's. As a result, the Weisses were invited now and then to the Levines' summer place, a rather shabby rented railroad flat in Atlantic Beach, Long Island. Those evenings, as Arlyne later recalled them, were unremarkable. She played with Red's well-behaved children, Murray and Alice, while May, a thin, consumptive woman, cooked and chatted with the women in the kitchen. In the parlor at the very front of the house the men would usually be arguing loudly. The discussions would cease at dinner. Jewish racketeers never discussed business at the table. Then, after dessert, Red would fold his napkin and announce that he had to go to "work." It occurred to Arlyne years later that it must have been during one of these nocturnal shifts that Red Levine shoved Abie Reles out of the window at the Half Moon Hotel.

If Red's business was never discussed in Billie's household, neither

were the affairs of Irving Weiss. Over time, Irving had expanded his
business from touring cars to locating and acquiring luxury cars for
wealthy clients. Soon after, he and his brother Henry opened a car
dealership on Manhattan's Upper East Side (they called it Chester
Motors after the ever-present Chesterfield King that hung from the
corner of Irving's mouth) where they dealt in Cadillacs and Rolls-
Royces. Irving liked to say that if he sold one Rolls a month it was
enough to keep his family fed. He was entirely too modest. The Weiss
family lived extravagantly, indulging in their custom-made clothes and
fine cars. Four years after the arrival of Arlyne, Billie gave birth to a
second daughter, but Irving, who was ever solicitous of his wife, never
allowed her to be burdened by domestic cares. The children were
watched and the household run by a series of black maids while the
Weisses made the rounds of fashionable nightclubs.

Irving Weiss's already sizable fortune swelled during the war years,
when he managed to obtain steaks, eggs, nylons and other luxuries in
short supply among the general population. Arlyne heard her father tell
her mother that she needn't bother with rationing coupons. Looking
back on those days, Arlyne was later to surmise that her father and his
brothers, as well as a certain Uncle Sidney from the old Williamsburg
neighborhood, were dealing on the black market.

During the war, the Weiss family spent their winters in Florida,
taking a private plane, courtesy of one of Irving's "friends." For Arlyne
those sojourns were infused with magic. There was the pleasure of
stepping off the plane in Miami and feeling her skin caressed with the
warm, moist air. She would fill her lungs, because in those days Miami
smelled clean. Years later whenever she heard the strains of "Moon Over
Miami" she would grow weepy with nostalgia.

The Weisses usually rented a small apartment in what is now the
Art Deco District. Billie sunbathed while Irving looked after certain
business interests. He owned a piece of a bar on Washington Avenue in
Miami Beach. As the place was usually crowded with sailors, Irving
would not let his older daughter come inside. Instead, she would meet
him outside, under the awning, and walk him back to the apartment
each day. Irving was also an investor in a night spot called The Paddock
Club. This too was a rather sleazy establishment, which boasted for
entertainment a foul-mouthed comedian named B. S. Pulley. It was a
"dirty club." Irving and Billie, who were accustomed to frequenting
classier joints, were nonetheless required to put in an appearance there
from time to time, largely because one of the other co-owners was one

of Lucky Luciano's friends, Giuseppe Antonio Doto, also known as Joe Adonis.

Adonis was aloof and to Arlyne, a mystery figure. She managed to catch a glimpse of him one night as he sat outside the apartment waiting for her father. Although she was not yet a teenager, the sight of Adonis's indistinct profile visible through the Caddy's smoky glass aroused in her stirrings of sexual interest. His thick sensual features seemed as exotic as they were forbidden. Although the subject had never been explicitly discussed, it was clear that any daughter of Irving Weiss was expected to steer clear of Italians, who were widely acknowledged to prey upon Jewish girls and broadcast the details of their conquests on street corners and clubhouses throughout the Lower East Side. On one hand, Adonis was attractive because he was so strange, the utter opposite of the pallid Jewish racketeers who hung out at Blum and Oxman's. At the same time there was something familiar about him. Something that reminded Arlyne of her father. Not that they were physically similar. Beyond their dark features, the heavy, weary-eyed Adonis had little in common with the slender, sleekly coiffed Irving Weiss. It was more a similarity of attitude, a commanding, powerful presence, which made them, in Arlyne's favorite expression, "dangerous."

From the time she was small, Arlyne had observed that her father, while a man of few words, made his presence felt wherever he went. On Sundays when he took his family to dinner at the Grotta Azzurra on Mulberry Street, the valet would snap to attention when they pulled up in a Rolls and the staff would whisper audibly "The *Weisses!*" They never had to wait for a table, and the waiters always hovered solicitously, eyes lowered and necks crooked in an attitude of deference. It gave Arlyne a shiver of pleasure to be under the protection of a man who commanded respect.

The feeling she got on those occasions was intensified by the knowledge that she was her father's favorite girl. While her mother was partial to Barbara, a sweet, dainty child to whom she routinely referred as "*my* Barbara," Irving favored Arlyne. No matter how she misbehaved, he turned a blind eye and seemed even to enjoy the vitality from which those pranks sprang. From the time she was small he would draw her now and again into his confidence. Not that he shared private thoughts with her. Looking back on her life from middle age, Arlyne could not recall a single extended conversation with her father. Their intimacy, rather, grew out of his willingness to include her in excursions with his closest associates.

Once, when she was around eight, he took her on a day trip to Palm Island with Red Levine. Even at that young age, Arlyne was aware of how privileged she was to be taken along, since the object of that outing was an audience with Al Capone, recently released from prison and rumored to be insane. During Capone's reign as crime boss of Chicago, Red Levine had enjoyed Al's trust, serving as a courier of personal messages between him and Lucky Luciano. Now, in Capone's retirement, Red served as a sort of legate-at-large, refreshing the fallen leader's ties with the underworld. Her father's meeting with Capone was uneventful from Arlyne's perspective. As they entered the house, a dreary place with bars on the windows, Irving told her to sit on a bench in the foyer. Then a door opened. She could not see who was inside but Red ushered her father in, saying, "I want you to meet Irving. You know who Irving is." The door closed. The little girl waited in the foyer until it got dark. When her father and Uncle Red reemerged, she craned her neck to see the third man, but the door closed before she could catch a glimpse.

Excluded as she was from the main arena of action, Arlyne, nonetheless, felt proud to be considered one of the boys. As time went on she became less eager to share her mother and sister's bond, from which she was perpetually excluded, and was drawn more and more to the male camaraderie of her father and his associates. Irving obliged by taking her along to the Jamaica Racetrack on Saturday mornings. It would be her, Uncle Red Levine and sometimes Uncle Sidney. Irving would drive them all to Queens in a touring car, which they would park in the enormous lot. The men would leave her in the grandstand eating hot dogs as they conducted their business at the betting windows, and from a distance she would admire her father as he threaded his way elegantly through the crowd in his white suit. In those days nobody wore a white suit except Bugsy Siegel. Irving Weiss rarely won. He was not a lucky bettor, but his losses, though sometimes substantial, never seemed to put him in a bad mood.

As Arlyne entered her teen years, Friday night dinner at The Grandmother's ceased to exert its irresistible pull on her and she would sometimes accompany her father and Red to the fights at Madison Square Garden. In those days people dressed to the teeth and Arlyne would show up on her father's arm wearing something tight and strapless. She would secretly imagine that she was her father's date, or if she was feeling particularly daring, his wife. Irving Weiss always got ringside seats because he had a connection. All the prestige that surrounded him enveloped her. In the company of the boys, she felt important.

Still, the intimacy that Irving Weiss offered his daughter always had limits, which frustrated her intolerably. And no place were these limits more strictly imposed than at the very seat of Irving's business affairs. In a practical sense, the doors of Chester Motors were open to everyone. And on Saturday afternoons Billie, Barbara and Arlyne sometimes went up to 116th Street to pay the Weiss brothers a visit. On those occasions they put on their best dresses, because Irving never liked to see his family wearing casual clothes in public, particularly not at the showroom of Chester Motors, where the Weiss brothers strove for a certain elegance to showcase their selection of fine automobiles. The floors were tiled with faux marble and several fat columns were covered with mirrors. Arlyne came to call it the "House of Mirrors."

Chester Motors' pretensions to class were belied to some degree by its clientele, Italian hoods from 116th and Pleasant Avenue who were always in the market for big cars. After they finished browsing among the Cadillacs they often stopped by Irving's office. Arlyne could see them through the high panels of glass arguing spiritedly with her father and Uncle Henny. She could not hear a word. The Weiss brothers had regular visitors who conducted their silent, energetic and unfathomable business. Among these were James Plumeri and his nephew, John Dioguardi, also known as Jimmy Doyle and Johnny Dio. These two hoodlums had been close associates of Lepke and Gurrah and had themselves done time on convictions for racketeering in the Garment District. Johnny and Jimmy seemed to have assumed the role of the Weiss brothers' special protectors. Once when Chester Motors was robbed and thieves took Henny's large diamond ring, Irving put in a call to Johnny Dio and the following evening the ring was returned under the door in an unmarked envelope. Another time, Irving's brother Joey stole some money from the safe and left town. At Irving's behest, Jimmy Doyle and Johnny Dio tracked him down to a resort in the Catskills where they found him holed up with a girlfriend. They dragged Joey back to face his punishment, but Irving, who had a soft spot for his younger brother, forgave everything.

Over the years Chester Motors served as a base of operation for racketeers from the teamsters and meat cutters unions. For a while it was even appropriated as an office by a corrupt narcotics cop who used it to collect graft payments. At all hours of the working day, men from the neighborhood would run in to make calls from a pay phone hanging on the wall. Often the phone would ring and ring. Arlyne's father and uncles would hear it, but no one would answer. Irving Weiss had given his daughters strict instructions to leave that phone alone.

One spring afternoon when Arlyne was in her early teens she was hanging around the showroom when the phone began to ring. It continued to ring and with each ring the temptation grew stronger to lift the receiver. She tried to imagine the party on the other end. Jimmy Doyle or Johnny Dio? The narcotics cop? She was overwhelmed by the urge to hear the voice. As she reached for the phone, however, she heard the sharp report of her father's voice calling "Arlyne!" She withdrew her hand. In one brief command he had excluded her firmly from the heart of his life. That was the way it always was with the Weiss family. Doors slammed shut. Mirrors stared back. And every ring of the phone concealed a secret.

TWO

MOB GIRL

If Irving Weiss appeared to draw his daughter into his circle of confidence only to push her away again, it was not because he intended to be cruel. He was, rather, ambivalent about his own life. Having done well for himself in the rackets, he nonetheless shared his wife's pretensions to respectability, particularly in regard to his children, for whom he envisioned a quiet, affluent life in the mainstream. "Even the worst mobster," Arlyne would later observe, "wants his child to be wonderful."

Ironically, Irving Weiss's two daughters mirrored the contradictory sides of his nature. Barbara, who had submitted herself dutifully to her mother's tutelage, learned everything a little lady should learn. She took dancing lessons and horse-riding lessons and applied herself to her studies. Even in grade school she seemed well on her way to the country-club set. Arlyne, on the other hand, routinely cut classes to haunt the basement of Knickerbocker Village, which was catacombed with dark storerooms. There she and her chums would smoke cigarettes, which her mother, an unrepentant chain-smoker, had strictly forbidden. Billie once caught her daughter in the act and resolved to break her of the habit. She locked her in the bathroom with a cigar and didn't let her out until she had smoked the whole thing. Arlyne found the experience sufficiently sickening that she never touched tobacco again. For the most part, however, the reform was superficial and she continued to cut classes.

Barbara also shone more brightly at play. Each summer the two girls would be shipped off to Camp Roosevelt for the Discriminating, a venerable Catskills outpost that catered to the offspring of rich Jews. There, Barbara Weiss became the youngest member ever inducted into the Blue Dragon Society, which honored the all-around best campers. Arlyne never made the cut. She was too busy sneaking to the milk bar at night for furtive necking with boys from Camp Winston across the lake.

By her early teens, Arlyne was already a striking girl, tall and thin with a precocious and ample bust. It was a figure that invited advances. She was only twelve when she lost her virginity. This occurred inauspiciously in her grandmother's funeral parlor. One Friday evening, her cousin, Solly, only slightly older but infinitely more experienced, lured her into a tiny guest bedroom to play "doctor." He guided her to the bed and, removing her panties, tried putting his fingers inside her. They wouldn't go. Arlyne recalled experiencing no particular physical sensation. She was sufficiently intrigued, however, that the following week, when Solly once again beckoned her into the little bedroom, she followed willingly. This time he climbed on top of her and pushed his thing inside of her. She felt a sharp pain, then began to bleed. She ran to the bathroom crying.

Arlyne told no one about this and, thereafter, avoided Solly. She hoped to put the episode out of her mind, but curiously it kept resurfacing. She wasn't sure why. The sex itself hadn't brought her any pleasure. Quite the opposite. There was another component to the experience, however, that held an irresistible attraction. Arlyne recalled that during the time that Solly was luring her to bed, she had enjoyed his full attention. And that filled a deep and curious need. Arlyne was hungry for attention, perhaps because she was excluded from her mother's affection and shut out of her father's confidence. As long as she could remember Arlyne was crying to be noticed and admired. Now she discovered that sex, as unpleasant as it might be, made her feel important.

After the episode with Solly, Arlyne longed to find that sensation again. Her next encounter was with a short, thin fellow named Stamey, an automobile salesman who drove cars up from Georgia and other points south for her father. Stamey, with his southern accent and polite manners, was unlike any man she had met. Whenever he was in town, Arlyne hung around Chester Motors a little longer than usual, making sure she attracted his notice. With Stamey, she discovered the sport of man teasing. One afternoon, she asked him if he would drop her off by the subway. He agreed. En route to the station, she began to run her forefinger up and down his thigh. To her surprise, Stamey drove her to his hotel and asked, "Why don't you come on up?" Arlyne had not anticipated he would call her bluff, but she agreed. After stopping into a liquor store next to the hotel, Stamey led her to an ugly room illuminated by the intermittent blink of a neon sign outside the window. The two of them got drunk on bourbon and crawled into bed. With a grown man, Arlyne had hoped sex would be more romantic. She had to undress herself and when she touched Stamey's naked body, she was disappointed to find it bony. What mystique there was disappeared entirely the following morning when she awoke to the smell of stale liquor. Everything seemed dirty. The room, Stamey, her own body. Leaving her lover in a dead sleep, she dressed and took a cab home, where there was a terrible scene. Irving Weiss had done a little detective work and discovered that Arlyne had left Chester Motors with Stamey the night before. After calling his colleague and informing him he had just had sexual relations with a minor, he turned his wrath on Arlyne, warning her never to see the man again. Strangely exhilarated by the tongue-lashing, Arlyne ignored her father's warnings. She and Stamey met two or three more times after that, not because Arlyne enjoyed the sex, but because she took pleasure in defying her father.

After Stamey, there was Sal, who owned a bakery shop on the corner. They would go up to his mother's house in the middle of the afternoon to have sex. Then there was the son of a senator who lived at Knickerbocker Village and whom she met for quick, stand-up sex in the cellar. There were other boys from the Village. There were the boys at the milk bar at Camp Roosevelt. There were boys, boys, boys. By the time she was fourteen, Arlyne had what was politely termed "a reputation."

On afternoons when they were supposed to be in school, Arlyne and her crew, a clique of Jewish girls named Teddy, Elaine and Hope, hung out on the corner by the K&K Candy Store. Hopie, whose father owned a prosperous bar on the Bowery, was older and drove a red Jaguar. As a result, the girls had the entire city at their disposal. They would go to Little Italy to have their fortunes told. Arlyne was fiercely superstitious and could never resist a palm reader. Then they would drive uptown, heads thrown out the window, hair streaming behind them, shouting taunts at men. In Times Square they would hang out at the hotels, flirting with the band members. Later they would follow the guys to after-hours joints in Harlem, arriving home at two or three in the morning.

Arlyne always had an explanation. She had been out with "the girls." Irving Weiss tended to accept his daughter's story because he refused to believe the worst of her. Billie was more skeptical, but with a little artful deception she, too, could be gulled. Before going out for the evening Arlyne would present herself to her mother wearing the most demure skirt and blouse in her closet. Once out the door, she and her chums would drive to a movie theater, and there buy tickets so they could use the restrooms to change into their cruising clothes.

Black satin skirts with high heels were their trademark. Arlyne wore her skirts so tight that she would have to wiggle out of them. Naturally, she could not risk a pantyline, so she dispensed with underwear. Over time her taste in clothing became even more flamboyant as she emulated the photos of showgirls and movie stars. Once she saw the starlet Marilyn Monroe in a pink linen halter dress with coat to match. She had her mother's seamstress make her an identical outfit. Even on sweltering summer days she paraded down Monroe Street in off-the-shoulder furs, turning every few steps to see who was watching. In her own mind, she was "Stella Stunning," a teenager's incoherent ideal of glamour.

And then, Arlyne Weiss discovered Virginia Hill.

Arlyne was not much of a reader. She did, however, make it a point to scan the papers to see what the rich and beautiful were wearing. She happened one day across a photo of Virginia Hill, the fabled beauty who had been the girlfriend of the late Bugsy Siegel. She was wearing a tailored two-piece suit and a large picture-frame hat. Arlyne thought she had never seen a woman with so much class. She was not just a mob girl. She was America's premier mob girl, and as such she seemed to enjoy the status of royalty. One publication went so far as to call her "the most successful woman in America."

Miss Hill, it seemed, had clawed her way up from poverty in the finest American tradition. Born in a wretched Alabama steel town, she claimed to have neither worn nor owned a pair of shoes until the age of seventeen—the year she ran away to Chicago, where she found a job waitressing at the 1933 World's Fair. There she happened to come to the attention of a big-time bookie and gambler who became her lover, financial advisor and ultimately her entree into the fast life of the Chicago Mob.

Virginia's timing was fortunate. She arrived on the scene just as the Lansky-Lucania crew in New York was linking arms with Capone's Chicago operation to form a national crime syndicate. That meant the bosses needed some reliable method of getting messages to one another. Talking on the phone was too risky as the wires were frequently tapped. Since most states had statutes making it an offense for two or more known criminals to consort with each other, the racketeers needed a courier who would not arouse suspicion. Who better than a bosomy redhead who was presumed to be some mobster's brainless girlfriend? There were, after all, dozens who fit that description and law enforcement considered them harmless. In this innocuous guise, Virginia shuttled unmolested between Chicago and New York City.

But Virginia, as it turned out, was neither brainless nor harmless. As one contemporary commentator explained, she was "more than just another set of curves. She had . . . a good memory, a considerable flair for hole-in-the-corner diplomacy to allay the suspicions of trigger-happy killers and a dual personality, closelipped about essentials and able to chatter freely and apparently foolishly about inconsequentials." Even the government eventually concluded that she was a "central clearing-house" for intelligence on organized crime. As such, Virginia enjoyed an independent power base within the Syndicate.

The bosses found other uses for Miss Hill. She became the underworld's personal emissary to café society. When Virginia arrived on the scene in New York in the late thirties, she contrived a new history for herself, one that would be sure to find its way into the gossip columns. The story circulated that she was a southern society girl who had gone through four rich husbands—all divorced or dead—and she had gotten $1 million from each. Authentic socialites saw through this ruse. Even so, it became fashionable to be seen slumming with her. Virginia made the circuit of Broadway clubs, picking up the check for an entourage of hangers-on and Latin gigolos. It was on one of these nightly swings that she supposedly contrived to meet Joe Adonis, the handsome hood who was later to become the business partner of Irving Weiss. She became Adonis's girl. And in time, she became Bugsy Siegel's girl. According to the popular lore of the underworld, it was Adonis himself who unwittingly brought Siegel and Hill together. Virginia carried a note of introduction from Joe to Bugsy, who was then eluding New York authorities in Los Angeles. The attraction was immediate and mutual. Although Virginia tried to placate both lovers by flying from coast to coast, she finally settled into Beverly Hills with Bugsy, whom she preferred to call "Ben."

Virginia cut as flamboyant a figure in Hollywood as she had in New York. She and Siegel gave fabulous parties attended by celebrities like George Raft who were perversely flattered to be courted by a mobster and his moll. When Meyer Lansky ordered Siegel to open up Nevada for gambling, Virginia and Ben took their road show to Las Vegas to oversee the construction of the fabulous Flamingo Hotel. It was there that Virginia's fairy tale career hit the skids. Bugsy was no businessman and he plowed the most expensive materials into the hotel without regard to cost. The overruns infuriated his Syndicate backers in New

York and Cincinnati, particularly when rumors began circulating that he
and Virginia were skimming construction dollars and socking them
away in a Swiss bank account.

On June 16, 1947, Virginia Hill took an unannounced trip to Paris.
Four days later, as Bugsy was sitting on the couch in Virginia's Beverly
Hills home, he was killed by the blast of a .30 caliber carbine fired
through the living-room window. During the months thereafter, rumors
concerning Virginia Hill's role in the Siegel hit proliferated wildly. One
school of thought held that Virginia knew Bugsy was in deep trouble and
had flown to Europe to plead for his life, the reasoning being that she
could place a call from Paris to Lucky Luciano, then in Italy, without
worrying about her line being tapped. More cynical speculation held
that she knew Bugsy's days were numbered and simply wanted to be out
of the line of fire.

After Siegel's death Virginia made a series of highly publicized
suicide attempts. These too admitted alternative interpretations. Senti-
mentalists concluded that she was undone by grief. Others professed
that Virginia took just enough pills to make her attempts at suicide
appear serious; that she kept a safe deposit box in which lay a packet
addressed to the district attorney of L.A. County. That this packet
contained evidence that could send ten Syndicate bosses to the chair for
Siegel's murder. That the document was supposedly to be delivered in
the event of Virginia's death. That after each suicide attempt she
received a substantial payment from the Syndicate to assure her
continued good health.

Four years later, the Kefauver Committee would call Virginia,
whom it hoped might be sufficiently grieved by Bugsy's death to divulge
the names of his killers. They were mistaken. Virginia was unshakable.
She claimed to know few of the men about whom the committee was
inquiring. She knew nothing about the source of Bugsy's money, had
never heard of his being involved in any illegal activity, and seemed not
to care one whit who had killed him. As far as she was concerned all of
Bugsy's friends were "perfect gentlemen."

Virginia Hill made it clear to a nation of fascinated onlookers that
a mob girl was no rat.

Arlyne was enthralled. Every day she combed the papers for some
new shred of gossip about Virginia. "In my eyes," she would later recall,
"here was a broad that really made it good." Here was a woman who
had clothes, money and all the attention any human could hope for. Not
only was she widely admired as a sex goddess but she seemed to enjoy

respect as well. What impressed Arlyne most deeply was that Virginia Hill had been admitted into the bosses' confidence. She had been accepted as one of the boys.

As a practical matter, Arlyne Weiss, the pampered racketeer's brat, did not enjoy much in common with the young Virginia Hill, barefoot 'til the age of seventeen. Nonetheless, Arlyne felt a curious kinship with her. There were certain aspects of Virginia's career that reminded her of Ida Blum, a sort of mob girl in her own right. Like Virginia, Arlyne's adored grandmother enjoyed beautiful clothes and was always surrounded by men who admitted her to their private counsel. Not that Arlyne ever thought of her grandmother as a common mobster's moll. She was a *lady*. But so in some strange way was Virginia. She was half tomboy, half whore, but always a lady. And that, Arlyne Weiss decided, was what she wanted to be. At the age of fourteen, she set out to become a mob girl.

The stylistic considerations were easiest to effect. Arlyne retired her Marilyn Monroe imitations and instructed the seamstress to make her a set of form-fitting two-piece suits, which she wore with a picture-frame hat. Although Virginia Hill's hair was a bright red, Arlyne never saw anything but black-and-white photos, in which it looked dark. Acting on this misconception, she dyed her own hair jet black. When the physical transformation was complete, she set about cultivating the one thing that distinguished Virginia most. Fast company.

Arlyne had always been attracted to "dangerous" men. Men like Joe Adonis who emanated a seductive aura of menace and power. Curiously, she did not find that quality present among the Jewish racketeers in her father's circle. It was certainly well known that individuals like Izzy Smith or Red Levine had the ability to pick up the phone and get someone killed. In the wisdom of her mature years, she would conclude that Jewish racketeers had more class than the Italian wiseguys. They certainly dressed better and they weren't always trying to kill one another off. But there was a certain sterility in the way they wielded their power—like executives. It was the Italians with their pretty-boy looks and passionate vendettas who attracted Arlyne. When a wiseguy was dangerous, he was truly *dangerous*.

The streets around Knickerbocker Village abounded with wiseguys, some of them made men, and others just punks in their Danny Anfang shirts and Benedetti shoes aspiring to membership in a local neighborhood crew. Arlyne and her girlfriends had considerable experience flirting with the punks, as one stop of their nightly circuit was likely to be Sullivan Street, where Italian boys congregated on the street by a church. Hopie would slow the Jaguar to a crawl, giving the girls, who had shoved their upper bodies out the window, an ample opportunity to flaunt their bosoms. The Italians proved to be easily aroused, but when they ventured close to the car Hopie sped away.

Teasing punks was one thing, going out with them another. These were not the sort of hoodlums who would meet Virginia Hill's high standards. And Arlyne had resolved to go after only those wiseguys who had made a name. At the top of her list of prospective conquests was Tony Mirra.

Arlyne was around fourteen when she first noticed Tony. He was much older, his jet-black hair already beginning to show the white streak that would become his distinguishing trait. Tony's midriff was already beginning to expand, a fate that seemed universally to befall wiseguys once they reached the age of twenty-five. But Arlyne found him "gorgeous." As with Joe Adonis, his dark good looks and commanding manner reminded her of her father.

Tony lived near Knickerbocker Village on Monroe Street with his old Italian mother, to whom he was passionately devoted. That filial solicitude stood out in sharp contrast to Tony's widely held reputation as a sexual brute. It was not uncommon for Tony, while cruising through the neighborhood, to pick up an attractive woman, nail her in the back seat and then push her out of the car. Tony was, furthermore, reputed to be an enforcer for the Bonanno crime family. She heard he was a bodyguard for a very big boss, she didn't know who. But he was definitely dangerous.

Tony's path had crossed the Weisses' at only one point, when he had come to Chester Motors with his uncle, Al Walker, looking for a car. They bought a black Cadillac with yellow doors. Irving had acquired it from the owner of a liquor store who had had signs hanging from the sides. Arlyne found the choice a little odd, but Tony and his uncle Al loved their two-tone Caddy. They drove it all around the Lower East Side. Wherever Arlyne saw it parked, she knew Tony could not be far away.

On most afternoons, Tony parked the Cadillac on Madison Street in front of one of his favorite watering holes, the Black Horse Saloon. He usually came there to conduct some unspecified business with two union officials. They would hang around on the street outside the bar's blue door before going inside to eat. Having noted this routine, Arlyne embarked on a campaign to get Tony's attention. Donning her Virginia

Hill garb, she would strut majestically down Madison on the pretext of visiting Savarese's corner drugstore. If her timing was good, she would catch Tony outside, in which case she would stop dead cold in front of him, turn slightly and give him a seductive glance from beneath the picture-frame hat.

For weeks, all she got for her trouble was indifference. Tony Mirra was simply not impressed by a fourteen-year-old dolled up like a high-class hooker. At length, Arlyne abandoned this tack in favor of a more direct approach. Enlisting Hopie's company for moral support, she took her usual tour down Madison one afternoon, but instead of continuing to the corner, she stopped before the blue door and, grabbing the handle resolutely, opened it and marched inside. The Black Horse was dim, even with the late-afternoon light streaming through its street-front window. When her eyes adjusted to the darkness, she scanned the length of the bar but failed to find Tony. Finally, she spotted him sitting at a table in the back with a union official having a plate of pasta.

"Come on over here, kid," Tony called. "I wanna talk to ya."

Thrilled at finally having attracted his attention, Arlyne steered Hopie toward Tony's friend and took a place beside Mirra. But things did not unfold as she had hoped. She had envisioned herself impressing Tony with her tough talk, then maybe he'd take her out to dinner where she could be seen with him. Just being *seen* with Tony Mirra was an honor in those days. But Tony had other things on his mind. Without warning, he began playing with her, feeling around her waist, thighs and breasts. Caught off guard she complained, but in fact she found herself becoming excited. It was rush hour when Tony took her out for a ride. He drove for a while then pulled over next to the *Journal-American* building on South Street and started to unzip his pants. "Tony, I can't do that," Arlyne objected, keeping a nervous eye on the stream of people exiting from the *Journal*.

"C'mon. I wanna show you how to do something," he said. And with that he grabbed her by her long dark hair and pushed her face toward his penis. When she resisted, he slapped her, growling, "You're nuthin' but a cockteaser." It was then that Arlyne allowed herself to be instructed in the art of oral sex. Tony taught her how to hold it and how to rub it up and down. She found the whole process revolting, but at that moment, nothing in the world seemed so important as pleasing Tony Mirra.

Afterward, Tony dropped her back on Monroe Street as if nothing

had happened, leaving her stung by his indifference. When the hurt
passed, she became angry and her anger took the form of a renewed
assault. Every day after that she showed up at the Black Horse wearing
the tightest outfits she owned. If Tony wanted to feel her up, she offered
no resistance. If he wanted to take a ride and park, she accepted docilely.
It was not, she imagined, how Virginia Hill had done it—or maybe she
had. But Arlyne felt this was all a necessary part of becoming a
true-to-life mob girl. Tony, in turn, allowed her the privilege of being
seen with him. She was allowed to come into the Black Horse when
Tony wasn't talking business. And if he was really feeling generous he
would take her for a ride in the two-tone Caddy with his uncle Al
Walker and cousin, Angelo. Tony, Arlyne would later recall, became her
"protector." If she ever needed money, she could get it from him. If she
found herself in a situation she couldn't handle at two in the morning,
she called Tony and he'd send someone over to pick her up. In return,
she ran errands for him. The nature and purpose of these errands were
never explained. Tony would simply give her a sealed envelope, which
she surmised contained cash—or sometimes a larger packet of undisclosed contents—and she would deliver it to one of his friends across
town. Whenever duty called, she would dress to the hilt, always wearing
a fox stole off the shoulder, Virginialike. She was thrilled that Tony
trusted her with his business. It made her feel important.

Arlyne knew that her parents would definitely not approve of Tony,
which, of course, was part of his charm. She enjoyed provoking her
mother by arriving home at three in the morning. Even at that hour,
there was no way Arlyne could make it to her bedroom unobserved,
since Billie would be waiting on the couch in the foyer. She would never
know for sure where Arlyne had been, but she was sure she had been up
to no good. And as soon as she heard the door close, she began
screaming, "You tramp! I've never had a good day with you. I've never
had anything right with you." Billie screamed until the muscles on her
neck stood out. Arlyne would just smile and say, "Hit me." After Billie
landed a blow, Arlyne would turn and walk into her own room.

During these brawls, Irving Weiss would not leave his bedroom.
And in the morning he would never let on that anything out of the
ordinary had occurred. He was a man who saw only what he wanted to
see. And for a long time, he turned a blind eye to Arlyne's relationship
with Tony Mirra. One evening, Arlyne told her father she was going out
with a Jewish boy and instead went drinking with Tony at a Chinese
restaurant called the House of Chan. When Tony dropped her off in

front of her house at five in the morning, Irving was waiting. He had recognized the black-and-yellow Cadillac. That night Irving Weiss gave his daughter a beating. It was the first of only two times Arlyne could ever recall her father raising his hand to her.

The Weisses concluded that Arlyne's wildness was attributable to the influence of the Lower East Side. Billie wanted find a "better environment," someplace where her daughters could grow up to be ladies. For several years, other families—both proper citizens and racketeers with yearnings toward respectability—had been moving out of the old neighborhood. If they had any money at all they settled across the East River in the borough of Queens. This exodus further hastened the decline of the Jewish quarter. East Broadway began looking neglected. Grocers, milliners, haberdashers and family restaurants went out of business. Even Blum and Oxman suffered when the Clinton Street Boys found another hangout in Queens.

When Arlyne was sixteen, the Weisses joined the exodus, moving to a posh second-floor apartment in the relatively stylish residential neighborhood of Forest Hills. But a "better environment" did not have the desired effect upon Arlyne Weiss. Despite the fact that she was now cut off from Hopie, Elaine, Teddy, Tony and the entire Monroe Street crew, she had a gift for finding bad company. In Forest Hills, she found Sophie.

Sophie was a pretty little girl with bright red hair, which she wore in a flip like Hedy Lamarr. It was always so perfect it looked like a wig. Her father, an Eastern European Jew, owned a neighborhood grocery. But he was sufficiently prosperous that he could afford to indulge his only daughter. Sophie was spoiled and lazy. Arlyne found in her a highly congenial companion.

Like Arlyne, Sophie cut school routinely. Every day Sophie would sleep until noon. Then around two o'clock she would get into a cab, swing by to pick up Arlyne, and the two would set out to make mischief. Largely through Arlyne's reconnoitering, they discovered the Carlton Terrace, a shady bar on Queens Boulevard, which served as the new hangout for the Clinton Street Boys. At any hour of the day you could walk into the Terrace's dark interior and find the old crowd from Ida's place and several other faces as well, including that of a union official named Moishe.

In the Blum and Oxman days, these had been The Uncles, who had given Arlyne quarters and affectionate tweaks. At the Carlton Terrace, however, they were usually in the company of women who were definitely not their wives. And when Arlyne and Sophie walked in like a couple of molls, they were greeted with lustful glances. During the ensuing seductions Arlyne managed to sleep with Moishe (whom she knew to be one of her father's friends). Sophie slept with a handful of her own. The girls enjoyed picking these old men off for the sheer sport of it.

Some afternoons, they would not go out at all. Sophie came to Arlyne's house. (Irving would be at work, Barbara at school and Billie off playing Mah-Jongg.) They turned on the television and if they saw a handsome celebrity, they would try to reach him by phone with the intent of seducing him. These overtures were usually unavailing. One day, however, while watching a rodeo, they saw a bronco buster named Casey Tibbs. Arlyne turned to Sophie and said, "I'll bet we can get to this sonofabitch." With that she dialed Madison Square Garden and told them it was an emergency and she needed to reach Mr. Tibbs. When she got Casey on the line, she proceeded without much prologue to describe the things she would do to him if he visited her in Forest Hills. The next morning he sent her a dozen red roses.

Casey went on the road, and over the next few months they talked a lot on the phone. When, finally, he returned to New York, Arlyne put on her silk sheath and went to meet him at his hotel. When he opened the door, she was crestfallen. However handsome Casey looked on a bucking bronc, in the flesh he was just a broken-down old cowboy. When he took her to a steak house, she was embarrassed by his cowboy clothes and the gaudy championship belt buckle that sagged around his thin waist. That night she and Casey had quick sex, and she fled to Forest Hills.

Other than this fleeting contact with celebrity, Arlyne wasn't meeting the type of big-name big spenders with whom an aspiring mob girl could hope to make a reputation. What she lacked was some grand stage on which to play out her role. Then, almost by chance, Arlyne discovered an entree into the world of prizefighting.

The opportunity arose during the summer of her fourteenth birthday. She and her family customarily spent the hottest days of July and August on Long Island in Atlantic Beach. There they rented a cabana, a little house with a bar and two shower stalls, at the Capri Beach Club, which was favored by racketeers, union officials and dress manufacturers from the Garment District during those years. Every day the Weisses would arrive from the city in a rented, air-conditioned limousine— Irving indulged in this luxury so that his beloved wire-haired terrier, Paula, would not risk heatstroke. While the chauffeur watched the dog, and Billie and Irving took their place at the cabana to play cards with old cronies, their daughters settled in by the pool. Arlyne, like her father, tanned quickly and, like him, she always wore a white or black suit to show off her color. By midafternoon, she would tire of the action poolside and ride her bike through the maze of residential streets that lay off the dunes.

On these outings, she passed by the brick beach home of Irving Cohen, best known as the manager of Rocky Graziano, who, that year, was about to make his bid for the middleweight title of the world. Cohen's place was the subject of much interested speculation among the Capri crowd, since Graziano and his friends were frequent visitors. That beach house with its promise of celebrity exerted an irresistible pull on Arlyne Weiss. She took pains to pedal past it on her afternoon rounds, knowing full well that Cohen and the fighters would be sitting on the porch drinking.

In fact, Arlyne passed by several times during the course of an afternoon, always slowing down to show off her tanned, suited figure to best advantage. For days, she failed to elicit so much as a hoot from the porch until one afternoon someone finally called, "Hey. Come over here!" Cohen was beckoning her to join him on the porch where he was sitting with Rocky and another fighter, named Al Pennino. Sitting down, Arlyne did a quick study of the two fighters. Rocky was a well-built if not conspicuously handsome man. His nose had been flattened by punches, which made him look a little stupid. Al was slightly younger than Rocky. Thin, handsome, with thick, curly hair, he was a minor talent compared to Graziano, but nothing to be sniffed at since he himself was a contender for the featherweight title. As Arlyne sat on the porch that day trying to catch Rocky's attention with her tough-girl talk, she became aware that it was Al who was making eyes at her. A few weeks later, Arlyne ran into Al by chance. Entering a lingerie shop on Second Avenue, she saw him standing with Rocky outside a fighters' bar called Foxie's. She got to talking to Al, who invited her to visit him where he worked out at Stillman's Gym.

Arlyne did not need a second invitation. With Sophie in tow, she made daily trips to Stillman's to watch Al train. The two vamps would get off the subway near Madison Square Garden and walk up a stairway to the gym to a big room where the men worked out. No matter how good a fighter's concentration was, he turned around and stared when a couple of pretty girls walked into the room. On those occasions Arlyne and Sophie wore the tightest skirts and sweaters they owned. Al or one of his several brothers would come over and offer them chairs, but they usually declined since their skirts were too tight to allow them to sit comfortably.

Arlyne and Al would rendezvous near the gym at a place called the Hotel America. Afterward, they would sometimes take a subway to the Red Hook section of Brooklyn to visit his mother. While Arlyne was flattered that Al thought enough of her to take her home, she was always uncomfortable. The Penninos' walkup was a "real wop house," the air redolent of simmering sauces and full of chatter. Mama Pennino glowered in the background, clearly displeased that her son had brought home a Jewish girl, but silent in deference to his wishes.

After an uncomfortable dinner, which Arlyne and Al usually ate alone, they would go out to sit on his stoop in the twilight. There he would take his guitar and sing lyrics he had composed for her. "Oh, honey baby, say you'll be mine. Don't tease me, baby. Say you'll be mine." It was a silly song, but Arlyne found it so touching that for a while she was convinced she was in love with Al.

Their affair continued through October as Al prepared for his fight with Sandy Saddler. Although conventional wisdom held that a boxer should refrain from amorous pursuits during the critical weeks before a fight, Al was so smitten that he tossed caution to the wind. Arlyne, for her part, was so intoxicated by the attention Al was receiving that she demanded every free moment of his time. She monopolized him up to the very eve of the Saddler fight when she took the initiative of checking them into the Hotel America. Unfortunately, Arlyne had made the mistake of confiding her plans to Sophie, who, perhaps jealous that her friend had bagged a minor celebrity, squealed to the Weisses. That night's interlude was interrupted by a knock on the door. When Al opened it, he found himself face to face with Irving and two of his brothers, who dragged Arlyne, protesting, into a waiting Cadillac. That incident apparently took a toll on Al's concentration. Saddler knocked him out in the fourth round.

The Saddler fight had been Al's best shot, and now Arlyne was worried that she might have done him irreparable damage. Although she did not ordinarily suffer over the pain she inflicted upon others, she was now wracked by guilt. For a time she undertook to "support" Al and his whole family by pilfering money from her father's wallet. She would take the subway to Brooklyn on missions of penance, and, arriving at the house in Red Hook, would hand Al several hundred-dollar bills. These gestures, however, did not make things right between them. The old sweetness was gone, as Al came to regard these reparations as his due. In time, Arlyne began to feel that they were laughing at her, Al, his brothers, Old Lady Pennino. Arlyne had to admit to herself that Al was considerably less attractive now that he was a nobody. He really was—and always had been—just a punk kid. It was time to move on to more ambitious conquests.

Each of the next four summers, the Weisses returned to the Capri Beach Club. During the early weeks of the 1951 season Arlyne waged a campaign for the affection of a young man about five years older than herself. Larry was a rich boy, his father a big bookmaker in New York, and Arlyne had him pegged as a very good catch. Larry's mother had other ideas. She wanted her son to marry a "sweet girl," and Arlyne Weiss, in her estimation, was "too goddamned wild." At his mother's request, Larry backed away.

Arlyne did not wallow long in self-pity before she was distracted by yet another potential conquest, one which promised to be the affair of the summer. Nathaniel Nelson was a friend of her father and Uncle Henry. Though nearly forty-eight, Natie was a Jewish pretty boy. His features were dark and sensual like Bugsy Siegel's. He also reminded her a lot of her father. Natie's thick wavy hair was combed back so that it formed a plateau. Everybody called him Flattop, after a bad guy in the comic strip *Dick Tracy*. He wore a large cat's eye diamond ring, a gold watch and a belt buckle with the insignia "NN" set in diamonds. He was clearly loaded.

Arlyne knew from overhearing conversations between Irving and his brothers that Natie Nelson was a clothing manufacturer from the Garment District and owned a company called Advance Jr. Dress. He was "secret partners" with Jimmy Doyle, who handled his shipping through a company called Elgee Trucking. (Elgee was presumably a coy derivative of Lepke and Gurrah's old logo, "L&G.") Their partnership was formed when Jimmy came to him threatening sabotage if he didn't ship through Elgee. But Natie didn't seem to bear any ill will. There were considerable benefits to that alliance. Besides the fact that his shop was safe, he was in a position to do certain favors for The Boys, and for this he was paid a lot of money. He also enjoyed the privilege of being seen with Jimmy Doyle and by virtue of that association was considered a heavyweight.

Natie was a frequent guest at the Weisses' oceanfront cabana. He never joined Irving Weiss and the other men at cards, however, preferring to drink at the bar accompanied by his sidekick, Heshie. Arlyne kept a lookout for him and would then strut past the bar in her swimsuit hoping he'd notice. He didn't. Once within earshot, she would try her tough-girl talk, thinking he'd be impressed. He wasn't. Some racketeers, she knew, did not like their women hard. It didn't look good, for instance, for a woman to be holding a cigarette or a glass of booze, nor was it good for them to be mouthy or forward. Figuring Natie might fall into this category, Arlyne took to standing at the bar demurely sipping soda, waiting for him to make the first move. He didn't. One rainy afternoon as Natie was preparing to leave the beach club, Arlyne followed him back to the cabana, and when he stepped inside to change clothes, she slipped in after him. Natie turned and smiled as if noticing her for the first time. Without much conversation, they made love on a chaise longue.

Irving Weiss noticed the attraction between his middle-aged friend and his seventeen-year-old daughter and he warned Arlyne to stay away from Natie. Arlyne gave her earnest promises that she would behave. Then she would promptly sneak away from the club to give Natie a blow job in his car. Or she'd pretend to be cycling and spend the afternoon with him in a motel. It was very romantic. That summer she heard Tony Bennett sing "Because of You." Because of you, there's a song in my heart. Arlyne couldn't get it out of her head. It seemed to speak directly of her and Nat Nelson.

As the weeks went by, however, Arlyne became a little worried about him. He began demanding more and more of her time and smothering her with effusive professions of love. He was also talking marriage, which Arlyne found a little odd. Natie had been a bachelor for forty-seven years. If he had resisted marriage that long, why would he now lose his head over a girl almost thirty years his junior? Arlyne found it very pleasant fooling around with him on hot summer days. She enjoyed getting gifts from him—he was extremely generous with money and jewelry. But she was not sure she wanted to get married. Finally, she told him that they had better not see each other for a while.

Arlyne intended to make the decision stick, but this was more difficult than she had imagined. Natie did not pester her to reconcile as she rather thought he would. Instead, he took up with a short redhead at the club. It was a very uncomfortable situation. Arlyne was becoming jealous. Eager to get away, she arranged to spend her eighteenth birthday at the Concord with her grandmother.

When she stepped out of the limo onto the big front lawn, Ida greeted her with arms and tapered nails outstretched. "Dahhhling," she crooned. "Tell Gam all about it." Over dinner, Arlyne poured her heart out to the one person who listened to her uncritically. Ida did not scold Arlyne because Natie was so old or because she had continued to see him behind her father's back. No, Ida Blum was very open-minded in those matters. Instead, she recommended an evening of dancing, which was her remedy for any heartache.

As she was dressing in her grandmother's suite, there was a knock on the door. Arlyne answered it and was shocked to see Natie standing before her. He handed her a gift box containing a diamond bracelet. She spent the next three weeks in the rooms Natie had taken at the hotel. Her grandmother turned a blind eye. Ida had taken an immediate liking to Natie, who also gave her small gifts and included her when he and Arlyne went out to dinner. When Natie confided in Ida that he loved her granddaughter, Ida got Arlyne alone and said, "Marry him!" If she married Natie, Ida argued, she would have everything she wanted, and she wouldn't have to run around wild anymore.

This idyll came to an end during the last week in August when Irving Weiss arrived at the Concord to take his daughter home. Natie had slipped off to New York with Heshie. Neither Arlyne nor her grandmother let Irving know he had been there. Although Natie's earlier promise of marriage technically stood, he had stopped mentioning it. Arlyne suspected that this was because he was getting everything he wanted without the vows. She agreed, nonetheless, to continue seeing him which was easy to do since she had dropped out of school and now had a job as a model at a company called Letty Doyle Dress.

Every morning she took a subway to the Garment District carrying a big hatbox. For most of the day she sat in a smock at the back of the showroom waiting for buyers to come in so that she could model the dresses. The work was not as glamorous as she had hoped, and she was eager for quitting time when she could take a cab to Natie's apartment on West Fifty-fifth Street. Arlyne loved that place. The living room was done in beige and brown with enormous couches and pillars like "something out of the movies." She always felt safe there. If her father were to come looking for her, he would have to buzz up from downstairs. She could always see who was in front of the building through Natie's large picture window. That would have given her time to compose a plausible explanation.

No one came looking. When she arrived home, however, Billie was waiting as usual and mother and daughter would have their customary screaming match. This went on for about five months. During that time, Arlyne became more brazen about appearing in public with Natie. They would sometimes go out to eat with Jimmy Doyle at Patrissy's or Patsy's or the Weiss family's old haunt, the Grotta Azzurra. On Friday nights they would go to La Fontaine, a nightspot favored by Jimmy and Johnny Dio. There Natie would have the opportunity to play the big shot and impress her with his connections.

As time went on, Arlyne couldn't help noticing that Natie was getting too big for his britches. He had always been something of a showoff, but he had had the good sense to keep his mouth shut in front of Jimmy, Johnny and their friends. Now he was bragging openly about favors he was doing "The Boys." He talked about people in the trucking business. About deals that were being made. The particulars went over Arlyne's head, but she could see the effect that Natie's behavior was having on the crowd at La Fontaine. Whenever he approached, Jimmy would turn his back.

One Saturday morning in January, Arlyne and her grandmother had set out in a taxicab for a day of shopping when Arlyne realized that Natie had forgotten to give her any money. She directed the cab to the apartment on Fifty-fifth Street, intending to hit him up for a couple of hundred dollars. Leaving Ida in the cab by the curb, Arlyne took the elevator to the fifth floor. When the door opened, she was taken aback to see Jimmy Doyle standing before her. Their eyes met. Jimmy's betrayed a flash of alarm, but he recovered quickly and slipped into the elevator as Arlyne walked out.

She stood in the hall for a moment trying to make sense of this peculiar encounter. No matter how mad Jimmy was at Natie, he would normally have said "hello" to her. Her sense of uneasiness grew as she looked down the hall and saw that Natie's door was ajar. She walked slowly toward it and called his name. There was no reply. She pushed the door open a little further and recoiled in shock. There was Natie lying lengthwise in the foyer. He was wearing a casual shirt and pants and all his jewelry. Arlyne's eyes rested for a while on his belt insignia, fearful of continuing further. Finally, she looked at his face. There was a bullet hole between his eyes.

For a moment she didn't know whether to cry or scream. All she knew was that she had to get out of there. She raced to the elevator and began pressing the buttons madly. Her grandmother was still downstairs, and as Ida was an eminently recognizable figure, Arlyne, in her panic, imagined that Jimmy might spot her and do to her what he had done to Natie. She was overwhelmed with relief to see Ida waiting in the cab.

"C'mon," Arlyne whispered to her grandmother, "we're getting the hell outta here! I'm taking you home!"

After dropping Ida off at the funeral parlor, Arlyne hurried home, locked her bedroom door behind her and turned on the radio. All afternoon she listened for news of Natie's death. The whole event had such a nightmarish quality that she thought it was possible that she had dreamed or imagined it. Even after she heard Billie and Irving arrive, she did not leave the room. She remained in solitary, her ear to the radio, until she heard the news. A prominent Garment District dress manufacturer had been gunned down in his apartment. In some ways it was comforting to hear the worst confirmed. But that temporary relief was quickly replaced by dread. Jimmy Doyle had seen her. He had looked right into her eyes. And now he would be coming for her.

Arlyne did not tell her parents about her predicament. Ida, who had doubtless put two and two together, had good enough instincts not to inquire further about it. The only person in whom Arlyne confided was the black maid, Sadie, who helped her keep a vigil. Three days passed and there was no word. Arlyne, who had not left the apartment since Natie's death, was going crazy with the suspense. Finally, on the fourth day, Sadie took a call from Jimmy Doyle. She passed Arlyne the receiver.

"Why d'ya want to see me?" she asked.

"You know what I want to see you about," Jimmy replied.

He told her to meet him at the Hotel Forrest in the Theater District and Arlyne agreed. After she hung up she gave the conversation a moment's thought, then made up her mind what she must do. Arlyne went to her closet and took out a pea green satin skirt and a strapless top. As a final touch she added her platina fox stole, her "drop dead" fur, as she called it. As she stood in front of the mirror studying the effect, she said to herself, "Well, if I'm going, I'm going like this." She told Sadie that she was going out and that if the maid didn't hear from her by nightfall she was to call the police.

The taxi got caught in traffic and Arlyne arrived late. She rushed into the lobby to find a scowling Jimmy Doyle. "When you meet me, you be on time," he said. Jimmy then took a key from the desk clerk and she followed him upstairs to a plain little room. Minutes passed. Jimmy said nothing. Arlyne could not read the expression on his face. Made uncomfortable by the silence, she took the initiative and asked point blank, "Jimmy, are you going to kill me?"

Jimmy smiled.

"What for?" he replied. "You're not going to say nuthin' to nobody." .

"That's right," she affirmed. "I'm not going to say nuthin' . . ."

"You know," Jimmy continued, "I always liked you. And now, you're going to do me a favor."

There were no preliminaries. The sex was rough and quick. Afterward, Jimmy paced around the room smoking a cigarette. After Arlyne had dressed, he muttered, "Get the fuck outta here. I'll call ya."

After that Arlyne was on call whenever Jimmy wanted to get laid. At first they met only at night because Jimmy didn't want to risk being seen with her, but as the weeks passed, he became cocky and started taking her out in public to La Fontaine and other haunts she had visited with Natie. Jimmy never once mentioned the murdered man.

The sessions with Jimmy were as instructive as they were disorienting. For Arlyne, sex had always seemed a means of getting control over a man. The control might be only momentary but she found it exhilarating nonetheless. "Control," Arlyne would later say, "is the most important thing in a person's life." The two women she admired most—Ida Blum and Virginia Hill—controlled everything in their orbit. Particularly their men. And in playing Little Miss Sexpot, Arlyne imagined that she, too, was in the catbird seat. Now, it was quite clear that she was a servant and sex was part of her servitude. Her degradation deepened when Jimmy began passing her around to Johnny Dio and Johnny's brother, Frankie.

Arlyne did not tell her parents what she was being forced to endure. She still felt she could manage the situation. That Jimmy would tire of her and release her with no one being the wiser. But Jimmy did not tire. And gradually, the strain took its toll. Arlyne was consumed by the idea she was being punished for all the bad things she had done. She was constantly frightened. She lost her appetite, became listless and had spells of weeping. When her mother asked what was wrong, Arlyne would whimper, "I can't tell you."

Billie conferred with Ida, who offered the opinion that Arlyne's sickness had something to do with Nate Nelson's death. It was decided that she should see a psychiatrist. Over Arlyne's objections, her mother and grandmother made an appointment for her to see Dr. Max Helfand. On the day of their first visit, the three took a cab into Manhattan, and stopping at the address on Central Park West, walked through a pair of swinging gates to Dr. Helfand's apartment, which also served as his office. A uniformed maid admitted them to a living room overfurnished with antiques. Arlyne and her guardians took seats on the brocade couches to wait for him. After a few moments, the doctor appeared.

Max Helfand was a short, balding man who wore spectacles and an expensive suit. He was energetic, charming and quite apparently a bon vivant. It took only a few moments for him to reveal that he was an enthusiastic dancer, which endeared him to Ida. The two carried on a subtle flirtation throughout the course of Arlyne's treatment. Arlyne, herself, did not care for Dr. Helfand. She did not like the way he probed to get at her secrets. It seemed to her that he was as intent as Jimmy Doyle upon robbing her of her control. And so she threw up barriers to him every step of the way. Before each session, she would concoct phony stories to throw him off track.

But Dr. Helfand with his unshakable goodwill began to wear her down. Little by little certain details of her life, which she had resolved to keep from him at all cost, slipped out. She told him about Cousin Solly and Tony Mirra. About Stamey and Sal and all the others. Confessing, however, did not make her feel better. The more honest she became with Dr. Helfand, the more exposed and powerless she felt. There were times that she longed for death and was tempted to jump from her bedroom window. At other times she was terrified of death and was afraid to cross the Queensboro Bridge—the route to Helfand's office—for fear it would collapse.

The one secret Dr. Helfand had failed to extract from her was the truth about Natie Nelson's death. And Arlyne clung to that like a life preserver. At length, Helfand, seeing that he and his patient had reached an impasse, conferred with Billie and sought her permission to give Arlyne an injection of strong sedative. It was necessary, he argued, to get to the root of the patient's trauma.

On the next visit, Dr. Helfand administered the injection and Arlyne let go of her final secret. As she slept off the drug in a little antechamber, Helfand urgently recounted to Billie Arlyne's story of the death of Natie Nelson and her involvement with Jimmy Doyle. That evening Billie conferred with her husband. In the days thereafter, Irving went to see Jimmy and struck a bargain. Arlyne would never tell what she saw. The Weiss family would never go to the police. In exchange Jimmy would leave her alone.

Arlyne was kept in the dark about the details of her father's intervention. All she was told was that she was safe and must now try to get better. Dr. Helfand recommended that Billie take her out of town, to Florida perhaps. There she could sit by the ocean. Salt water, he felt, soothed the nerves. Billie agreed and within the week, she and her daughter set off for Miami.

As Dr. Helfand predicted, the trip had a tonic effect upon Arlyne. She responded not only to the tropical sun, but to the care her mother lavished upon her. It was the first time in her life she could recall having Billie's undivided attention. And the weeks they spent together during Arlyne's convalescence were among the most tranquil they would ever enjoy. At the end of a month, Arlyne returned to New York, tanned, healthy and resolved to turn over a new leaf.

THREE

AN HONEST
WOMAN

Arlyne had not worked out all the details of her reform. The centerpiece of the plan, however, involved giving up men. For a good month or so after the return from Miami, she was virtuous. The memory of her humiliation at the hands of Jimmy Doyle was still fresh in her mind and she gave her old haunts a wide berth. She stayed home nights, deferring to her parents. Gradually, however, virtue began to wear on her nerves. She thrived on the excitement generated by discord. She would rather receive a cuff on the ears than a pat on the head. She missed the rush.

Arlyne renewed her old acquaintances at the Carlton Terrace, partying there until 3:00 A.M. Billie resumed her vigils in the foyer but became more resigned with the knowledge that Arlyne, now eighteen, was slipping beyond her control. The daughter grew wilder, until a trick of fate temporarily clipped her wings in a way her mother never could.

Arlyne had been having a bed affair—she coined the term "bed affair" to indicate a more serious involvement than a roll in the back seat of a Cadillac—with Moishe, the racketeer who was a regular at the Terrace. Arlyne was not serious about Moishe. She found his thin, angular body and pale skin revolting. Moishe, furthermore, was a serious cheater. At the time they met, he had not only a wife but a girlfriend. Arlyne could see cheating on a wife, but a man who double-crossed his girlfriend was beneath contempt. Moishe, however, was high up in the unions and he got her around to places where she wanted to be seen. The arrangement was tolerable until Arlyne missed her period.

For several days she lay around in a kind of stupor. How could it have happened? she wondered. This was no real mystery, since she had never in her six preceding years of sexual activity used birth control. But just the fact of having gone so long without a mishap had left her feeling she led a charmed life. Now she was caught. Mustering her resolve she called Moishe and arranged to meet him at the Terrace. She laid out the problem calmly.

"Moishe," she said. "I'm pregnant."

Moishe did not blink and he replied without emotion, "Do what you gotta do."

He did not believe the child was his and he clearly did not intend to help her.

Arlyne walked out of the Carlton Terrace in disbelief. Taking a cab home, she was relieved to find that Sadie had not yet left for Harlem. She burst into a tearful confession. Arlyne had found that she could count on Sadie at times like these. A little wild in her own right, the housekeeper proved a willing partner in crime and together they decided that they should try to take care of matters without telling Billie, who was vacationing in Florida. Sadie had a few time-tested remedies up her sleeve. First she made a trip to the druggist and came home with a bottle of enormous black tablets that she called "elephant pills." Arlyne didn't ask what they contained. She just swallowed a couple of them with water. She did the same thing the following day and the day after. A week passed and still her period did not materialize.

So Sadie came up with another plan. Taking out a tin of turpentine with a long nozzle, she squeezed three drops into a spoonful of sugar and told Arlyne to swallow it. If she did that for nine days, Sadie promised, the blood would return. Before the treatment was complete, however, Arlyne was seized with violent stomach cramps and fever. Sadie became frightened and allowed as it was time to get help. It was decided that the wisest course was to tell Ida and have her relay the news to Billie, since Billie would not dare yell at her mother. The plan worked admirably. The unflappable Ida issued her usual comforting assurances. "Dahhl-ling, don't worry. I'll take care of everything." She summoned Billie from Florida and the two arranged for a discreet visit to a reputable doctor located through a family friend.

Thanks to her abundant natural vitality, Arlyne recovered from both the turpentine poisoning and the abortion in a matter of days. Her father, whom everyone agreed should be spared the facts, was none the wiser.

The episode frightened Arlyne. But having come through it without any apparent consequences curiously increased her sense of invulnera-bility. She resumed her promiscuous habits, disdaining birth control, convinced against all reason that the odds were with her. But she was ever the unlucky gambler. Over the next four or five years, she was to become pregnant eight more times, each time, she was convinced, with a Jewish racketeer (a pattern that increased her preference for Italians). Each time she came home crying that she had gotten caught, Ida and Billie would mobilize their forces. They found her a doctor in Philadelphia. They found her a doctor in Manhattan. They found her a Cuban doctor who had dirty instruments. Each time, Arlyne limped home to spend several days in bed sipping soup and meditating upon her crimes. During the fever and pain that followed each of those furtive operations, she would vow to be good. But as soon as she felt better, she was back on the circuit.

The last of these illegitimate pregnancies occurred when she was twenty-three. She had been sleeping with one of her father's friends, a car dealer from Manhattan, when she discovered that she was once again "caught." The father, like all the others, denied responsibility. And once again, Arlyne appealed to her mother for help. This time Billie, who by now knew her way around the medical underworld, turned up a physician known as Dr. Sunshine. He performed only abortions and made a fortune at it. Billie made the necessary arrangements and one gloomy winter morning she accompanied her daughter to Dr. Sunshine's office located in a hotel next to the Roxy Theater.

The doctor's waiting room was rather small and soon after arriving Arlyne noticed a man sitting across from her. He was in his late thirties, with wavy hair turning a premature gray. While short, he was a stylish dresser. He was with a woman who appeared to be more than ten years his junior. Out of habit, Arlyne threw him a seductive glance. Soon, he was engaged in animated conversation with her mother.

His name was Norman Brickman. He and his father, he said, owned a fur business in Midtown. As Norman and Billie found they knew people in common, they exchanged phone numbers. Then Arlyne heard her name called by the receptionist, and she put the furrier out of her mind.

A few days later as she was convalescing, Arlyne received a call from Brickman, who asked her if she would like to go out. She found this a little odd in light of the circumstances of their meeting. Norman, she assumed, was involved with the young woman in the waiting room. (Arlyne had to admit that the sight of a man standing by a woman he had knocked up was endearing and certainly without precedent in her own experience.) The woman, Norman explained, was just a "friend." Over dinner he elaborated on his personal life. He was married but unhappily. He and his wife were legally separated. After dinner he took her home early and asked if he could see her again.

Arlyne liked Norman Brickman. He was courteous, attractive and impressively generous. Shortly after they started to date he began giving her furs. A white fox stole. A platina fox coat. Then a mink jacket. What's more, he reminded her in some inexplicable way of her father. There were no physical similarities except for the fact that Norman was approaching middle age. But the presence of an older man was enough to evoke in Arlyne Weiss the yearnings of her youth.

In early January, less than two months after they had met, Brickman proposed marriage. At the time Arlyne did not stop to ask herself why he might be moving so fast. She was preoccupied by her own agenda. Her sister, Barbara, had just announced her engagement to a very good-looking boy from a straight family. This impending union was, of course, everything that Billie and Irving had wanted for their daughters—both of them—and there was a great stir in the Weiss household in anticipation of an August wedding. The prospect of Barbara monopolizing the family's attention for an entire summer galled Arlyne. She reasoned that she might steal her sister's thunder by marrying first. With this invidious intent, she accepted Norman Brickman's proposal.

On hearing the news, Billie was alarmed. Norman, she felt, was inappropriate on several counts. First was the obvious age difference. Beyond that was his complicated personal situation, which included, as far as she could see, both an estranged wife and a once-pregnant girlfriend. Arlyne assured her mother that Norman's divorce was due to become final soon, but that did not put Billie's mind at rest. At the bottom of her uneasiness, however, lay a suspicion that she could not verify: that Norman was hoping to get his hands on Irving's money.

Billie pleaded with her daughter to reconsider, but Arlyne was adamant. In the face of Arlyne's resolve, the family set a date during the first week of April. It was nothing special, just a "hit-and-run" wedding in Greenwich, Connecticut, where there were marriage statutes favorable to the recently divorced. Arlyne wore a beige Chanton suit with mink stole. Bride and groom trudged through a snowstorm to a justice of the peace. After the ceremony, the wedding party gathered at an inn for a champagne breakfast. Everyone got drunk, less out of high spirits than to take the edge off the discomfort. Billie wept continuously. The only one who seemed happy was Ida, whose years as a funeral director had steeled her to rise to any emotion that convention demanded.

Although Irving was dubious of his new son-in-law, he put the best face on things, unveiling his wedding gift to the newlyweds—a pink Cadillac. Amid the farewells of well-wishers, Arlyne and Norman climbed into their new auto and drove off into the blizzard.

They honeymooned at the Concord, Ida's old haunt and a spot that Arlyne had always associated with gaiety. But the mood was sour. Norman drank and sulked. She had never seen him that way. Arlyne attributed it to the uncivil treatment he had received at the hands of her family and redoubled her efforts to raise his spirits. She was determined to be a good wife, although her motives were not altogether pure. On one hand, she had seen enough of the two-timers at the Carlton Terrace to realize that a good marriage was something worth having. Her own parents had a relationship to envy. They were loving and fiercely loyal to each other. Like any other couple, they had gone through some rough times. When Arlyne was in her early teens, she had learned that Irving was having an affair. The phone had rung one evening and a woman asked for Irving. Billie came on the line and delivered the coup de grace. "*I* am still Mrs. Irving Weiss." After that, Billie never let on that anything had happened. At the time Arlyne marveled at the cold-blooded cruelty of a mistress who called a man at home. But she never thought less of her father. It was only, she figured, a momentary lapse in an otherwise exemplary marriage.

But there was a more pressing reason why Arlyne could not fail. If she gave any impression that her marriage was in trouble so soon after the wedding, Barbara's August nuptials would appear all the more glorious. With this in mind, Arlyne threw herself into being Mrs. Norman Brickman. Upon their return from the Catskills, she found an apartment on Manhattan's fashionable Upper East Side. She prevailed upon her mother to loan her Sadie for a couple of days a week, but it was Arlyne herself who oversaw the management of the household. All of her slovenly habits disappeared. Where she used to toss her custom-made clothes in careless piles behind the door, she would not now suffer anything to be out of place. She became a fanatic about cleanliness, getting down on her hands and knees to scrub. Every day she ordered fresh flowers from the neighborhood florists and filled the rooms with huge, aromatic bouquets. Flowers always suggested innocence.

Though Arlyne waited on her husband like a servant, he was not an easy man to please. He was particular about his shirts, which had to be hand-washed and hand-ironed. It took both Sadie and Arlyne working full-time to keep Norman's wardrobe in the condition he demanded. He was equally fussy about his meals. Sadie did most of the cooking but every so often Arlyne, who was no mean cook herself, would make him his favorite dinner of veal cutlets and mashed potatoes. Then she would sit and wait for praise, which never came. Instead, if she tried to make conversation, Norman would raise his hand as if to strike her.

Arlyne could have taken her husband's cruelties in stride had it not been for one peculiarity that threatened to drive her insane. On Friday nights she would normally send Sadie home early and prepare what she hoped would be an intimate dinner for two. Only a few weeks into the marriage, however, Norman started leaving in the middle of dinner. He would rise from the table, his meal half-eaten, to announce that he was going out for a pack of cigarettes. Arlyne would sit alone listening to the clock strike nine, ten, eleven. Midnight. Norman would not return that night nor, indeed, the next day. It was not until Sunday that he would wander back, cigarettes in hand. Without a word of explanation he would walk to the phonograph and put on his favorite song, "Let there be you. Let there be me. Let there be oysters under the sea." Then he would ask for the rest of his dinner.

Arlyne was mesmerized. Either Norman was crazy or he was engaging in this charade to drive her over the edge. Whatever the case she felt she needed independent verification of his bizarre behavior. One Friday afternoon, she asked Sadie if she could stay the weekend. "You're going to see he's going to come back Sunday night like nothing happened. He's trying to do a *Gaslight* on me." Sadie thought it sounded queer, but she stayed in the shadows and bore witness as Norman walked out on Friday night and returned two days later.

Satisfied that she had the forces of reason on her side, Arlyne seized the initiative. She hired a detective to follow her husband. The private eye tracked Norman to a Brooklyn apartment right around the corner from where Arlyne went to the beauty parlor. The apartment belonged to a woman named Chickie. Arlyne studied the photos of her purported rival. Chickie was a real Brooklyn broad with long silvery-white hair. Nothing special to look at except that she was conspicuously pregnant. Arlyne decided it was time to sit her husband down for a little talk.

Norman Brickman professed outrage that his wife had hired a private eye to spy on him. Arlyne, however, was not to be diverted so easily and did not let conversation stray from the subject of his pregnant girlfriend. After much arguing, Norman promised to give the other woman up. But the situation proved not entirely within his control. When she didn't hear from Norman for a few days, Chickie showed up in front of the Brickmans' apartment, in broad daylight, brazenly flaunting her stomach. When she did not get an answer to the doorbell, she stood under the window shouting, "Norrrrman!" Arlyne watched from behind the curtain, fascinated and appalled. Norman sat in his armchair reading, as if nothing was happening.

Finally, Arlyne opened the window and shouted "go away," but Chickie ignored her. She was determined to get at Norman and she would not be deterred by his wife's opinion of her. In short, Chickie had no shame and showed up several times in weeks thereafter, standing under the window, calling Norman's name. When Arlyne asked her husband what he intended to do about this situation, he insisted that he had already ended the affair. Arlyne earnestly wanted to believe this and in her heart she hoped that Chickie's determination would simply burn itself out. She never asked Norman if the baby was his. If he said "yes," he would be acknowledging an obligation that he might feel compelled to honor. Arlyne worried that her husband might be a man of scruples. However, those fears were soon dispelled by the appearance of a new caller.

There had been a temporary pause in Chickie's siege. Still, every ring of the doorbell gave Arlyne a start. One afternoon it rang and she peeked out from behind the curtains. Standing in the doorway was a tall, very attractive blond. Not a cheap blond like Chickie, but a broad with some class. Arlyne opened the door and found herself staring into the forlorn face of another very pregnant woman.

Arlyne invited her in for a cold drink and learned that her name was Frances. She was an Irish girl from the Bronx. She had met Norman two years earlier in the fur district where she was working as a model. Now, she was pregnant and Norman wouldn't return her calls. She wouldn't have imposed, she explained, but she was about to deliver and had no money. Arlyne was moved. Unlike Chickie, who had stormed the gates like a Hun, Frances was simply trying to find some justice. Rather than a rival, she seemed more like a fellow sufferer.

Without telling Norman about this visit, Arlyne gave Frances some money to tide her over and sent her back to the Bronx, calling every few days to inquire about her condition. When Frances went into labor, Arlyne took her to the hospital and, seeing that the girl did not have a decent nightgown, went out and bought her one. On the Feast of St. Jude, the saint of impossible causes, Frances had a son. Arlyne held the baby briefly. Then, giving Frances another substantial sum of money, she walked out of the hospital never to see her again.

Arlyne could not bring herself to discuss Norman's mistresses with her parents. That would be an admission of failure. Instead, she invited her parents to dinner on Friday night with the intent of presenting a tableau of domestic bliss. Throughout the meal she was in a state of nerves, wondering if her husband might not wander out for cigarettes. But in the presence of Irving Weiss, whose wealth and influence he admired, Norman behaved like a model husband. Although the Weisses earnestly wanted to believe in their daughter's marriage, in the hopes that it would settle her down, they were not so easily fooled. Rumors of Norman's wrongdoing had filtered back by way of Sadie. Arlyne, however, refused to discuss her troubles, until events forced her hand.

Soon after their marriage, Arlyne had realized that Norman's business was in trouble. He and his father had fought about something, she wasn't sure what, and for days at a time Norman stayed away from the shop. One afternoon in mid-June the doorbell rang. Norman was lounging around the apartment relaxing in his favorite blue boxer shorts, so Arlyne answered the door. She met two New York City detectives with a warrant for her husband's arrest.

Norman did not seem surprised. He calmly pulled on his pants, gave her instructions for arranging bail and left with the detectives. That night after she had managed to retrieve him, he explained his difficulties. He had taken a bundle of furs on consignment, sold them and pocketed the money. In the process he had ruined his father and now he himself stood to go to prison.

Norman related all this dispassionately. Still, the prospect of her husband behind bars was so disturbing to Arlyne that she threw herself on her father's mercy, begging him to intervene. Accordingly, Irving prevailed upon one of his own friends, a congressman, to take on his son-in-law's case.

Convinced that her husband at last needed her, Arlyne felt closer to him than at any time since their marriage. When he came out on bail, his behavior was exemplary. He was thoughtful, kind, attentive. In early July, she discovered she was pregnant. For once she was happy about it. It was not a sentiment shared by Billie Weiss, who, sensing impending disaster, begged her daughter to get another abortion. But Arlyne would hear none of it. Although she had regarded her previous pregnancies with fear and revulsion, she now felt maternal yearnings. She wanted something of her own. As usual, Arlyne's motives were not unalloyed. Having a baby, Ida Blum's first grandchild no less, would assure her of a position of esteem within the family, one that Barbara could not preempt.

When Arlyne told Norman about the baby he seemed delighted and, concerned for her delicate condition, suggested she should remove herself from his legal troubles as far as possible by spending a few weeks with her grandmother at the Concord. Arlyne agreed, but once there she was restless and worried about her husband. His next hearing was approaching and she felt guilty that he would be facing it alone. It would be a nice surprise, she thought, if she showed up to meet him after he got out of court.

When Arlyne's rented limo pulled up next to their apartment on the Upper East Side, the lights were out. She turned her key in the lock and called Norman's name. There was no reply. The place looked much the same as when she had left it. Norman, unlike many men, was no clutterer. The instant she passed from the living room to the bedroom, however, she could tell something was wrong. Her favorite nightgown, a turquoise peignoir, was thrown across the bed. She would never have tossed it so casually, nor would Sadie, who knew her mistress required her lingerie to be laundered after each wearing, have treated it with such disregard. It had been worn by another woman.

She was enraged with Norman, who, it was now clear, had tricked her into leaving town so he could play house with Chickie. Repenting any sympathy, she waited in the darkened house until she heard him walk in the door. He was alone. When he turned on the light, he saw her and froze. Arlyne had no intention of giving him the opportunity to explain himself. Brandishing the incriminating nightgown, she launched into a tirade against his lechery. Norman struck her. Then he stormed out the door.

All that night, Arlyne nursed her wounds and seethed. By morning, she had decided upon a course of action. She called the assistant district attorney in charge of prosecuting Norman's case and told him she had information to offer concerning her husband's misconduct in the fur business. The prosecutor ushered her into his office, where she recited a litany of Norman's "crimes."

Arlyne had not reckoned with the consequences of her own revenge. Years later as she tried to reconstruct the tumultuous aftermath of her trip to the prosecutor's office, she would recall that Norman was taken back to the city jail. She had ratted out her own husband. She was mortified. She would set things right, she decided. She would recant her statement. But first she would bail her husband out. That, she learned, would be impossible until the next day. All night long she sat outside the Tombs in her pink Cadillac waiting to do penance. In the morning when she finally got in to visit Norman, he told her he never wanted to see her again.

In the days to follow, Norman and the state struck a bargain. He pleaded guilty to charges of grand larceny second degree and was sentenced to a brief term at the state maximum security prison in Ossining.

In every practical sense, Arlyne's marriage was over. She moved from the Upper East Side back to her parents' apartment in Forest Hills. The retreat was humiliating, particularly since it came only two weeks or so before Barbara's wedding, a fairy-tale extravaganza in the Grand Ballroom of the Plaza Hotel. At that point, news of Norman's conviction was not common knowledge and the Weiss family hoped the news would not leak out to spoil Barbara's big day. It would be best, they decided, if Arlyne and Norman would show up together, smiles on their faces, putting rumors of their domestic problems to rest. This was difficult to arrange since Norman, out on bail, was living with Chickie.

Getting him to that wedding was a feat that required the skills of a trained diplomat. Arlyne rose to the occasion. She called him in Brooklyn and explained that in his precarious legal position he had as much to gain as anyone by appearing to be embraced by his influential in-laws. Their continued goodwill, in fact, might prove useful to him come time for parole. Enticed by this appeal to his self-interest, Norman attended the wedding, where he was a shadow, if a *necessary* shadow. He appeared in only one photo, an obscure figure seated in the background.

Arlyne did not see her husband again before he left for Sing Sing.

The full weight of her misery did not settle upon Mrs. Brickman until after the wedding, when the contrast between her circumstances and those of her sister became all too clear. While Barbara and her new husband honeymooned in Europe, Arlyne was back at home with no husband and a baby on the way. Pregnancy, furthermore, was not the glamorous interlude she had imagined. She suffered from morning sickness. She suffered from nerves. Despite the former and to assuage the latter, she ate ravenously, gaining fifty-five pounds. As her depression deepened, her mother thought it might be a good idea for her to go to work for a few hours a day at Chester Motors to keep her mind off her troubles. Irving Weiss had recently lost his secretary and could use the help. This arrangement, however, caused Arlyne still more discomfort. She knew her father despised people who let themselves go. There was never an excess pound on his frame. Billie, too, was always reed-thin.

Now, waddling around under his critical gaze, Arlyne felt she was repulsive to him. She wished for two things only: that the hateful pregnancy would end, and that she could regain her freedom from Norman Brickman.

Given their stormy history, she had believed that Norman was as eager to be out of the marriage as she was. When a decent interval had passed, she wrote him at Sing Sing asking for a divorce. She received a reply that said, in essence, "As long as I'm rotting, you're going to rot." Arlyne's already precarious emotions now swung wildly between depression and hysteria. Weeping, she went to see her father's old friend, the congressman, to ask if he would handle her divorce. He informed her this wouldn't be proper since he already represented Norman in a criminal matter. Noting her distracted behavior, he warned, "Arlyne. You keep acting this way and you're going to have a very nervous child."

Arlyne's disposition did not improve. Her delivery date came and went without a sign of a contraction. The days dragged by. One week. Two weeks. Still no baby. The Weiss family kept a vigil. For hours on end, Arlyne played gin with her sister and new brother-in-law. Occasionally, someone would break the silence with a polite query into her condition. Arlyne felt she might scream.

Seventeen days late, Arlyne went into labor, a painful, arduous labor that lasted more than twenty-four hours. Late in the evening she gave birth to a daughter. When the nurses tried to bring her the baby, Arlyne did not want to see it. For several days after delivery, she suffered from postpartum blues. All of her parents' friends sent bouquets. But Arlyne, who had always loved flowers, was now terrified by the sight of them. They reminded her of the wreaths at her grandmother's funeral parlor. In her troubled state, she reasoned that she had died.

When the black mood passed, she sent for her daughter. Little Leslie Rebecca Brickman was an undeniably beautiful child. Arlyne studied her white skin and plump limbs with pride. Before Leslie's birth, Arlyne had worried that Irving might not accept the baby. Her fears were soon laid to rest. From the moment he saw her, Irving Weiss fell in love with his little granddaughter. He carried her home from the hospital and ensconced her in a nursery where she was tended round the clock by a nurse. The baby was denied nothing. Whenever she cried, her grandfather demanded she be given a bottle. As a result, she grew fat. When she was old enough to sit up, Irving bought her a custom-made baby carriage with a window in the back. It looked like a Cadillac. He took her shopping at Little Royalty, one of the finest baby shops on Queens

Boulevard. By her first birthday, Leslie had a closetful of little velvet dresses with pantaloons.

Leslie returned her grandfather's affection. When she took her first step, it was to him. After that, she toddled after her "Poppy" wherever he went. He would take her with him to Chester Motors, where she played on the leather seats of his vintage Rolls-Royces. When she was older, he would take her to ride ponies in Oyster Bay. As time went on, Irving Weiss began to think of himself as Leslie's father. The thought of her real father returning at some point to claim her was more than he could bear. He offered Arlyne a deal. If she would get a divorce from Brickman, he would take care of Leslie for the rest of her life.

Arlyne called Sing Sing and asked to be put on the list to see Norman Brickman.

"Who are you?" the guard asked.

"I'm his wife," she replied. "Mrs. Brickman."

"What kind of game are you playing, lady," the guard replied. "You've been coming up here to see your husband every week."

Organizing a war party that included both Billie and Ida, Arlyne—dressed in her most provocative ankle-strapped shoes and her furs—set out for Ossining to pay a visit to the warden, who, as it happened, had once bought a car from Irving Weiss. The warden received the delegation politely.

"Now tell me," he asked, "are *you* Mrs. Arlyne Brickman?"

Arlyne showed him her birth certificate and marriage license.

"Well, wait a minute," the warden replied. He called a guard. "Is this the woman who sees Norman Brickman every week?" he asked. "No," replied the guard. "That's a blond."

Arlyne knew she had Norman dead to rights. The false Mrs. Brickman had to be Chickie. It was time, Arlyne felt, that Norman be made to realize the power she had over him. She informed the warden that her husband had been sneaking in a mistress with false identification. The arrow struck its mark. Norman was punished with a transfer to an even less congenial maximum security prison in Auburn. But if he was chastened by his wife's guerrilla tactics, he didn't show it. When she asked, once again, for a divorce, his reply remained: As I rot, you shall rot.

Arlyne had no choice but to wait for her next opportunity. It arose approximately one year later when she went for her weekly appointment at the beauty parlor in Brooklyn. While she was having her hair teased, she heard a woman next to her telling the beautician about her "son-in-law," Norman. Arlyne shot a glance at the speaker. She was a haggard bleached blond. Arlyne did not need to be told that this was Chickie's mother. Norman was apparently out on parole and living in Brooklyn with his old paramour.

When Arlyne relayed the news to her father, Irving Weiss was decisive. They must somehow catch Norman in the act of infidelity. That would provide the evidence Arlyne needed to start divorce proceedings against him. Wasting no time, Irving hired a pair of private eyes who set about planning a "raid" on Chickie's apartment. They would need a family member or a close friend to accompany them for the purpose of establishing that the woman with whom Norman was living was not his wife. This gave the Weisses pause. Irving and Billie were not willing to compromise their dignity by participating in this sordid outing. Arlyne was the logical person to go but to pit her in the same arena with Chickie was asking for a nasty scene. The family decided to send Sadie.

Late one evening Sadie and the detectives left for Brooklyn. When they knocked on the door, one of the private eyes instructed her, she was to look for an opening to slip inside and head for the bedroom. Norman answered the door in his favorite blue boxer shorts. Sadie, seizing her chance, slipped past him to the foyer where she nearly collided with Chickie, who was wearing a short nightgown and dangling a baby over her arm. Sadie fixed Chickie in her gaze. Chickie shouted, "Get out of here!" Having the proof they came for, the party retreated.

The raid put Norman in the mood to negotiate. In the days thereafter, he and Irving met to discuss the matter like gentlemen. The upshot of this summit was a solution satisfactory to both. Norman would grant his wife an uncontested divorce and give up all claim to the baby; in return, Irving Weiss would assume all responsibility for their support. When Arlyne went to court to formalize the dissolution of her marriage, the judge asked her if she didn't want at least one dollar, as this would leave the door open for future support payments. "No," she replied adamantly. "I want to be rid of him."

Norman Brickman made only one more appearance in Arlyne's life. Several weeks after the divorce became final, she was strolling the baby, by now over two years old, down the sidewalk in Forest Hills. She looked up and saw Norman crossing the street in her direction. Her first instinct was panic. She was very happy with the promise her father had made to support Leslie and she was afraid that if he saw her talking to Norman, he would be so angry he would renege.

"What do you want?" she hissed.

"I want to see what my daughter looks like," he replied. He glanced at the child in her stroller, then turned his attention back to Arlyne. He was leaving, he said, for California and she would never see him again. And with that he walked down the block and out of her life. That night, Arlyne went through her photo albums destroying images of Norman. The Weiss family held council and decided it was best to tell Leslie that her father was dead.

FOUR

WISEGUYS

At first, Arlyne had been very pleased with motherhood. When she wheeled the sleeping Leslie down Queens Boulevard, passersby would peer through the rear window of her carriage and coo, "Isn't she sweet? Isn't she gorgeous." Arlyne basked in the reflected glory. At home too, she enjoyed new status. Irving's adoration of his infant granddaughter seemed boundless and, as Madonna in residence, Arlyne could do no wrong.

Arlyne felt a fondness for the baby and enjoyed certain aspects of mothering, such as giving Leslie her bottle after their afternoon stroll. But the attachment was uncertain. Arlyne would realize in later years that she did not understand what it was to bring up a child. "She was beautiful," she recalled, "but why the hell did I have her. I was tied down. I couldn't run."

As months passed, Arlyne's restlessness grew. She had lost the weight she had gained during pregnancy. Her stretch marks disappeared. She missed carousing with Sophie. Billie Weiss was alert enough to perceive that her daughter had to be kept occupied or she would give in to the siren call of the East Side. She talked it over with Irving and they decided that Arlyne should have a job. Accordingly, they appealed to Irving's brother, Henry, whose wife's sister's son was a manager at Saks Fifth Avenue.

Arlyne, though not at all eager to give up her lazy life to punch a timeclock, was nonetheless intrigued by the idea of Saks. She had always shopped on the Lower East Side at boutiques favored by the wives and girlfriends of racketeers. Saks, sitting high on Fifth Avenue, was distant and mystical terrain. The Kennedys shopped there. So, too, did the Supremes. Working as a salesgirl seemed to her an honor, a little like being a lady-in-waiting to royalty.

Arlyne arrived for her first day of work in a Rolls-Royce, in a tight

sheath and wearing one of her mother's diamond bracelets. She soon
learned that this was not what Saks considered style. For the first few
days, she and a handful of aspirants attended a class taught by the floor
manager, Miss Panserell. Miss P. was a spinsterish sort who took one
look at Arlyne and announced firmly that the correct attire for a Saks
girl was a simple skirt and blouse. Miss P. generally did not approve of
the ostentatious newcomer, who, she felt, had come by this exalted
opportunity through family connections. Moreover, Arlyne seemed to
lack the discipline required of a Saks employee. She could not seem to
master the subtleties of filling out a sales slip. She would leave her station
and wander the floor. Under the circumstances, she sold little.

Her lack of success did not bother Arlyne in the least. Her attention
was diverted entirely by the tempting selection of merchandise that
surrounded her. During her unauthorized ramblings, she undertook to
"learn the floors." She was particularly fond of the perfumes and
pocketbooks on the main level. She delighted for a while in the junior
shoes on the seventh floor but then found the "better shoes" on the
second. Discovering new treasures became an obsession. So, too, did
acquiring them. Arlyne went on a spree—buying dresses, coats, shoes,
belts and bags and putting them on her mother's charge card. At the end
of the month, Billie Weiss received a bill for three thousand dollars.

Her parents recognized belatedly that sending Arlyne to work at
Saks was like putting an alcoholic to work in a distillery. They arranged
with a willing Miss Panserell for their daughter's quiet resignation.

Now liberated, Arlyne slipped back into her old ways. With Sophie
at her side, she sought out new habitats for mischief. They hung out for
a while at a club on York Avenue, drinking and partying with models
from the Garment District, then worked their way downtown, accumu-
lating lovers along the way. There were so many, in fact, that years later
when Arlyne tried to reconstruct the inventory, they blended hopelessly
into one another. The only ones that stood out in her memory were
those who had given her extraordinary pain or pleasure, or those who
had a "name."

Arlyne was the first to admit that Babe did not have much of a "name."
In fact, in retrospect, she was hard put to recall anything beyond his
nickname. He belonged to the South Side crew on the Lower East Side.
It was a small-time outfit into the numbers racket and not much more.
Within that insignificant enterprise, Babe himself was just a gofer. But he
was a nice-looking fellow who had impressive family connections. His

sister owned a gambling club on Bradford Street in East New York and his uncle was a big racket guy from Williamsburg. Most important, he offered Arlyne a means to get out of the house.

The tension at home was growing intolerable. Billie started suffering from spells of depression and spent a lot of the time crying. She had stomachaches and muscle spasms in her neck. Irving was constantly summoning Dr. Stein, a handsome young physician who had an office on the same block. He would come to the apartment and give Billie something to knock her out. During those episodes, Irving was very solicitous of his wife, closing the blinds and shutting off every appliance that might disturb her. It seemed to Arlyne that he was almost in mourning. This irritated her because she suspected that her mother's spells were calculated to get his undivided attention. Billie, Arlyne speculated, felt displaced by all the excitement over the baby and was now struggling to regain her position as queen of the roost. The screaming matches between Arlyne and her mother escalated to the point that they were pulling out each other's hair. One winter night, after a nasty brawl, Arlyne called Babe, asking him to come rescue her. When he arrived, she grabbed Leslie and the three of them sped away in his borrowed Pontiac.

Just why she took Leslie that night, Arlyne was never sure. Perhaps it was because she feared her own departure would have no impact. She had stormed out of the house on a number of occasions, only to return, tail between her legs. Taking the baby would sound a note of finality. At any rate, Babe checked them all into a suite at the Forest Hills Inn. After putting Leslie to sleep on a couch, Arlyne went to bed with Babe. She hadn't been there long when there was a knock at the door. A key turned in the lock. A moment later her parents rushed in. Her father, Arlyne assumed, had spread a few bucks around to locate her. Billie bundled up the baby and hurried back out. Irving looked at his daughter and said, "Get dressed."

Babe did not take this intrusion kindly and as he pulled on his socks he muttered, "What kind of shit is this?" As Arlyne dressed, her rage grew. To have her grand departure end in such a humiliating scene was more than she could tolerate. Impulsively, she grabbed the keys to Babe's car and ran out the door. It was snowing hard, but she found the Pontiac parked on the street. She pulled out of the parking spot and stepped on the gas. Almost immediately, she lost control of the car on the slippery surface. The Pontiac careened into a wall beside a railroad trestle.

Arlyne was conscious but stunned. She was aware of a deep, dull pain in her stomach where it had been jammed into the steering wheel. Now she was starting to bleed. The blow had brought on her period. Irving Weiss was the first one to reach his daughter and he helped her gently out of the mangled Pontiac into his own Cadillac. He settled with Babe, then took Arlyne home and put her to bed. Dr. Stein came to examine her and announced she had suffered no serious injuries. Over the next few days, Irving hovered over her.

Just as Arlyne had been nettled by the care her father had lavished on her mother, now Billie was put out by Irving's indulgence toward Arlyne. "No matter what she does, you don't care," she accused him. Billie's nerves took a turn for the worse. As Arlyne grew stronger, her mother grew lackadaisical. She forgot to wash her hair and change her clothes. She took to wearing a housedress, which Irving hated. Even at home, he always liked to see his wife in fashionable attire.

One evening, several weeks after the incident at the Forest Hills Inn, the Weiss family was suffering another uneasy evening at home. Arlyne was in the kitchen with Sadie. Uncle Sidney had dropped by to talk business with Irving. The men were in the living room. Billie seemed disoriented, pacing from the kitchen, to the study, to the foyer, to her bedroom.

At one point, Arlyne went into the living room to share a joke with her father. Billie appeared in the doorway and called her daughter's name. Arlyne ignored her. That was the final straw. Billie lost control. "You think your daughter is so wonderful," she shouted at Irving, "let me tell you about her." The rage and resentment she had held inside for years poured out. Billie told her husband about Arlyne's wiseguy boyfriends, that she had had affairs with his old racket friends, that she had had nine abortions. A look of horror passed over his face. Irving Weiss was a very proud man who never wanted other people to know about his problems. He was disgraced in front of Sidney. He slapped his daughter's face.

Arlyne went to her bedroom and slammed the door, not daring to come out until morning, and by then Billie's condition dominated the household. She was confined to bed with muscle spasms. When Arlyne saw her father at breakfast he said, "Leave your mother alone." Dr. Stein was summoned to give Billie her usual injections, but the treatment had no effect. That evening she was taken to Mount Sinai Hospital in the throes of a nervous breakdown.

Over the next month, everyone went to see her. Irving, Barbara, Ida. All but Arlyne. There was a tacit understanding that it was Arlyne who had made her mother sick. Her presence, it was decided, would be too upsetting. Arlyne passed those weeks in anguish, not so much out of concern for her mother as out of an awareness that she had been cast from grace. Her father would not look at her, let alone talk to her. She felt dirty.

When Billie came home, she was changed. The breakdown had frightened her, and she was determined never to lose control again. She extended her domination more completely over the household. Arlyne knew that her mother had won. There was no point in fighting her openly. But Arlyne decided that her parents had to be punished. She chose the tactics of her revenge.

To that point, her affairs had been conducted in East Side bars and suburban cheaters' clubs. Now she brought the insult home. While Irving was at work and Billie was off playing Mah-Jongg, Arlyne invited men to the apartment. Not just anybody. She was still embarrassed at having sunk to the level of Babe, and was determined to upgrade her choice of men.

Her opportunity arose one evening when she got a call from a fellow named Benny, an automobile dealer and one of her chums from the nightclub circuit. Benny was at the Boulevard Club in Queens, and he wanted her to come on down. "I've got a friend of yours here," he said seductively, "Rocky Graziano."

Arlyne was delighted at the prospect of a rematch with Rocky. When she was fourteen, he was middleweight champion of the world and out of her league. Now he had lost the title and was not such a big deal anymore. Still, some of the old cachet remained and Arlyne was eager to make an impression that Rocky would not soon forget. She did not choose from among her wardrobe of skin-tight sheaths. When she showed up at the Boulevard in a mink coat and heels, she walked to the bar where Benny was sitting with Rocky. "Hiya, boys," she grinned. She threw open the mink to reveal her nude body. There was silence at first. Then nervous laughter. Although Benny and Rocky seemed to enjoy the joke, Arlyne had the uncomfortable feeling that she had gone too far. The two men had intended to take her clubbing in Manhattan. Under the circumstances they chose to remain in more out-of-the-way precincts of Queens. Arlyne had had the foresight to bring along a bra and pair of panties, and having pulled them on in a ladies' restroom, joined Benny and Rocky for dinner and a floor show, her mink wrapped tightly around her.

After they dropped Benny off, Rocky said, "C'mon. You wanna

take a ride?" There was no doubt in her mind why she had been summoned that evening. Rocky wanted to get laid. That expectation had been implicit in the invitation. Having accepted it, she felt she had no choice but to go along. As she allowed herself to be driven to a parking spot near LaGuardia Airport, the prospect of sex was becoming less and less appealing. It was cold. Not wanting to take off the fur coat and climb into the back seat, she took the initiative and gave Rocky a quick blow job.

She saw him only twice more. Once he took her to dinner. Then one afternoon, he visited her at the apartment in Forest Hills, where they had sex in her parents' bedroom, a sumptuous chamber that Billie had outfitted with a French Provincial bed that was reflected in a long gilded mirror. Arlyne felt it was a good deal more impressive than her own room, which she shared with Leslie and which had the air of a girls' dorm. Rocky did not call again.

On his heels came the politician, a state assemblyman who summered in Atlantic Beach. The politician was Italian. In those days, Italians were not welcomed at the clubs, so they sunned instead on their own little strip of beach. Arlyne sometimes strolled by, straining to see notables. One afternoon as she was riding her bike past the assemblyman's house, she skidded on the gravel, cutting her palm. He had come down from the porch to see if she was all right and after that returned her greetings on the beach. That had made her feel important.

Ten years or so after their first meeting, when Arlyne had developed a keener awareness of the desirability of having a politician as a friend, she met the assemblyman again while strolling the sand in Atlantic Beach. This time she invited him for a ride and gave him a blow job. After that they became "very good friends." He would come to visit her at her parents' apartment every Monday around 11:30 A.M. Sadie would take Leslie with her to the laundry room. In exchange for that courtesy, Arlyne's suitor brought the housekeeper a bottle of liquor. When Arlyne suspected her mother was getting wise to the visits, the assemblyman invited her to his own apartment. Arlyne was shocked and more than a little disappointed to find that he lived in a cramped, cluttered bachelor pad, accommodations she considered unbefitting such an influential man. She cringed at the idea of making love in his bed. At the head, hung a crucifix; at the foot, the portrait of a saint. The painting's somber eyes seemed reproachful, so she would turn its face to the wall before taking off her clothes.

The novelty of making it with a politician finally palled. He would never take her anywhere, since he couldn't risk being seen with a woman of her reputation. Arlyne preferred to be out partying, the center of attention. As always, when she needed diversion, she took up with Tony Mirra.

Her relationship with Tony had survived the move to Forest Hills. They saw each other periodically, mostly when she needed a favor from him. She came to think of Tony as her guardian angel, someone she could call at any hour to get her out of a jam. In the circles she ran in, Tony's presence was ubiquitous. When she had been married and smarting under Norman's insults, she would invite Tony to her Upper East Side apartment. Having sex with him made her feel she was evening the score.

Tony had contempt for Norman, whom he clearly considered a small-timer. One night when Arlyne was a few weeks pregnant she and Norman were out nightclubbing at the Copacabana. He was in a foul mood. They had an argument and he raised his fist to her in full view of everyone. Tony, who was standing at the bar, called Norman outside, where he and another hood worked the furrier over. Tony escorted Arlyne home, leaving her battered husband to find his way back in a cab.

After her divorce, she saw Tony more frequently. Although she did not flatter herself that she was Tony's girlfriend, he was good to her and did, on occasion, show a proprietary flash of jealousy. One afternoon she went with him to a barbershop in Queens. He got out of the car and hurried inside carrying a package. Arlyne could only guess what the parcel contained. Hot jewelry. Drugs, perhaps. In those days drugs had a dirty reputation and she tried not to think too much about that. In a little while, Tony walked out in the company of Alphonse Mosca.

Funzie, as he was known on Queens Boulevard, was a down-at-the-heels old man who, in spite of appearances, enjoyed a powerful reputation as a Gambino crew chief. Out of habit, Arlyne lifted her skirt, crossed her legs and addressed him. "I see you all the time when I walk with my girlfriend," she told him. Funzie seemed amused by her audacity and as he bent over to talk to her, Arlyne could see Tony getting hot under the collar. When he got back in the car, he growled, "Keep your mouth shut and act like a lady." They fought and she ended up walking home. Just as she was turning into her street, a car pulled up beside her. It was Funzie. He invited her to go for a drink and to her surprise, didn't ask for sex that afternoon. Instead, he invited her to come to his apartment, just off the Brooklyn-Queens Expressway. Sometimes, he explained, he would leave his car parked out front even when he wasn't there. That was to throw off cops, who often had him under surveillance. When the porch light was on, he said, that meant he was home and she should come on up.

Arlyne began hanging out at Funzie's place, which, though shabby, served as a bustling transfer point for hot jewelry and other contraband. She became Funzie's lover. After that, she spent most of her time at his apartment lounging on the couch, filing her nails, watching a stream of wiseguys come and go, straining to hear the murmured details of deals that were going down around the dining room table. After a while, Funzie was trusting her with little packages wrapped in cord destined for a jeweler named Tillio on the Lower East Side. Tillio was a short, terse little man who did not like her much. Arlyne concluded it was because he considered her a wisemouth Jewish broad. But Tillio and his pals had to put up with her because she was under Funzie's protection.

At the Jewelry Exchange, Arlyne expanded her circle of contacts to include Tillio's partner, Eddy; Tillio's gofer, Jilly, and assorted wiseguys like Butchie, a first-rate bank robber from New England. She hung around listening while they discussed their scores, reveling in the atmosphere of intrigue. She loved being around wiseguys because each day was different. "In mobsterland," Arlyne later explained, "you took things as they came. You couldn't plan your days because you never knew what was going to happen. Nothing was usual, but then again, nothing seemed unusual. It was exciting."

Funzie was a strange man. At the end of the day, he hid his money in the walls and ceilings. He slept with a shotgun by his bed, which Arlyne found only slightly less inhibiting than her assemblyman's crucifix and saint. Funzie was a patient lover, but after a while it was clear to Arlyne that he got his thrills by listening to her describe her affairs with other wiseguys. He did not demand sexual exclusivity. Arlyne's new encounters provided more grist for her storytelling. He encouraged her to make new conquests. Arlyne was happy to oblige.

One rainy winter's evening Arlyne found herself stranded in Manhattan, unable to find a cab back to Forest Hills. Swallowing her pride, she took a subway to Queensboro Plaza. Then, braving the downpour, she started walking home. Hurrying down the sidewalk, she became aware that she was being followed by a black Cadillac. The caddy pulled up beside her and the driver leaned out to say, "Goin' my way?"

Arlyne could tell at first glance that the driver was a wiseguy. He wore the telltale black pants. There was something in his voice when he said "Get in" that clinched it. Wiseguys never said, "Please get in." They gave orders.

His name was Joe. He didn't seem inclined to tell her more about himself. He certainly had money, though, so when he invited her to dinner, she accepted. He took her back to Manhattan to a restaurant at the St. Moritz Hotel on Central Park South. During dinner Arlyne crossed her legs suggestively and began to drop names. Funzie, Rocky Graziano and, of course, Tony Mirra. Joe said he knew Rocky and Tony well. He claimed to have business dealings with Funzie. The more they talked, the more at ease he seemed.

Arlyne grew progressively more uncomfortable. There was something in Joe's manner that irked her. He seemed distracted. Even as he conducted this supposed seduction his attention was elsewhere. He seemed to be hurrying her through dinner so he could get her into bed. While Arlyne had known from the moment she got into Joe's car that they were going to have sex, she still expected a man to go through the formalities of courtship. "With a mobster who had class," she explained later, "you would go out with 'em a few times. You'd give 'em a blow job in the car. Maybe they'd buy you a piece of jewelry. Maybe they'd give you a few hundred-dollar bills. 'Here, go buy yourself a dress.'" This Joe, however, seemed interested only in eating and getting laid.

After dinner he brought her without ceremony to a suite upstairs, one he apparently kept for such occasions. The shabby furnishings reminded her of a cheap motel. Joe went straight to the bedroom and began to undress. Her revulsion increased when she saw that he was wearing unhemmed boxer shorts. Normally, a wiseguy's wife would have taken the trouble to stitch them up. Arlyne felt there was no excuse for such sloppiness. There was, however, no way out. When Joe said, "Get into bed," it was an order.

The sex was mechanical, but mercifully quick. Afterward, lying in bed, Arlyne became aware that Joe hadn't taken off his socks. That disgusted her. She thought a shower might make her feel better but when she emerged, hair wet, no makeup, she felt even worse. Joe, however, was cheerful and hungry for ice cream. He insisted she accompany him to Rumpelmayer's for a sundae.

"You know, I like you," he said, licking his spoon. "I'm gonna call you again."

"How do I tell Funzie who you are?" she asked.

"Tell Funzie you were out with Joe Colombo."

The name meant nothing to her. The next day, however, she went over to see Funzie.

"Hey, Funzie," she said, "who's this Joe Colombo?"

"What are you, crazy?" Funzie looked stunned. "He's a boss. He's a button."

Joe Colombo, Funzie explained, was a lieutenant of the ailing Joe Profaci.

Arlyne would not have gone out with Colombo again if Funzie had not told her he was important. When Joe called, she agreed to meet him on Queens Boulevard. Once again, they ended up at the St. Moritz. This time Joe did not even accord her the consideration of a meal in the dining room. Instead it was room service in the same dismal suite. He didn't wait until the plates were removed before he got undressed. The sex was even worse than before. No little trinket, no hundred-dollar bills. Joe Colombo was cheap. She met him once more a few days later, thinking he might cough up some gifts. But Joe was bent on the same bleak routine; dinner and bed. This time, as he started to undress, she walked out the door leaving him standing there in his foolish boxer shorts.

When Arlyne took a cab back to Funzie's place, he asked as usual, "Was he a good fuck?"

"He's the worst fuck in the world!" she replied. "Not like you, Funzie." As they lay in bed, she reduced Joe Colombo's manhood to rubble as Funzie cackled appreciatively.

Arlyne took advantage of Funzie's indulgence by coming on to several of his friends, including Fred Santaniello. Farby, as he was called, ran with a crew that operated out of Pleasant Avenue at 116th Street. They had the reputation for being a particularly bad bunch, heavily into junk. Every Thursday, Farby would drop by Funzie's apartment with a package. Arlyne assumed it was hot jewelry. Then he would return the following day to pick up money. She could see him and Farby through the kitchen door counting out fifty- and hundred-dollar bills. It was more money than she had ever seen paid for jewelry. In Farby, Arlyne saw a catch.

After flirting with him for a few weeks as he passed in and out of Funzie's place, she called Farby at a phone booth on 117th Street and invited him to her apartment. She fixed him a cup of steaming Cuban coffee and they went to bed. For a wiseguy, Farby was an extremely good lover. She figured it must be because he hung out with Spanish broads. Better still, he was a free spender who seemed to take a liking to little Leslie. He bought the child a black poodle.

The affair with Farby, however, was short-lived, since he was picked up in New Jersey for dealing swag and ended up doing time at the state prison farm. When he went away, Farby put Arlyne on a retainer. In exchange, she visited the prison with containers of pasta from one of his favorite restaurants on Pleasant Avenue. She, Sadie, Leslie and Farby would sit talking in a courtyard. Then, at a prearranged signal, Sadie would take Leslie to the bathroom. Arlyne would pass money to Farby by putting her hand on his crotch. He would put his hand over hers and take the bills.

She had learned long since that doing favors was the surest way into a wiseguy's confidence. She was proud that her industrious errands had placed her in good standing with at least three of New York's major crime families. By carrying the little brown packages for Funzie, she had served the Gambinos. Her missions of mercy for Farby stood her in good stead with the Genoveses. And her association with Tony Mirra had shored up her stock with the Bonannos.

Arlyne hardly suspected the demands that would soon be made of her. On the morning of September 26, 1959, she opened her *New York Times* to discover that Little Augie Pisano and his girlfriend, Janice Drake, had been killed in a gangland hit.

Little Augie, whose real name was Anthony Carfano, was an old-time bootlegger and union racketeer who was reputed to have been a Capone lieutenant as well as an intimate of Lepke and Gurrah. Like so many other East Siders, Little Augie had summered in Atlantic Beach. He was sufficiently aloof to elude Arlyne's youthful wiles. She had, however, met his girlfriend, Janice Drake, when one of Billie's friends, Shirley Segel, had brought her over to the Weiss cabana. Janice was a cute little blond, a former Miss New Jersey, and winner of a more obscure title for having "the most beautiful legs in the United States." Janice was married to a nightclub comedian named Alan Drake, who apparently did not know about his wife's affair with the gangster.

In the fall of 1959, Arlyne saw Tony and Little Augie together occasionally. They were supposedly still friends, although watching them from a distance at bars and clubs, Arlyne perceived that something was wrong. It was nothing you could put your finger on, just a coolness. She saw Tony adopting the same distant, dismissive attitude with Augie that she had seen in Jimmy Doyle before Natie was killed.

These observations assumed a pressing importance as she read the news accounts of September 26. She had seen Janice and Little Augie just the night before. That Friday evening, she and Sophie had taken a cab into the city hoping to meet up with Tony Mirra. Tony had told her that he would be at Marino's, an Italian restaurant on Lexington Avenue. After checking her pink fox coat, Arlyne had scanned the room. There was no sign of Tony, but she was surprised to see Little Augie having dinner with Janice Drake and Shirley Segel. A few moments later, Tony arrived with a man she didn't recognize. Tony went to Little Augie's table, pulled up a chair and talked briefly. Then he joined his companion at the bar. Arlyne waved to him, but he seemed preoccupied. When she persisted, he came over to her table, threw down a few hundred dollars and said, "Get the fuck outta here. I'll catch up with you later." Annoyed, Arlyne and Sophie moved on to a club on York Avenue.

The following morning, Saturday the twenty-sixth, she read that Janice and Little Augie had been found dead in a parked car near LaGuardia Airport. Both had been shot in the neck. Little Augie had taken a second slug to the temple. A witness had supposedly seen two men fleeing the car. (From accounts in succeeding days, Arlyne was even more surprised to learn that Janice had been questioned seven years earlier in the murder of Natie Nelson. She had apparently been nightclubbing with him the night before his demise.)

Arlyne had to steady herself as she took in the news. Why would anyone kill harmless little Janice Drake? She had an uneasy feeling about Tony. When she tried to reach him at his familiar haunts, it seemed he had dropped out of sight. That afternoon, or the day thereafter, Tony called her at home. He sounded tense. Would she come to a hotel on Lexington Avenue and make sure she wasn't being followed?

With her toddler tucked under one arm, Arlyne took a cab to the hotel, took the elevator as far as it would go and walked up a short flight of steps to the top floor. Tony's room was small, with only a bed, a dresser and a mirror. This seemed odd, since Tony liked nice things. He was sitting on the bed and for the first time he looked frightened. She asked him what he was doing here. He said he was hiding.

"What are you hiding from?" Arlyne asked.

"Do you read the papers?"

"Yeah, I read the papers."

"Well, you know who killed Little Augie?"

"*You?*" She was incredulous.

Tony was silent, but his silence said a lot.

"And Janice. Why Janice?" she asked finally.

"She was in the wrong place at the wrong time," he replied blankly. Arlyne scrutinized his expression but could not detect any remorse.

He had called her, he said, because he needed her to run two urgent errands. She agreed without hesitation. He gave her two items. One was a small package and the other was an envelope, which felt as if it contained a piece of paper. She left, hailed a cab and rode to Central Park West where she left the parcel, as instructed, at the bar of a steakhouse. After that, she visited a wiseguy named Jimmy to whom she handed the envelope, saying it was from "our friend." Her errands completed, Arlyne discovered she had money left over from the wad of bills that Tony had given her. She swung down by Tillio's to see Jilly and his crew.

It was late afternoon by the time a cab dropped her off at her parents' apartment in Forest Hills. No sooner had she gotten into the house and begun undressing Leslie than the doorbell rang. Billie answered it. Two plainclothes detectives were asking to see "Mrs. Brickman."

Rattled, at first Arlyne thought it must have something to do with Norman. "He's in prison," she replied. But the cops took her down to the station house for questioning, and it soon became clear that they were not interested in her jailbird husband. Somewhere during the day's travels—possibly as early as the hotel, possibly after the drop at the steakhouse—she had picked up a tail. In the process the police had figured out that all the guys she had seen that afternoon were associates of Tony's. Cursing herself for her carelessness, she struggled to remain cool.

One of the detectives, who was sitting with his back to a large window, was holding a list of names with small photos beside them.

"Do you know Tony Mirra?"

He proceeded down the list of Tony's friends.

Arlyne knew them all.

Finally, the detective stopped, looked her in the eye and asked, "Who do you think you are, Virginia Hill?"

The remark was not intended to flatter. But she was enormously pleased. Even after the cops had despaired of learning anything useful and released her into the custody of her father and Uncle Henry, Arlyne was still savoring the accolade.

For the next few days Arlyne endured her parents' silent disapproval. They knew she was involved in something serious, but as she seemed to have escaped with few apparent consequences, they did not inquire too pointedly. She waited for a call from Tony, but none came. Word of her brush with the police had apparently gotten back to him and he couldn't risk further contact. She read in the paper a couple of days later that the district attorney had found and questioned Tony Mirra, then, apparently lacking evidence, dropped pursuit.

Little Augie's murder and its aftermath left Arlyne feeling more connected, more important, than she had ever felt in her life. She was a keeper of secrets. She knew who had killed Natie Nelson, but even her psychiatrist hadn't been able to drag it out of her without the assistance of drugs. Now, Janice and Little Augie were dead. Her revulsion at their murder was overshadowed by a sense of purpose. She was the guardian of Tony Mirra's safety. Knowing too much was always dangerous, of course. Tony might reconsider the wisdom of that offhand confession he made at the hotel and move to silence her permanently. But, naively perhaps, Arlyne trusted Tony's affection for her. If she kept her mouth shut, she could only increase her own reputation as "good people."

To that point in her career, Arlyne's attempts to invent herself in the image of Virginia Hill had been hit and miss. Now, in her mid-twenties, however, her career took a more purposeful turn as she fell under the sway of Ethel Becher.

Arlyne met Ethel at Albert and Carter's, an uptown beauty salon that catered to prostitutes and showgirls. Ethel, in fact, looked like a showgirl. She was tall, slender and always tanned. She wore her reddish-brown hair cropped short like Eydie Gormé. Ethel was not young. She had been married twice, once to a Garment District magnate by whom she had two children, and again to a hotelier named Becher. Both marriages ended in divorce. Arlyne suspected that Ethel was in her late thirties. But she waged a fierce and successful struggle against advancing years. At the first sign of a wrinkle, she had it plumped out with silicone. Her skin appeared flawless. Ethel, too, had great style, always smoking her cigarette in a holder because it was "effective." She appeared to have an endless supply of clothes, and rarely wore the same dress or suit twice. She was always decked out in jewels, which, she took pains to let one know, had been exacted as homage. This, Arlyne Brickman decided, was a woman who could teach her something.

It did not take many minutes of idle chatter for them to realize they both knew, and had slept with, Tony Mirra. Curiously, this knowledge did not arouse their competitive impulses. Rather, it produced an almost instant camaraderie, such as that between two strangers who find they belong to the same exclusive club. No one, after all, went out with Tony expecting him to be faithful.

Ethel took no pains to conceal the fact that she was a call girl. Quite the opposite, she took pride in her clientele, which consisted of influential mobsters, lawyers and judges. She was strictly outcall and every day she set out on a round of appointments that took her to uptown penthouses, judges' chambers and the backs of cruising limos. Ethel, in Arlyne's words, was a "traveling sex machine." No matter how wide a swathe she cut during the day, however, Ethel was always back at her apartment by 5:30 P.M. to be with her children. Then, after putting them to bed, she readied herself for an evening of entertaining. Shortly after making Ethel's acquaintance, Arlyne began receiving invitations to these soirees.

Ethel lived in a smart, doormanned building on Central Park West. Whenever Arlyne went up there, she dressed to the teeth because she never knew who she might meet. Frank Costello, Bugsy Siegel's right-hand man, lived in the same building and often dropped by. So too did Aniello Dellacroce, a rising star in the Gambino family. Neil was a friend and steady patron of Ethel's. And, of course, there was Tony Mirra, who had weathered Little Augie's murder and now seemed miraculously beyond suspicion. The gatherings were animated by the anticipation that one of the hostess's Vegas friends would turn up. Ethel boasted that Frank Sinatra and Shecky Greene were among her crowd. Arlyne always kept her eyes peeled for Frank or Shecky, but they never showed.

There were always plenty of women at Ethel's parties, and it didn't take Arlyne long to realize that her new friend was running an escort service. This aspect of Ethel's diversified enterprises, Arlyne noted with admiration, was carried off with consummate discretion. Prostitution, to Ethel's way of thinking, was just a set of favors exchanged among "friends." Her girls were all "friends." Several, in fact, were the current or former wives of Ethel's wiseguy lovers. If one of these women needed money, she would contact Ethel, who would fix her up with a date.

Arlyne needed little persuasion to allow herself to be drawn into this incestuous family. For years she had been dispensing blow jobs and other favors with the expectation of receiving some expensive trinket. Sometimes, as with Joe Colombo, a guy took advantage of the ambiguity and stiffed her. That never happened when Ethel served as go-between. Not that there was a strict schedule of payment. The amount was subject to courteous negotiation, as befitted a transaction among old cronies. If, for instance, a guy gave you five hundred-dollar bills, telling you to go out and buy yourself a dress—a standard courtesy—you gave Ethel whatever you felt like giving her. If two hundred dollars was too little, she simply froze you out. Ethel created the incentive to be generous.

Often payment came in the form of commodities, usually swag. If a guy offered you a case of liquor, you made sure that he gave you another for Ethel. No means of payment was beneath consideration. Ethel set Arlyne up with numerous purveyors of commodities. One of those dates was in the refrigeration business. Afterward, she and Ethel split the take—one hundred packs of frozen vegetables. Arlyne never considered Ethel her madam, but—as the credo demanded—her friend. In time, she came to think of her as her "best friend." True, Ethel used people and was not above throwing you to the wolves if she could gain advantage by it. Out of her earshot, Ethel's girls gossiped that she was "a fucking whore" who couldn't resist making a play for other women's husbands. Arlyne knew all of this was true. But there was also a more generous side to Ethel's nature. She was happy to impart the wisdom she had gathered from her years in the trenches. And Arlyne was an eager pupil.

On some afternoons, if Ethel had gotten back early from her rounds, she would invite Arlyne over to the apartment for a cocktail, but more particularly to drink in her hard-won wisdom. First and foremost, Ethel told her, a woman must decide what impression she wants to leave, then direct her every thought and movement toward creating it. In pursuit of that goal, there were a few rules she must observe.

Rule number one. Think big. Live in the most luxurious apartment. Wear the most expensive clothes. "To make money," Ethel counseled, "you have to live like you have it." *Rule two* (a corollary to the first). Spend *other* people's money. *Rule three.* Never appear to have a care in the world. Men do not want to see that a woman has troubles. If you can control yourself, you can control others. *Rule four.* "Be a lady in public but a whore in bed." Ethel may have been the biggest whore going, Arlyne would later say of her friend, but she was always a lady.

Some of Ethel's advice was more down to earth. When you go out with a guy, she admonished, you must never allow him to see you undress. That reveals too many secrets about padding and girdling. It went without saying that he was not allowed to see you in rollers or without makeup. This ruled out casual moments, but then a woman bent upon recreating herself as a legend could not afford to be casual.

Arlyne tried her best to implement Ethel's precepts. Creating an impression of wealth was no problem, since she had been plying her Virginia Hill routine since the age of fifteen. Using other people's money was second nature. Self-control was a taller order. Arlyne admired cool women. The image of Ida Blum, serene and unflappable, dispensing food and good cheer on the Sabbath still occupied a hallowed spot in her imagination. In recent years, Ida had gone into decline. The exodus of Lower East Side Jews to the suburbs had caused her to close the funeral parlor. When the Clinton Street Boys defected to the Carlton Terrace, Ida found herself a queen without a kingdom. She developed hardening of the arteries. Nowadays, she was often confused and frightened. Arlyne preferred to remember her as she had been, always in command of herself and others.

In some ways, Ethel reminded her of her grandmother. That was odd, since Ida was as good-hearted as Ethel was treacherous. Still, both had the relentless poise of self-made aristocrats. As she thought back on it, Ida too had been intent upon creating an impression. A plain woman, she was nonetheless able to convey the impression of enormous grace and beauty. She, too, had been playing a role—that of an East Side racketeer's moll. She never slipped out of character. As warm and giving as she was, she never let her feelings show. Ida, like Ethel, could get what she wanted from men. Which, after all, was the name of the game.

Try as she might, however, Arlyne could not seem to govern her own emotions. Not a thought popped into her mind but she had to share it with a lover. Every heartache—indeed, every irritation—was an invitation to hysteria, which she indulged with abandon. There were times, of course, when weeping paid off. Certain men, like her father, were either moved or cowed into submission by these spectacles. God knows Billie had kept Irving, and the entire Weiss household, in line for years with her tantrums. More often, however, Arlyne would end up squandering her capital. Whatever gains she made with her sexual prowess were dissipated by needless outbursts. She could be "a whore in bed," but attempts to be "a lady in public" found her struggling against her basic nature. As a result, her hold over men was tenuous.

With Walter Perlmutter, Arlyne hoped things might be different.

Arlyne met Walter at the bar of the Pan American Hotel. Walter was no button, just a roly-poly Jewish businessman who thought he was a gangster. He was into "structural anodyzing," a process for fortifying aluminum. That brought him into contact with the construction trades, hence onto the fringe of racketeering. He often allowed his offices to be used as a meeting place for politicians who had shady business with union officials.

While Walter was not the catch of the century, he nonetheless flashed a big bankroll. Ethel, with whom Arlyne conferred on her new lover's merits, opined he seemed cheap, but Arlyne thought he could be managed. And during the first weeks of their courtship, Arlyne found this to be so. Walter was so courteous, so sweet, there seemed nothing he wouldn't do for her. Every afternoon they would meet for lunch on Queens Boulevard and he would confide his woes. His marriage was hell, he said. Soon, he began talking about leaving his wife to live with her.

Arlyne certainly had no intention of becoming the next Mrs. Walter Perlmutter. Still, the idea of a man leaving his wife for her was flattering. Inasmuch as living with Walter would bring him and his checkbook more firmly under her control, she encouraged his fantasies. It was decided that she should go to Miami and take an apartment where he would join her later.

"What about Leslie?" Arlyne asked. "Can I take Leslie down?" Leslie was now going on six.

"No, not now," Walter replied.

On the morning she was to leave, Arlyne accompanied Leslie and Sadie to the playground. She bent down and kissed the little girl. Mommy, she said, was going shopping. Then she hailed a cab to the airport.

Arlyne knew her way around Miami and since Walter had given her loads of money, settling in was no problem. She rented a suite with an ocean view at the Seacoast Towers. While luxurious, it was not particularly homey, so she added a few personal touches like an electric organ, thinking that Leslie might enjoy it when she arrived. Then she waited for Walter. Weeks passed. Money kept arriving, but no Walter.

Arlyne placed repeated phone calls, asking, "When are you coming down? When are we going to get married?" Walter always had an excuse. Finally, Arlyne's anxiety gave way to hysteria and she threatened to come home. This gave her lover pause. Walter, Arlyne figured, was nervous because she had been making threats to call his wife. To assure that she did not return inopportunely, he sent one of his lackeys down—ostensibly to protect her, but in actuality to see that she stayed put.

Georgie Futterman, also known as Georgie Muscles, was an improbable bodyguard. A slight man with spectacles and false teeth, his appearance hardly inspired fear. Nonetheless, he was an ex-con and former officer in the International Jewelry Worker's Union, and he was rumored to be a tough guy. To Arlyne's dismay, Georgie moved right into the apartment with her, in fact, into the bedroom she had been decorating for Leslie. After that, she couldn't go anywhere without

Georgie on her heels. Every morning, they had breakfast together, then he followed her to the beach, where she had taken a cabana. They sunbathed together. If she went into the water, he was not far behind. Only once did he let her temporarily slip out of his sights. That was when he lost his dentures in the surf. In the evening she would put on one of the many beautiful gowns that Walter had bought her and go downstairs for dinner—with Georgie as escort. Arlyne began feeling that she was a kept broad in a mink-lined prison.

Relief, if not freedom, came unexpectedly with a call from Ethel Becher. Four or five months had passed since Arlyne had last seen Ethel. At that point, she was still reigning supreme over the soirees on Central Park West. Now, Arlyne learned, her ambitious friend was in Miami, encamped next door at the Fontainebleau. Ethel seemed to be a little down on her luck. She claimed she had come to Florida with Shecky Greene, to whom she was "almost engaged." But then Shecky, she said, had called the whole thing off. Now she was badly in need of a place to stay and a friend to talk to.

Without hesitation, Arlyne insisted that Ethel be her guest. She did not even bother asking permission from Walter, who kept sending money and never asked for an accounting. She was fairly certain that Georgie would also welcome the diversion of Ethel's presence, and she was right. From the moment Ethel had her bags sent over from the Fontainebleau, life became one long-running party. Ethel seemed to have recovered quickly from her broken heart and now ordered cases of champagne and gourmet goods, turning the apartment into an open house for racketeers. Some were old friends Georgie had bumped into on the beach. Others were new acquaintances, like the big-time bookmakers who did business out of the Eden Roc. Word reached as far north as New England that Arlyne had a new headquarters. Tillio's friend Butchie, who was on the lam after pulling a bank job in Boston, showed up on Arlyne's doorstep looking for a hideout. When Walter caught wind of the house party he was inadvertently sponsoring, he flew to Miami on weekends to join in the fun.

Everyone, it seemed, was having a good time but Arlyne. She missed her privacy. During the day, the apartment was crowded with wiseguys hanging around drinking and playing the organ. At night, they would simply crash unceremoniously on one of the many couches in the living room. In the morning Arlyne had to pick her way through the jumble of bodies like Scarlett O'Hara at the Siege of Atlanta.

Ethel, too, was getting on her nerves. Far from being the grateful,

humble guest, she had moved in and taken over, running up astronom-
ical telephone, food and liquor bills. True, Ethel moved discreetly to the
Fontainebleau every time Walter came down for a visit—at Walter's
expense, of course—but she always came back and showed no signs of
leaving. Of course, there was no way to throw her out unless you wanted
her as an enemy. And the thought of Ethel as an enemy was too awful
to contemplate.

But there was another concern that was weighing even more heavily
upon Arlyne's mind. And that was Leslie. It had been nearly six months
now since she had seen her daughter. She had never been the most
attentive of mothers, but neither had she endured a separation this long.
Now she found herself missing the little girl. Throughout her stay in
Miami, she had made frequent calls home asking to talk to Leslie, but
Billie, who was furious at her desertion, would not bring the child to the
phone. On those occasions Arlyne would have to endure harangues
about what an unfit mother she was. At one point Billie threatened to
charge her with abandonment and see that Barbara got custody of
Leslie.

The merest suggestion that Barbara should get something that was
hers startled Arlyne into action. She was still on a leash, but Georgie was
enjoying himself so thoroughly that he had relaxed his guard of late. She
was now allowed to go shopping by herself and this new liberty
presented an opportunity for escape. The only problem was cash. While
Walter had placed no limits on her spending, Georgie controlled the
purse strings, taking care that she never carried more than pin money.
The question of how to finance her getaway perplexed her until one day
she found herself confiding her troubles to a woman she had met on the
beach. When she finished the stranger advised, "Don't you know that
you can charge your plane fare to your cabana?"

Ethel's partying had recently gotten them thrown out of the
Seacoast Towers and the whole crew had moved into the Fontainebleau,
where they had also taken a cabana, but Arlyne had not realized all of
the privileges renters enjoyed. With this new information, she immediately put a plan into action. She made a plane reservation to New York.
That afternoon she joined Georgie at the cabana, going for a swim as if
nothing were happening. Then, without even bothering to shower the
salt off, she told George she was going to the hairdresser and went back
to the hotel. Hailing a cab she set off for the airport and caught a plane.
It was still early evening when her cab arrived in Forest Hills. She had no
money, so her mother had to pay the driver. Arlyne humbled herself. She
begged for forgiveness, secure in the knowledge that no matter how

awful she had been, Irving Weiss would never turn his own daughter out on the street.

The fact of the matter was, Arlyne was far less worried about how her family might receive her than about how Walter would respond to the news of her return. Arlyne couldn't quite imagine Walter ordering a hit, but he did command muscle. In her more anxious moments she had visions of being dipped in a vat of chemicals. She had taken pains to obscure the fact of her departure as long as possible, going so far as to leave all of her beautiful clothes hanging in the closet of the Towers. What woman, after all, would skip town leaving behind a million-dollar wardrobe? When a week passed with no word, she became anxious and called Walter.

He did not threaten. He did not beg. All he said was that she was no fucking good and to lose herself.

This got Arlyne good and mad. Once again she called her old friend Ethel, who, ousted from her sinecure in Miami, was now back in New York. "Ethel, what am I going to do?" she whimpered. "I have to live at home. I have no money." Ethel graciously imparted another of her trade secrets.

"Tell him you're pregnant," she said.

This made no sense at all to Arlyne, who recalled all the times when she actually *had* been pregnant and no guy would lift a finger to help her. But Ethel insisted. "You gotta be daring. If he doesn't listen to you, you call the house and you tell the wife that you want to see her. They never let you get to see their wives."

Emboldened, Arlyne called Walter back. "I need ten thousand dollars," she informed him. (Ethel had told her to start high because he would certainly try to negotiate it down.) "If you don't see me," she threatened, "I'm calling your wife and telling her I'm pregnant."

"You don't have the guts," Walter said, and hung up.

That night Arlyne called the Perlmutter residence and spoke to Walter's son. "Have him call Arlyne Brickman," she said.

"Who's Arlyne?" the boy asked.

"Your father will know," she replied.

The following day, Walter coughed up eight thousand dollars. Arlyne split the score with Ethel right down the middle and the two of them flew to Las Vegas to celebrate.

That was how it was hanging around wiseguys. One moment you feared for your life; the next you were rolling in cash and compliments. The danger, to Arlyne's way of thinking, was not a drawback but one of the attractions of the life. She loved the rush. The prospect of violence gave her a sensation approximating sexual pleasure. Her concentration, normally shattered by petty anxieties, was never keener than when she found herself having to talk herself out of a tense situation. In her heart of hearts, she never believed that anything would really happen to her. It was all a game really. The game lasted for over ten years. During that time Arlyne went from one wiseguy to the next. Tony Mirra, Funzie, Farby. They were all her friends. She felt sure that they loved her—not only as a broad but as a pal—and if the game turned nasty they would come to her rescue.

In later years, Arlyne would recall an unmistakable pattern of evil leading up to the event that would shatter her illusion of invulnerability. The first of these omens came when she took up with Joey Russo, a wiseguy she had met through Farby. Fatty, or Joe Fats, as he was called, was grotesquely overweight. He perspired heavily and he had boils between his thighs so Arlyne had to take a good stiff belt of booze before giving him a blow job. Joey, however, had an uncle who was a button. And underneath his ugly exterior, he was a gentle, generous man who gave her many gifts. One evening, when he picked her up to take her to the fights, he handed her a tiny jeweler's box. She opened it to find a large pearl ring. It was all she could do to hide her dismay. Well-intentioned as he was, Joe apparently did not realize that pearls brought bad luck. This oversight was strange, since wiseguys were usually fanatically superstitious. But since refusing to accept a gift was also bad luck, Arlyne took the ring without protest. Then when she got home, she flushed it down the toilet. It was too late, however, for the damage was already done. Within weeks, Joey had a heart attack. It did not kill him, but he disappeared from the scene. She had lost her meal ticket.

As a satisfactory boyfriend is not replaced on a moment's notice, Arlyne had to settle for a temporary stand-in, Tillio's gofer, Jilly. There was no danger of falling seriously for Jilly. He was a "short, fat piece of shit" without the soul or generosity of Joey Russo. Furthermore, he was the lowliest mob guy she had dated since Babe. But Jilly did have access to Tillio's possessions, including his Cadillac and yacht. Wherever they went, they went in style.

Arlyne trusted Jilly. And that was why when he phoned her one night asking if she wanted to go out, she was surprised to feel a stirring of uneasiness. She didn't know why. The invitation was straightforward enough. They would go to a club called the Wagon Wheel Bar. Jilly wanted her to meet the owner, a friend of his named Sally Burns. Arlyne had never met Sally, whose real name was Salvatore Graniello, but she knew he, too, was a friend of Funzie's and, therefore, "good people."

Arlyne nevertheless felt inexplicably uncomfortable at the prospect of going out that night and told Jilly she was tired. But he would not let the matter drop. "No. No. No," he said. "You've gotta come with me. I'm going to pick you up. We're going to have a good time." Finally, she relented.

The Wagon Wheel was located just off Times Square, near the Peppermint Lounge, which had become one of the most popular discos in town. There was also dancing at Sally Burns's place but the joint was not nearly as classy. It had a bar, a few tables and far in the back a cramped little dance floor where a few couples bobbed to the tinny throb of a jukebox. Arlyne took an instant dislike to the place and wanted to go home, but Jilly took her by the waist and steered her to a table in the corner where Sally Burns was holding court.

Sally was yet another unwholesomely fat Italian, with wavy gray hair and sullen demeanor. Upon being introduced to him, Arlyne's gaze fell promptly upon his chest to an enormous diamond-studded cross. For some reason, she could not take her eyes off of it. Sally grunted a salutation, but did not seem overly taken with her. As the evening wore on, however, and he downed more drinks, he became increasingly attentive. Arlyne, who had also drunk too much, found herself flirting with him. Sally asked her to dance and she agreed. While undulating in his sweaty grasp, she heard him say, "Let's go downstairs. I want to show you some things."

Arlyne followed Sally down a stairway that led to a subterranean office. Hopping up on the desk and crossing her legs, she waited to see what he meant to show her. As she was tipsy, she could not make complete sense of events that followed, but she was aware that someone named Joey had walked in unannounced and was now arguing with Sally over a collection. Sally left to make a phone call and she found herself flirting with the newcomer. Then Sally returned with another guy named Tony and the three men started arguing loudly. The disagreement seemed to concern money, but Arlyne wasn't sure.

She was confused by what was going on. For a moment it seemed as though Sally was going to hit Tony. She wondered where the hell Jilly was, for he must surely be missing her by now. Then, she became aware that all three men were staring at her. Suddenly, Tony grabbed her and demanded a blow job. Arlyne was stunned. Never in her experience with wiseguys had one taken her by force. Despite the fact that she slept around a lot, she had felt sure that the guys respected her. Now this nobody, Tony, had her arm in a lock.

"Sally?" she asked imploringly.

Tony and Sally just looked at each other. Then Tony pushed her backward onto the desk and started to pull down her underwear. Sally said "No!" In her terror, Arlyne interpreted this as a reprieve and she tried to run for the stairway. But Sally himself caught her and knocked her to the floor. After that, all she could remember were fragments from a dreadful dream. Sally on top of her, his pants rolled down to his knees, his enormous penis ramming upward into her insides. She was screaming and he hit her again to quiet her. All through the frantic struggle, she could see Sally's huge diamond cross swinging just above her eyes.

After Sally dismounted, Joey and Tony each took their turn. When they finished, all three buckled their pants, laughing as if it had all been a good joke. Then they went upstairs, leaving her half-conscious and bleeding on the cellar floor. Arlyne was not sure how long she lay there. But she recalled wondering where Jilly was. He must have seen the three men come upstairs without her. He must be missing her by now. When the door finally opened, it was not Jilly but a young waiter who had come down to get a bottle of liquor.

"What happened?" he asked with concern.

She could not tell from the tone of his voice if he was surprised to see her there, or if someone had sent him to pick up the pieces. She did not answer him.

"Forget it," he said. "Come on. I'll help you."

The fellow went upstairs and brought down her blue fox stole, which he wrapped around her torn bodice. Then he led her, nose bleeding, lip swollen, past the table where Sally and Jilly and several women Arlyne had never seen before were sitting around laughing. As she crept by, she heard one of them hiss "Jew cunt."

The waiter hailed a cab, but once inside Arlyne realized she hadn't any money. Going home now would mean asking her parents to pay for the ride. That would rule out the possibility of sneaking into her room unnoticed. No, she decided. She would have to find someplace private where she could clean up and collect herself. She directed the cabbie to Funzie's place.

When Funzie opened the door and saw her, he exclaimed, "My God!" Paying the cabdriver, he sat her down on the couch, made her some strong coffee and listened as she poured out her incoherent tale. His expression was full of pity. For all his kinky habits, Funzie did not like to see a woman roughed up. "Get washed," he said. "Don't worry about it. I'll take care of everything for you."

When the cab dropped her off in Forest Hills, Arlyne turned her key in the door very silently and began tiptoeing down the long hallway. But she was out of luck. Her mother was waiting in the foyer. The lights were off as usual so as not to disturb Irving, and Billie did not see the cuts and bruises. She grabbed her daughter by the arm. Arlyne broke free and escaped into the bedroom with Billie screaming, "You dirty tramp. God should punish you." The noise, fortunately, did not wake Leslie, and Arlyne crept into the bed next to her daughter's and pulled the covers over her head.

The following morning, Arlyne listened to make sure Leslie, Irving and Billie had all left before she crawled out of bed. When Sadie arrived, Arlyne told her what had happened. They agreed that the rape must be kept from Billie at all costs. They would explain the bruises by saying that Arlyne had fallen down the stairs. Arlyne tried to douche, but her insides were too raw. So Sadie drew a bath and Arlyne soaked for a couple of hours. Her body felt so dirty, she didn't think it would ever be clean. After drying herself with four or five towels, she turned around and took another bath. This went on for days, until Billie, noticing the piles of wet bathtowels in the hamper, scolded, "You must be pregnant again!"

That was Arlyne's deepest fear. She tried to suppress the memory of the rape. Every time a detail floated to the surface, she would push it back down again. In doing so, she was able to deny for short periods that the event had occurred. If she were to become pregnant, however, it would be irrefutable proof of the attack. And it would be doubly hard to hide from her parents. When her period came a few days later, she nearly cried with relief.

There remained the question of her honor. Her shock and bewilderment had long since turned to anger. Who was this Sally Burns to treat Arlyne Brickman—friend of Tony Mirra, Funzie Mosca, and Joey Russo—like she was a piece of shit? Sally had to be made to pay. Funzie, after all, had promised that he would "take care of everything." Before she left his house, the night of the rape, he had told her he would call someone in Brooklyn who was supposedly very good friends with Sally. He wasn't specific about what might happen, but Arlyne took considerable satisfaction in fantasizing about Sally having his extremities lopped off and his carcass sunk in cement.

She waited for the call from Funzie. Days passed and it did not come. It infuriated Arlyne to think that the redemption of her honor was not the highest priority on his list. It was time, she decided, to haul out the big gun. She called Tony Mirra. Tony said he was sorry and promised that he would get to the bottom of this. But more days passed, and he too never got back.

The reality of her situation slowly began to dawn on her. It was a realization that struck her with less force but more revulsion than the rape. She was now well into her thirties. For the past twenty years that she had been playing at mob girl, she had worked tirelessly to make herself indispensable to mobsters. She had been operating under the illusion that they respected her, even loved her. That she was one of the boys. If push came to shove, they would protect her. Now she knew that was untrue. She was an outsider. A broad. She was simply, as Sally Burns had so vividly demonstrated, a piece of shit. Her powerful friends were less concerned with protecting her than they were with protecting one another.

No one would ever vindicate her honor. That realization marked the passing of innocence.

FIVE

TOMMY

The horror of the rape lingered for many months. Arlyne dreaded falling asleep for fear the detestable Sally Burns would appear in her dreams, smothering her, invading her with his fat tentacles. Even waking, there would be no relief. When she closed her eyes she could see the diamond cross swinging in slow motion above her head.

Worst of all, Arlyne could not shake the feelings of filth. The showers and baths continued unabated. Whenever she entered a room she sprayed it with perfume. As always, having cut flowers around made her feel cleaner. Now her yearning for them became uncontrollable. Every day the florist arrived at the doorstep delivering fresh blooms, but these succeeded only in giving her room an air of false cheer.

Arlyne's eccentricities grew more pronounced until her mother insisted upon knowing the truth. On learning of the awful events at the Wagon Wheel, however, Billie showed neither compassion nor anger. She simply withdrew into her own suffering. For comfort, Arlyne turned to her grandmother, longing to hear the familiar, "Don't worry, Dahllllling." But the old woman was growing weaker with each passing day. There were still glimpses of majesty in her bearing. Sometimes when she was taken for her afternoon walks, she would wear her ermine coat—one of the few valuables that had not been sold to pay her mounting medical bills. On those occasions, she was the Ida of old, making her way down East Broadway with an imperial gait. More often, however, she was bewildered and confused, invoking the names of Frankie and her dead children as though she expected them for Friday dinner.

That spring Ida suffered a heart attack and had to be taken to the hospital. The family, frightened by the suddenness of the seizure, was relieved to see her condition stabilize. For the next week they took shifts, assuring that someone was with her every minute during visiting hours.

Ida seemed to be getting better. On the morning of May 5, 1969, she asked that a manicurist be brought to the hospital so that she could have her nails done. Arlyne and her mother joked between themselves that there could be no better sign that Grandmother was on the mend and they each went home to get a little rest. That afternoon Ida Blum suffered another attack and passed away in her sleep.

The shock Arlyne felt was compounded by guilt that her grandmother had died alone. And when the pain and guilt passed, there came a sense of abandonment. If Arlyne's life had made sense to anyone, it was her grandmother. If anyone could appreciate the subtle artistry in a mob girl's mischief, it was Ida Blum. To her mother she might have been "no goddamned good," but to Ida she had been an adventuress in the most flattering sense of the word, a woman of daring who sneered at convention and grabbed for herself the best things of life. Now Arlyne felt she was standing on an empty stage, the audience gone home.

For months after Ida's death, Arlyne drifted aimlessly. Her longing for her grandmother grew so intense that she sometimes imagined she heard Ida clip-clopping in her high heels on the pavement below the window. When she ran to look, there was no one there. She took only occasional pleasure in mothering and would drop her responsibilities at a moment's notice if the opportunity for a good time presented itself. Promiscuity, however, had become less a vocation than a dreary habit. The qualities that had given wiseguys their allure now seemed ludicrous. For all of their macho posturing, racketeers were, by and large, vain and childish, unable to deny themselves anything. For all their talk about loving women, they certainly didn't like them much. The girlfriend—the fabled mob girl who had seemed in Arlyne's youth to rule the world—was infinitely expendable.

There were still men—many men—but no big love affairs. Now, at the age of thirty-seven, her looks fading and illusions shattered, Arlyne was desperate for anyone, anything, which might give her life form. It was during the winter of 1970 that fate—in its perversity—placed Arlyne Brickman on a collision course with an obsession.

That bitter February, Arlyne had been doing a bit of modeling in the Garment District. One evening after work she stopped into the Messina Restaurant in Queens. The owner, Paulie—known to his friends as "Paulie Messina"—was an old chum. Several years earlier, she had slept with Paulie. It was just a nice friendly roll, which had curiously cemented their friendship. Since then, he had adopted a protective attitude toward her, sizing up her boyfriends and giving her advice in matters of love.

On the night in question, Paulie kissed her on both cheeks and gave her a table by the window. No sooner had she sat down than she noticed a man having dinner with friends several yards away. He was in his early thirties, she guessed, but it was hard to tell because his hair was turning prematurely gray. There was something about his face, either the crooked nose or the boyish expression, that she found attractive.

Arlyne was not at her best that evening. A couple of days earlier she had cut her foot on a broken glass. As vanity would not allow her to wear a slipper, she had been hobbling around on high heels. The pain had taken its toll on her looks and under ordinary circumstances, she would have forgone all attempts at seduction. But the stranger, dark and reminiscent of Joe Adonis, Tony Mirra and all of the other "dangerous" men to whom she had found herself attracted over the years, stirred her involuntarily to combat. Drawing herself up into vamp posture, she walked slowly across the restaurant past the stranger's table. He was reading a racing sheet and did not look up. She walked past again. And again. And again. Until she heard one of his companions say, "Tommy, that broad likes you." Tommy looked up briefly and grunted, "Boy, she looks like she's had it."

Stung by the remark, Arlyne withdrew to her own table to pout. The next day she returned to the Messina and drawing Paulie aside asked him about the stranger at his table the night before.

"Oh," Paulie said, "you mean Tommy Luca?"

"Yeah, yeah," Arlyne replied. "When does he come around? Where does he hang out? What does he do?"

Luca, Paulie told her, had been a sometime bodyguard for a couple of brothers who were capos in the Genovese Family. Unhappily, Smitty and Frankie had been gunned down in a restaurant, presumably while Tommy was off-duty. Nowadays, Paulie said, Luca hung out with a guy who owned racehorses and had an automobile business in Queens.

For the next week Arlyne called the showroom asking for Luca. He was never there. Or if he was there, he could not be bothered. Her pursuit, however, was relentless, and at length he came to the phone and grunted an unintelligible greeting.

"Now listen, Tom," she began familiarly. "This is the broad that you saw the other night. You know, the one you said has 'had it.' I would like to see you. I've heard you do scores, and I've got a score for you."

Tommy told her to meet him at the dealership that afternoon. When she arrived, she found Luca, sitting in the office. He motioned to her to sit down. She began to tell him about "a very rich woman," a friend of her mother's she said, who kept jewelry at her house on Long Island. The woman spent a lot of time in Florida, and the gems were ripe for the taking. Luca didn't say much, but she could tell that he was interested. That afternoon, Tommy called the Messina, and Paulie assured him that Arlyne was "good people." Then he called and agreed to meet her at the apartment in Forest Hills. Conveniently, Arlyne's parents were in Florida, allowing her to leave the impression that the apartment, with its antiques and opulent furnishings, was hers. Tommy was visibly impressed. He sprawled on the couch, making himself at home.

Tommy had brought a couple of friends and the three men listened silently as Arlyne proceeded to describe the proposed robbery. The rich woman's home, she explained, was on the water, which meant it could be approached from either car or boat. In an upstairs closet, they would find a seven-carat diamond and emerald ring. The woman also had a large collection of silver dollars, which shouldn't be overlooked. The beauty of this job, Arlyne concluded, was that the proposed victim had no security system and spent most of the year in Florida.

In retelling this story years later, Arlyne would insist that she had no intention of going through with the robbery. She would claim that she had concocted the story of the rich woman—a character based loosely upon one of her mother's friends—solely to catch Luca's interest. Having succeeded in that, however, she was left with the awkward problem of how to disengage herself from the game. Luca and his friends had bought the story and had returned to the apartment several times to discuss strategy. Arlyne realized that she had possibly gotten herself in over her head, and hastened to apply the brakes.

It was during Luca's third or fourth visit that she hit him with the bad news. The rich woman, she said, had come back from Florida unexpectedly. What was worse, she had heart trouble. Arlyne knew that a piece of information like this would scare off a smart thief. For one thing, you could be prosecuted for murder or manslaughter if someone died while you were robbing them. Even if you escaped clean, goods taken from a house of death were considered bad luck and one might have a hard time finding a fence to handle them.

Luca grumbled but the heist was called off.

Arlyne figured she had seen the last of him, but in the weeks thereafter, he kept coming around. Wiseguys, she knew, were always looking for new hangouts. Most of them spent little time with their wives and families. (Tommy, she heard from Paulie Messina, had a wife and three children in Howard Beach.) They needed a secure, comfortable outpost from which to plot their mischief. Often this was one of several all-male "social clubs." Sometimes it was the business establishment of a friend, like the automobile showroom. (In the old days Chester Motors had served this same purpose.) Many times, however, it was the apartment of a girlfriend.

Tommy had made it clear that he was taken not with Arlyne, but with her apartment. No matter how provocatively she crossed her legs, he showed not the slightest interest. Arlyne figured this was because he had heard about all the guys she had been with and considered her soiled goods. The snub became more galling when he took up with one of her girlfriends. "Mary the Spic," as she was called, was a very pretty beauty operator who did Arlyne's hair. Since Arlyne had had a falling out with Sophie and needed someone to pal around with, she and Mary would go nightclubbing together. The beautician dropped by the apartment one night and caught Tommy's eye.

Arlyne fumed quietly, but chose to bide her time. Mary, she knew, tended to throw herself headlong at men, and Arlyne had Luca pegged as the skittish sort. Given enough rope, Mary would hang herself. The three of them settled into a strange camaraderie. Sometimes they hung out at Arlyne's, other times they all went over to Mary's place, a high-rise apartment in Forest Hills. As the spring wore on, the threesome spent more and more time at Mary's hatching schemes around the dining room table while Mary's aging mother served them fried bananas and chicken with rice.

Tommy's and Mary's affair continued into the early summer. Arlyne stayed alert, looking for a moment to insert the knife. By the end of June she was encouraged to see Mary demanding more of Tommy's time and complaining when he went home to his family. That, Arlyne knew, meant she was on the verge of doing something foolish. Sure enough, Mary drew her aside one day and asked her if she had Tommy's home number. A true friend would have told Mary that invading the sanctity of a wiseguy's domestic life is one of the most reckless moves a mistress can make. But Arlyne—intent upon watching the little beautician destroy herself—finagled the number out of Paulie Messina and passed it along.

After that, the affair unraveled quickly. Mary came to Arlyne weeping that she had called Tommy's house and he had shouted at her.

Luca had promised Mary that he would take her to Florida and she was living for that trip, but now, he was looking for a way to worm out of it. On the morning that they were scheduled to leave, he showed up at Arlyne's apartment and announced he was hiding from Mary.

This was the opportunity Arlyne had been waiting for. Excusing herself for a moment she slipped into her bedroom and returned wearing a royal-blue peignoir with an ostrich plume boa. The suddenness of the transformation apparently caught Luca off-guard and he allowed himself to be led to the bedroom to see what exotic sexual experience his seductress had in store. But things went badly. The phone kept ringing. It was Mary trying to find Tommy. Arlyne insisted she hadn't seen him. Anxious, nonetheless, that Mary might show up at the apartment, Luca tried to pull his clothes on. Arlyne lured him back to bed. Under the circumstances, she herself was having difficulty getting aroused. After minutes of futile grappling, a disgusted Luca got up to leave. Arlyne was suddenly seized with panic at the thought of losing him.

In fact, there was nothing so special about Tommy. For all of his boyish charm, he wasn't as good-looking as Tony Mirra. He wasn't a button like Farby or Funzie. In fact, Tommy wasn't even a made guy, but a low-level street hustler who had happened to enjoy a brief stint as a bodyguard. But Arlyne, in the sad confusion of approaching middle age, had chosen him as her savior and now all of her irrational hopes were pinned on getting him to stay. Stopping him at the bedroom door, she told him to sit on the couch and unzip his pants. Then she did what she did best. A blow job, Arlyne discovered, left Luca as content as if he had been laid. After that, he visited the apartment nearly every day to receive her ministrations. And when Billie and Irving finally returned from Florida, Arlyne and Tommy took to meeting at a cheap motel near LaGuardia Airport.

By now it was late summer and the Weisses were again spending their days at the beach club. Arlyne had approached her parents cautiously with the news that she had a new boyfriend—a disclosure met with baleful skepticism. Arlyne, nonetheless, got them to allow her to bring Tommy by the club the following weekend. On the appointed day, she drove to Atlantic Beach with her parents. Billie took her place at the canasta table. Irving and his friends sat down to play gin rummy. Arlyne donned her swimsuit and settled into a canvas tanning chair to wait for Tommy.

When he finally made his entrance onto the patio, conversation ceased, heads turned, and there was a mortified silence. He was wearing powder-blue pants and shirt, an awful white jacket and black shoes. Worse yet, his cheap nylon socks were bunched up around his ankles. When Arlyne had first seen Tommy at Paulie Messina's, he had struck her as dashing. Now, looking at him through the eyes of her parents and their peers, he looked like a lowlife.

Arlyne introduced Tommy to her mother, who greeted him icily. When he turned away she muttered, "Trouble again." Irving Weiss, dapper as usual in his summer whites, would not even look up from the gin table to acknowledge his daughter's new friend. To spare Tommy further humiliation, Arlyne whispered, "Let's get outta here. I want to go eat."

When her own embarrassment subsided, Arlyne was determined to do something about Luca. First, she took him to a stylist, who blew out his wavy hair for a smoother look. Then she steered him to a shop on Broadway where she bought him an ensemble of yellow pants and black sports jacket, a maroon jacket and matching tie, and of course a white suit, much like her father's.

Arlyne took Tommy to the club again decked out in his new clothes. This time he enjoyed more success. Irving Weiss still would not acknowledge him, but he managed to get a gin game going with one of Irving's friends, a shirt manufacturer from whom he won several thousand dollars. Tommy, apparently sensing there was money to be made in this crowd, comported himself like a gentleman. Still, there was one aspect of his behavior that continued to puzzle Arlyne. While the other men sat around in the blistering sun dressed in beach clothes, Tommy insisted upon wearing his suit. Whenever she urged him to change into trunks, he looked uncomfortable and changed the subject. Finally, it dawned upon Arlyne that the reason he insisted upon remaining dressed was that he didn't want to have to explain a suntanned torso to his wife.

Luca's marriage was a subject Arlyne dared not broach. She had seen poor Mary destroy herself by invading Tommy's private life and she was not about to make the same mistake. Since childhood, she had held conflicting opinions about "the other woman." During the period when her father's mistress called the house, she had felt that it was cruel to taunt a man's wife that way. In her own heyday, however, she chose men without regard to their marital status. It seemed to her that the mistress often got the better treatment. Now the specter of Tommy's wife, ensconced like a madonna out in Howard Beach, tormented her. She would not rest until she got a look at her rival.

Her opportunity arose a little over a year after she first met Luca when Paulie Messina happened to mention that Tommy would be bringing his family to the restaurant for Easter dinner. Without telling Tom of her intentions, Arlyne showed up at Messina's that Sunday and parked herself in a spot that offered a superior vantage point from which to observe the Family Luca. She saw the back of Tommy's blow-dried, salt-and-pepper thatch bobbing above the family gathering. If he noticed her, he did not betray any surprise. His two little girls, about three and four, were chasing each other around the restaurant. In the midst of their scurrying, they stopped dead still in front of Arlyne and smiled. Mrs. Luca was sitting across from her husband holding their infant son. Arlyne was pleased to see that she was fat with oily skin and dark features. A real wop wife.

Still, it bothered her to be held at arm's length, knowing there were recesses of Tommy's private life that she could not penetrate. Occasionally, he would tell her about his children, who were being brought up as proper Catholics. Even the worst gangster, she reflected, wants his child to be wonderful.

She knew little of Luca's parents except that they were second-generation immigrants who were eager for their children to succeed. Tom's father, as far as Arlyne could tell, had been an honest man and achieved some status as chauffeur to Nicky Hilton. Tom's older brother was also a straight shooter and worked as a super at an apartment building on Park Avenue. The youngest brother, Nino, was the object of Tommy's adoration.

At the age of sixteen, Nino Luca had apprenticed himself to the celebrated horsetrainer Johnny Campo. By his mid-twenties, he was a trainer in his own right. To Tommy, Nino was a kid who came from nothing and made it big. Tommy looked up to him as if he were the older of the two, and was constantly striving to find the big score that might place him on equal footing with his brother.

For months, Arlyne only heard stories about Nino. Although she and Tommy often went to Aqueduct to bet on the horses, he never offered to introduce her to his brother. When Arlyne finally insisted, Tommy reluctantly took her to the stables where Nino was stretched out on a bale of hay. He looked so young, Arlyne mistook him for a stableboy. Tommy introduced her as a "very rich woman" with whom he was doing some deals. But Nino, who was fond of Tommy's wife and children, saw right through that ruse and gave her the cold shoulder.

The snub from Nino only served to remind Arlyne of her precarious position. She would have a firmer claim on Tommy's affections, she felt, if she could get him to move in with her. But then that meant breaking ties with her family and, by doing so, forfeiting Irving Weiss's continuing support of Leslie, who was now entering her teens. It would be possible, of course, to go live with Tommy and leave Leslie with her grandparents. It meant giving up some of her natural prerogatives. Her territory, she felt, might be usurped by her sister.

Billie Weiss still talked openly of her hopes that Barbara would adopt Leslie. Indeed, as a child, Leslie had spent much of every summer with her aunt's family on Long Island in an environment far more strict than the one she enjoyed at home. Aunt Barbara and her husband treated her like one of their own children, whom they kept in check with affectionate discipline. Her aunt Barbara, Leslie would later observe, had a "real family," where rooms were inspected and stars given out for good behavior. Every good child had to drink milk before he got any soda. After a month at Barbara's, Leslie was dying to get home where standards were more relaxed.

Billie and Irving Weiss were not strict disciplinarians. Arlyne could not control herself, let alone her daughter. That task fell to Sadie, who every once in a while would take out a belt and give Leslie a good strapping. But the girl seemed impervious to pain. She was, in fact, a rather cold, indifferent child. Even in the face of her grandfather's effusive affection, she would never give him hugs. Her longing seemed reserved for her mother, who, of course, came and went like a cat. Even as a very little girl, she would suffer visibly throughout Arlyne's prolonged absences, complaining of stomachaches and headaches and crying for her mother. Nothing Arlyne could do seemed to alienate that affection.

Leslie had always felt protective toward her mother. Whenever Arlyne came home late and Billie launched into her customary invective, vilifying her as a "tramp" and a "whore," the little girl listened from behind her bedroom door and came to hate her grandmother. At one point she grew so sullen toward her grandparents that they took her to a psychiatrist, who, after one session, announced that the child had too many people trying to be her parents. Leslie wanted to be with her mother, and only her mother. So when Arlyne raised the subject of going to live with Tommy, Leslie had had enough of this prolonged strife and was ready to flee.

But breaking free was not so simple. Tommy was noncommittal. Arlyne herself was ambivalent about leaving the relative security of her parents' home. No matter how many times she had stormed out in the past, she had always come skulking back. The apartment in Forest Hills had the draw of a magnet for her. Arlyne might have vacillated indefinitely had she and her mother not had another knock-down brawl. In the heat of the screaming and wounded feelings, Arlyne grabbed Leslie by the arm and dragged her out the door into a cab.

Arlyne had no idea where she was going, only that she ought to find Tommy. She directed the driver to Brooklyn, where she knew Luca sometimes hung out in the late afternoon. Sure enough, she spotted him coming toward her on Atlantic Avenue. Confronted by the pair of refugees, Luca had no choice but to take them in tow. That evening, he checked them into a sleazy motel on Conduit Boulevard. Arlyne complained that the surroundings were a bad influence on Leslie and Tommy finally bowed to pressure, renting his two charges an apartment in a Queens high rise called the Executive House.

Arlyne would always say that this was the point at which her life with Tom Luca began in earnest. Except for the few hours a night he slept in Howard Beach, he spent nearly all of his time with her. Arlyne flattered herself they were now living together. Tommy, however, seemed less concerned with the domestic aspects of the arrangement than with the obvious professional advantages. He now had a permanent hangout from which to conduct business.

Tommy had not confided much about what he did day to day. Arlyne knew that for a while he supposedly worked for his brother-in-law, who painted lines on highways. But Tommy imagined himself cut out for better things. Early in their relationship, he had told her that he did "ribbons." At first she thought he sold hair ribbons, but as time went on she realized that he meant the numbers business. Tommy had a partner, a slick young hood named Vito. There was also a silent partner whose name was never mentioned. All Arlyne knew was that he was a button in the Genovese Family.

Every evening about five, Vito would arrive at the Executive House for dinner at the head of a motley entourage. There was Joey, an elderly man who, Arlyne figured, must have been very dapper at one time, but who now worked as a gofer for Tommy and Vito. There was Pete the Plumber, so named because he owned a plumbing business. Pete smelled so bad that she had to spray disinfectant around the place when he left. In addition to Joey and Pete, there was a goony fellow known as "Frankie Garbage" because he had once worked on a garbage truck.

On these occasions Arlyne had one function and one function only. To cook. Every day she would go to the Italian section of Queens to shop for sausage, pasta, fresh bread and cartons of tomatoes. She learned how to make tomato paste from scratch. Every meal had a salad, pasta and a main course such as Tommy's favorite roast pork with potatoes. For this she never received so much as a passing thanks or compliment. Throughout dinner the men ignored her while they discussed business. Arlyne found this extremely rude, since the Jewish racketeers she knew never talked shop at the table. As she cleared the dishes—of course, no one ever lifted a finger to help—the men settled in to do the numbers work.

Numbers, also called "policy," had flourished since the late 1800s in New York and its environs, particularly among blacks, and then Hispanics, in Harlem. It was an illegal lottery run by small-time racketeers and later crime syndicates. In the early days, bettors "purchased" a number, hoping it would match a winning number to be drawn later in the day, usually from a bowl in someone's attic or garage. The disadvantage of this system was that the drawings could easily be rigged. To convince bettors that their games were on the level, operators later turned to independently published numbers, such as the last three digits of the Federal Reserve Clearing House report. The policy racket finally linked its fortunes to the track, pegging the winning number to published horseracing results from Belmont, Aqueduct and even Saratoga Springs. This was called "the handle."

Tommy and Vito ran a variation on the handle, which was called "single action." Under this system, results were called in directly from the track, so that bettors could find out their number the same day they bet instead of having to wait for the morning paper. Luca had six black runners who made the rounds of bars, candy stores and tenements in Brooklyn's Bedford-Stuyvesant taking bets. Each customer would wager between one and five dollars on his favorite number. The runner would write the bettor's name, number and amount bet on a slip of paper, give the bettor a copy, and keep the original. The first race started at one o'clock and the runners had until 1:30 P.M. to get their betting slips and cash to collection points manned by controllers. No later than 2:00 P.M., Tommy and Vito along with Joe, Pete and Frankie picked up the envelopes containing the goods from the controllers and brought them back to the Executive House. There they would spread the envelopes out on the table and, after 5:00 P.M. when the three-digit number had been tallied, would start searching the work for "hits."

The ribbon, Arlyne was interested to learn, was nothing more than a seven-column steno pad. In the far lefthand corner, Tommy wrote down the names of the controllers, and beneath each, their respective runners. In the next column, he recorded the hits racked up by each runner's bettors. In the third column, he posted the critical number, the payout. A quick subtraction of the payout from the amount received told the crew if they had made or lost money.

Arlyne observed all this from a distance. Then gradually she began insinuating herself into the action. At first, she performed lowly tasks like opening the envelopes. Then as Tommy, Vito and the others grudgingly made room for her at the table, she began reading off the totals. Every now and then, when Tommy was tired, he would let her do the ribbons, a job that was exacting and tedious but one that she attacked with her usual manic enthusiasm. It finally occurred to Tommy and the crew that Arlyne could be put to some use.

Luca condescended to show Arlyne a few tricks of the trade. When they went to the track, he would point out the man, usually a black or Hispanic, who stood outside the track with a pair of binoculars watching the post board, figuring up the single-action number. She observed as the sentinel turned and signaled with his fingers to a battery of relay men who then sprang for telephone booths and sent the number speeding along the wires throughout the boroughs.

Late in the evening, after the hits were tallied, Arlyne would throw on her wrap and accompany Tommy and Vito to the "nigger neighborhoods" of Bedford-Stuyvesant to disperse the winnings. The streets were desolate. Packs of dogs leaped out of darkened alleys snarling like wolves. As they waited in the car for these attacks to subside, Tommy explained that there were black dogs and white dogs, just like there were niggers and white people. The black dogs could tell a white person by the smell and it made them crazy. Vito had no stomach for house calls, so he waited in the car while Tommy and Arlyne took the cash to the controllers. Their apartments almost always were shabby. For Arlyne Brickman, who kept her own surroundings immaculate, it took all the resolve she could muster to enter these rooms, sit on the couch and accept a drink if it was offered, in a filthy glass.

There was only one stop that she enjoyed and that was at the home of Sweet Rose, a controller who worked out of Bedford-Stuyvesant. Rose was a beautiful black woman in her mid-twenties who also danced at a nightclub that had a colored review. She moonlighted at numbers and was one of the best controllers Tommy had.

Sweet Rose was not a mob girl in the strictest sense. She did business with racketeers but did not sleep with them. Arlyne admired her for her beauty, savvy and self-respect. Rose radiated self-respect. You could see it in her grooming and the way she kept her belongings. Although the outside of her building looked, in Arlyne's words, like a "little nigger house," her apartment was like another world. The downstairs, where she received business associates, was spare and immaculate. The upstairs, where she entertained her friends—and Arlyne was pleased to be counted among these—was furnished richly but tastefully in green-and-white brocade. Her bathroom was outfitted in white marble with gold fixtures. What impressed Arlyne most, however, was Rose's relationship with her three children. Although they had grown up in the middle of the ghetto, they always spoke to their mother with respect and gave her no problems. Arlyne found this remarkable, since Leslie was beginning to get a smart mouth.

Arlyne would call Rose several times a day. Sometimes it was because she was lonely or having troubles with Tommy. Rose was full of comfort and common sense. More often, however, Arlyne would prevail upon her for psychic guidance. Rose was a spiritualist who rendered a very special service to her bettor-clients. If they told her their dreams, she would consult her "dream book" and come up with a number. Dreams of blood, for instance, signified "846." Death indicated "769." Numbers derived in this fashion were thought to be supernaturally inspired and especially lucky.

Arlyne found Rose's dream book irresistible. Superstitious by nature, she was forever susceptible to omens, and dreams opened a whole new vista of prognostication. If, for example, she had dreamed that her grandmother had visited her, holding out her hands with their long vermilion nails in a gesture of welcome, she would promptly call Rose the next morning with the details. Rose warned her never to take the hand of a dead person because you could be yanked into the underworld. Then she would tell her to play 769, which was the number of death.

Tommy did not discourage these preternatural dabblings. As a gambler, he was also governed by superstition. When he was winning, he would take care not to change anything in his routine for fear it might break his luck. If his hair was long when the streak started, he would let it grow until his black curls fell onto his neck and back. At other times, he felt it was lucky for Arlyne to cut his hair. She trimmed it at the kitchen table until he suffered a big loss. Then he blamed her and went back to his usual barber.

Tommy, Arlyne observed, "thought like a nigger." He observed their superstitions, one being that if you brought dirt from a cemetery into your house, it would bring good luck. Once, he had her run out to Mount Hebron where her grandmother was buried and collect some of the soil from the grave. They kept it in a blue jewelry box on the dining-room table. This bothered Arlyne a little since, religiously speaking, it was not right to steal dirt from a graveyard, but she overcame her qualms for Tom's sake. On one occasion, Arlyne dragged Tommy to Ida's grave and told him to pray for good luck. He bowed his head and mumbled, "I'm in trouble. I need help." That ushered in one of the luckiest periods Luca had ever enjoyed. For five weeks in a row he kept hitting numbers. Tommy covered the grave with bouquets of roses and gladiolas until the streak stopped.

On balance, however, Tommy was not a very lucky gambler. He could blow five thousand dollars like it was nothing. Arlyne had gone to the track all of her life with her father's racketeer buddies and she had never seen Jews bet money like that. Occasionally, Tommy enjoyed a windfall of ten thousand or twenty thousand dollars that would pull him out of the hole. But more often, he would have to resort to borrowing from loansharks, or "shocks" as he called them, to cover himself. When the vig, or interest, on those loans came due, he would pace the kitchen wailing, "I'm getting killed!"

Tommy had a gift for getting people to bail him out. To pay the shylocks he borrowed from friends and even the black controllers. "The Lord *looooves* a cheerful giver," he would say with a wink. He never paid those loans back, but the lender always forgave him. Getting Luca out of trouble became a personal mission to Arlyne. She never felt more needed—more *important*—than when Tom was about to be killed and she was able to pull his feet out of the fire. She pawned her jewelry. She sold a load of fur coats that Norman Brickman had given her. And after Tommy had tapped out all of his friends, Arlyne contacted hers, calling in old favors. Once, she approached Milty Tillinger at his customary hangout, the Luxor Baths, and reminded him that long ago her grandmother had hidden out his kin. Milty gave her five thousand dollars, with no mention of repayment.

The mystique of money had exerted its hold over her ever since she was a child when she had sneaked into the secret cache under Ida's mattress to fondle the bills. She had no real notion of their value. She had always been a little confused, in fact, about what money was really worth. If she asked her mother for sixty dollars, she received thirty. If she asked her grandmother for sixty dollars she got eighty. She would later observe, "I was always killing myself to get exactly what I needed." One thing certain could be said of money, however—it was the currency of excitement. As Irving Weiss used to say, "When you have money, every day is Christmas." When you had money you were never frustrated by longing. If you wanted a two-thousand-dollar fox stole, you bought it. If you wanted to spend a week at the Fontainebleau you did it without considering the cost. To Arlyne's way of thinking, those whose lives were governed by savings accounts and budgets were pitiable.

It was the source of considerable discomfort now that she often found herself in financial straits. Since she had left with Leslie, Irving Weiss had turned off the tap. She was reduced to wheedling cash from her mother. When Tommy was flush he was generous, often buying her expensive jewelry. But she knew that whenever he was into the shocks, she would have to place those same pieces in hock. These mad intervals of "money days" and "depression days" only served to increase her anxiety. As her anxiety increased, so too did her suspicion of Tommy.

She had reason to believe that Luca was holding out on her. There was one morning in particular when she had picked up a hot tip from Billy, the corner druggist, on a long shot named On the Rail. Arlyne passed the tip along to Tom, who was scornful. "That fuckin' nag," he replied. "I ain't bettin' that horse." Upon further reflection, he allowed that he might "throw a few dollars at it."

That evening as Arlyne was preparing dinner she was listening to race results on the radio and heard that On the Rail had come in paying 115 to one. Since Tommy normally bet between two hundred and three hundred dollars on a horse, a little hasty computation told her that they had won a small fortune. In her exuberance, she dumped the pots of pasta and sauce she had been preparing down the incinerator, got dressed to the nines and went downstairs to wait for Tommy. Six o'clock came and went. He didn't show. It was getting cold so she went upstairs. When Tommy finally arrived, his expression revealed no jubilation.

"Where's the food?" he asked glumly.

"What do you mean?" she cried. "Didn't you bet Billy's horse today?"

Tommy muttered that he had not.

They didn't argue much because they had the collections to do and they were already late. When they got back, they ordered in food for the crew. That evening, Arlyne didn't lend a hand with the numbers.

Instead, she went off to sulk, nagged by her conviction that Tommy really had bet that horse and had taken the winnings to pay off loansharks. Of course, she couldn't prove anything.

After that, the deception cut both ways. As her suspicion of Tommy grew, she found herself cheating him as a matter of survival. One unfortunate consequence of Luca's gambling was that he often did not have enough cash on hand to cover on the hits. Arlyne, who knew that a numbers business could not long survive if winners were not paid, confided her woes in Sweet Rose, who advised, "Tell him you're losing."

"Rose," Arlyne protested, "how could I steal from Tommy?"

"It's very simple," Rose replied. "Don't tell him how much you have on the number exactly, and put the money away. This way when you have a hit and he doesn't have the money, you tell him that you're going to a shock to get it."

It proved to be just as simple as Rose had said. Tommy spent most of his time at the track now and had turned the ribbons over to Arlyne. So she claimed more losses than there were and squirreled away the rest in a secret fund. From time to time Arlyne drew on this for personal luxuries and found herself clipping Tommy to line her own purse. When she got the "loan" from Milty Tillinger, for example, she failed to mention that Milty had given her the five thousand dollars outright. When Luca gave her the money for vig, she simply pocketed it.

In doing this, she was taking a considerable risk. Tommy had a nasty temper. When he lost control of it, he would become cruel. He knew, for instance, that she loved the little black poodle named Candy that Farby had bought for Leslie and he was always threatening to kill it. Once on a numbers run, the dog irritated him so he threw it out of the car. Arlyne retrieved the animal unharmed but after that always held it in her arms when Tommy was around.

More often, however, Luca's anger would be directed at Arlyne, whom he would punch in the face and arms. At first, she downplayed these incidents because she was embarrassed. None of the Jewish racketeers she had ever known beat women. Her father had always treated her mother with respect. Frankie always treated Ida like a queen. With the terrible exception of Sally Burns and his crew, Arlyne had never been manhandled by a wiseguy. The fault, she concluded, was her own. She talked back to Tommy. That was just her way, she couldn't help it. If she could just keep her mouth shut, she told herself, she wouldn't upset him. But often it seemed that her very presence irritated him.

No matter how much work she did in the numbers business, Arlyne remained an outsider at her own dinner table. That she was a woman and a Jew conspired to keep her on the fringe. Tommy was an unabashed anti-Semite and sometimes as she was clearing the dishes, she would hear him mutter "matzoh-grease bastard" and Vito, Frankie and the others would laugh. So she dyed her hair black and put on weight in an attempt to look more like the dark Italian women they all went home to. When Sadie saw her for the first time in several months, she was shocked. "All you need is black shoes and black stockings," she noted disapprovingly. It did no good. When Tommy got mad, she was still the "goddamned Jew."

Exacerbating tensions was the fact that she and Tommy did not have sex the normal way. Since the Sally Burns incident, she had not been able to perform naturally with any man. She had had bed sex on only a handful of occasions, but she would never get undressed in front of a man and never allowed the lights to be left on. Once after they had started going together, she had overcome her aversion and allowed him to take her the conventional way, but he soon learned this was the exception, not the rule. When she told him about Sally Burns, he seemed sympathetic and appeared to be content with a nightly blow job, after which he would sleep on the couch for a few hours, go home to Howard Beach to sleep for a few more, then return to the Executive House to shave. But as the relationship wore on, he began to nag her about sex. And if he wanted the upper hand, he would belittle her for not behaving like a "real woman."

These tensions simmered until one evening they exploded with a ferocity Arlyne could not have anticipated. It began innocently when Arlyne found some hot paintings that Tommy had brought home and stored in the closet. Tom wasn't a fence but he knew one so he sometimes served as a middleman if someone was looking to unload stolen property. The paintings had been delivered as canvas rolls, but Tommy had them framed by a friend of his to improve their value. When Arlyne stumbled across the paintings, she was taken with them. One was a portrait of an old man; the other of a girl in a garden. As the Executive House apartment had always seemed cold and impersonal, Arlyne thought she would try to warm things up by hanging the paintings. The effect was nice and she thought Tommy would be happy. When Luca walked in the door and saw the hot artwork hanging in full view, he turned white.

"Take down those paintings," he said quietly.

Arlyne protested. "No, I want to keep them. I love them. Tommy, can't we please have them?"

With no warning, Luca lunged for the paintings, pulling them off the wall and shattering the glass with his feet. Then he took a kitchen knife and slashed the canvases. His rage was still not expended. Turning on Arlyne, he began to beat her, not as a man hits a woman, but the way a man hits another man. Then, in an unexpected turn, he pushed her back onto the floor, and unzipping his pants mounted her. It was the nightmare of Sally Burns all over again, made worse by the fact that Tommy's saint's medal was swinging over her eyes. In the anguish of the moment, it was transformed into a cross.

When it was over, Tommy let himself out swiftly, leaving Arlyne stunned and aching on the living-room floor. She was not sure how long she lay there before finally managing to pull herself to her feet and stagger to the bathroom. When she looked in the mirror she was shocked. The face, purple and bleeding from a cut above the eye, did not look like hers. As she was dabbing the wounds with a cold washcloth, the phone rang. It was Tommy. He sounded sorrowful.

"Arlyne," he said, "why do you do these things to me?"

"I don't know," she replied numbly.

"Remember one thing," he said softly. "I'll always be there. I'll always be with you."

From that moment on, Arlyne assumed that Tommy would always be hers.

After that she and Tommy had a few good weeks. It was like a second honeymoon. There was nothing he wouldn't do for her. They went shopping together and he bought her clothes and things for the house. He had a workman come in and mend the holes where the plaster had been destroyed. It was as if he were intent upon wiping away all traces of his shameful deed. But there were scars in certain recesses of her mind where his goodwill could not reach. There the wounds were so deep that she could not look him in the eye. Besides, she knew that these good days would not last. Tommy would lose interest in being thoughtful, and they would be back to where they had started.

Sure enough, Tommy soon became distracted by a new worry. He was less noisy about it, forgoing the usual handwringing and moaning that he was being "killed." The very fact that he refused to talk about it made Arlyne think that it must be very serious. One day when they were out driving, he turned to her and said, "I'm in a lot of trouble, Arl."

"What do you mean, Tom?" she asked.

"Well, you know, I'm stealing. Vito doesn't know I'm stealing and I'm in trouble. I'm in a lot of trouble, Arlyne. Fritzy's going to find out."

It was the first time Tommy had brought up the name of Fritzy, but Arlyne guessed right away that this must be the silent partner. With a little prodding, she learned that Fritzy's real name was Federico Giovanelli. He was a Genovese soldier who ran an operation out of the Capri Lounge in the Ridgewood neighborhood of Queens. Fritzy acted as Tommy's banker, absorbing his losses and taking a cut of profits. He was also godfather to Tommy's son.

Now Tommy was telling her that he had been pilfering cash from the envelopes collected on the nightly numbers run. Since Vito never went into the nigger houses, he was in no position to verify the amounts actually received from the controllers. Arlyne herself had noticed a discrepancy between the cash on the books and cash in hand, but Tommy had told Vito that he was having trouble collecting from the controllers. In order to cover the shortfall he had borrowed more heavily from loansharks. When he couldn't extract any more from the white shylocks he started borrowing from blacks who exacted a stiff interest of "one for one." That is, if you got one thousand dollars, you had to pay back two thousand. The borrowing, however, was only a stopgap measure and did not cover the amount owed Fritzy, a sum which ranged between thirty thousand and forty thousand dollars.

This was serious trouble, indeed. If he didn't pay the black shocks he could be beaten until he was crippled. And if Fritzy found out what he was up to, Tommy might well end up with a bullet through the head. Seeing him now so timid and scared, Arlyne took pity on him and put her mind to work trying to come up with a way out of this mess.

A couple of days later, she and Tommy had dropped by Frankie Garbage's house and were sitting around waiting for race results when an idea occurred to her.

"Tommy," she blurted out suddenly, "why don't *we* write a number book?"

Tommy, Frankie and Frankie's wife all looked at her as if she had lost her mind. Keeping a numbers book was nigger business. The ledgers were all "written," that is to say the bets recorded, by the black controllers.

"No," she insisted. "If the niggers can hit numbers, why can't we?" She proceeded to outline an even more outrageous plan in which, instead of gathering bets from customers, they could dummy up a set of books containing numbers that they would play themselves. That way, if there were hits, they would keep all the winnings.

"Where we gonna get the money for it?" Tommy asked, referring to the necessity of producing the cash supposedly generated by the phony bets.

"We'll make it a weekly," Arlyne explained. If luck held, there would be earnings early in the week from which they could pay Fritzy at week's end.

The scheme was risky. Fritzy knew nothing about Arlyne and Luca was eager to keep it that way. Tommy would have a lot of explaining to do if it were discovered that he had let his girlfriend—a Jew at that—in on the business. And if it were discovered that the same interloper was running a scam? The consequences could be serious. Tommy, however, was intrigued by the prospect of a new supply of cash and encouraged Arlyne to put her scheme into the works.

Putting herself in the place of her imaginary bettors, she chose her own favorite numbers. There was 624, which had hit a couple of times before. There was Tommy's address and Leslie's birthday. She played not only the lucky numbers but also combinations of them, so 624 was also bet as 426, 264 and 246. For reasons no one could figure, it turned out to be a very lucky book. The first night they hit for $10,000. The next night $6,000. Then a run of $10,000 jackpots.

For several weeks thereafter, the money flowed. Tommy was starting to clear up his debts with Fritzy. The shocks were also off his back so he was playing the big spender, tossing around cash and jewelry as he always did during the money days. But not everyone was happy about this bonanza. Fritzy was getting hurt by the payouts on the extraordinary number of hits. Finally, Giovanelli's people downtown apparently called him in and told him there had to be an accounting. Fritzy phoned Tommy and said he was coming down for a look at the numbers work.

This development threw Tommy into a panic. Hoping to deflect suspicion from Arlyne, he told Fritzy that the book belonged to a black controller named Virginia. Luca then paid Virginia a few dollars to go along with the charade. When Tommy brought Fritzy and his two bodyguards over to Virginia's house in Bedford-Stuyvesant, she played her role with gusto, throwing herself on Fritzy's mercy, exclaiming, "Mr. Fritz . . . I can't help it. They're hitting left and right." Fritzy, who was reassured to see what looked like a legitimate operation, nonetheless informed Virginia that the book was too hot and he couldn't carry her anymore. No hard feelings.

That was the end of Tommy's dreams of glory. Arlyne, however, did not come away empty-handed. She had seen that Tommy was afraid of Fritzy and she now had a secret to hang over his head, a little extra leverage should he become hard to handle. Despite the promise that he "would never leave," Tommy was always threatening to return to his wife. Whenever they fought Tommy would storm out leaving the impression that he was returning to Howard Beach. One evening, after a particularly bitter brawl, he left, slamming the door behind him. In her fury, Arlyne picked up the phone and called the Capri.

Fritzy Giovanelli never answered his own phone, nor would he talk on one. Arlyne had heard that he had been picked up on a wire once and was scared of them. So when an unidentified man answered, she laid it on the line.

"Look," she said, "I'm a very good friend of Tommy Luca's. I know all about the numbers business and he's up to no good."

The man replied, "Gimme your number and I'll call you back."

Arlyne knew he would check the number against the one Tommy had given as a work contact. Moments later, the phone rang. When she picked it up a voice said, "Nine o'clock at the candy store on Continental Avenue."

Arlyne was very pleased with herself. The danger was exhilarating and she felt the old mob girl fever rising. She was once more Virginia Hill on a mission of intrigue. Accordingly, she put on a tight cashmere sweater dress and the blue fox coat and glanced at the clock, waiting to make her move. She was startled when she heard the key rattle and Tommy Luca walked in the door. He was contrite as a beaten puppy and bearing an amethyst ring as a peace offering.

Arlyne was thoroughly flustered. There was no doubt about taking him back. Making up with Tommy had become a reflex. The question was what to do about Fritzy. Having tossed the ball into the air, she could not just let it fall. If she did not show up at the candy store, Giovanelli was likely to come after them both.

Tommy did not ask why she was dressed to leave. Arlyne let him believe that she was making another of her furtive visits to her mother. When the clock read a quarter to nine, she told him she was going out for a racing sheet and would bring him back ice cream. Arlyne reached the candy store a little past nine. There was a black car parked at the curb. One of Fritzy's bodyguards got out of the car, pushed her against a wall and frisked her. Then he opened the back door of the car, motioning to her to get inside. She found herself sitting next to a short, stocky man who reminded her of Anthony Quinn.

"You're Eileen?" said Fritzy, unbuttoning his coat so that she could see the handgun he had stuck into his belt. "What is it you want to tell me?"

Arlyne had been considering that same question ever since Tommy walked back in the door. In light of the reconciliation, she could not now tell Fritzy about the phony numbers book or the fact that Tommy had been stealing from him. The only choice Arlyne had was to somehow insinuate herself into his confidence.

"Fritzy," she said confidentially, "I hope you don't mind, but Tommy's doing the number work in my house." Arlyne went on to explain that she helped out even though she had never been properly introduced to or okayed by Fritzy. "I hope that it is all right by you," she simpered.

Fritzy seemed a little perplexed, then disarmed, by this innocent admission. He suggested they all go for Italian food and discuss things at greater length. Over dinner Arlyne let it be known that she would happily serve as Fritzy's "little spy" on Tommy. When Giovanelli and his entourage dropped her off on Continental Avenue, she implored, "Please, Fritzy, don't tell Tommy or I'll get a terrible beating." He agreed.

The beating, she figured, was inevitable. Sooner or later someone would let something slip and Tommy would come home in a rage. After pondering this eventuality for several days, Arlyne concluded that a preemptive strike was called for. That evening, she approached Tommy and announced, "Guess who I ran into by Paulie Messina's? Fritzy Giovanelli."

Overlooking for a moment the utter improbability of such a meeting, Tommy queried, "You didn't say nothing to him, dija?"

"I told him that you were doing the number work in my house," she replied.

As she expected, Tommy lit into her, blackening her eyes and splitting her lip. But when he had finished, he let the matter drop. Perhaps he had been frightened by her audacity in approaching Fritzy and realized that she was in a position to do him considerable harm. At any rate, the Giovanelli caper left her feeling much more powerful than before. Fritzy would now call the apartment occasionally and ask for her, just to make sure that Tommy was treating her right. Tommy would even take her to meets at the Capri Lounge. Of course she had to sit in the car.

Arlyne worked tirelessly to make herself indispensable to Tommy. She did his numbers work, deflected shylocks, cooked for him and gave him sex. And while all of this might have passed as goodness, Tommy recognized her efforts for what they were—an attempt to control him. He resented this, complaining that their troubles were the result of her meddling. "If you would just step back," he insisted, "everything would be all right." But the more he resisted, the more she pushed.

For Tommy, the last word was violence. His beatings became more severe, until Arlyne began to worry about their effects upon Leslie. One night when Tommy was pummeling Arlyne with his fists, Leslie emerged from the kitchen holding a butcher knife and screaming, "Get the fuck outta here and don't ever hurt my mother again!" Arlyne screamed "Don't!" Tommy appeared stunned for a moment, then bolted from the apartment. Arlyne ran after him. Many years later, Arlyne would reflect ruefully, "I made him more important than Leslie. How could my kid have respect for me?"

But Leslie Brickman's own feelings toward Tommy Luca were far more complicated than the knife episode would indicate. On the fine days—that is to say the days when Tommy was playing the good-natured imp, or better yet, Daddy Warbucks distributing presents—she adored him. In his own way Tommy was fond of Leslie and showed her the attention for which she was starved.

Leslie was suffering acutely from the lack of a father. As a small child, she had been told that Norman Brickman had died and was buried far away in California. But in her imagination, he would not die. When she pressed for details, her mother and grandparents would change the subject. As she grew older and grasped the concept of illicit love, she had begun to believe that she was the product of one of her mother's flings. On learning this, Arlyne quickly produced a birth certificate showing that she was legitimate. Studying the document, Leslie noted that her father was a "furrier," and for years, that was all that she knew about him.

During the stormy scenes between her mother and grandmother in Forest Hills, Leslie had lain on her bed and fantasized that the doorbell would ring. She would answer and a very tall man, her father, would announce calmly, "I'm taking you away." Try as she might, she could never imagine his features. Over the years, she tried on many fathers for size. The first was her Poppy, but as she grew older and it became necessary to take sides in the domestic battles between her mother and grandparents, her affection for him turned to resentment. Although she respected her aunt Barbara's husband even as she resisted his attempts to discipline her, she certainly did not love him. Some of her mother's boyfriends had been thoughtful to her, but she generally viewed them as her mother did—as a string of patsies to be played for expensive gifts.

Tommy was different. For one thing, he had stuck around longer than any of her previous uncles. If Tommy could be brutal, he could also be tender. And when he and her mother weren't fighting, they seemed to be gleeful conspirators. She noticed that Tom never slept in her mother's room. For the few hours a night he spent at the Executive House he lay sprawled on the living-room couch. Once he had taken her aside to explain, "I don't sleep with your mother. Your mother and I are just good friends." Leslie found that a little weird but she never said anything.

Tommy seemed to care about her. If she got home late, he smacked her around. Once she had spent the night at a girlfriend's house without telling him and when she got home, he hit her in the head with a telephone. She did not hold it against him. She considered it a "father-type thing." But, of course, Leslie Brickman had no idea how a father should behave.

Leslie's conflicted affection for Tommy was not the only thing that worried her mother. When she lived with her grandparents in Forest Hills, the girl had fallen in with a group of Hispanic delivery boys who hung around the neighborhood. Leslie and one of her girlfriends would pretend to be going to school but once out of sight, darted into the back of a delivery truck to smoke reefer. One evening she came home wearing only her slip. Her grandparents appeared not to notice. Sadie smelled a rat when Leslie persisted in wearing sunglasses. She admonished Irving and Billie that if they made her take off those glasses, they would find her eyes were pink. They ignored the warnings.

Arlyne had seen her daughter so little during that period that the trouble signs escaped her as well. Arlyne was not a disciplinarian. There had been times when Arlyne was lonely and encouraged Leslie to stay home from school just so she could have company. Now, in the evenings when the girl should have been finishing her homework and getting ready for bed, Arlyne and Tommy would take her along on collection runs. Not surprisingly, Leslie's grades dropped so sharply that it appeared she might be left back a grade. Arlyne herself had dropped out of school before graduation, but the thought of her daughter not finishing alarmed her.

While she fretted ineptly over Leslie's problems, her failure as a mother was brought forcibly home by a call from Ethel Becher. Arlyne had stayed in touch with Ethel over the years. She had even taken Tommy to meet her. On that occasion, Ethel had sent her out on an errand so, Arlyne assumed, she could try to seduce Luca. Whether she succeeded, Arlyne never knew. Over time, Ethel's image had lost some of its luster. Arlyne discovered that many of her beautiful clothes had been loaned to her on consignment. Then she learned that her diamonds were fakes. Ethel had been little more than an illusionist, and she could no longer conceal her shabby tricks. Now, Ethel called her from Mount Sinai Hospital to tell her that she was ill. Her condition was rare. She had had so much silicone pumped into her flesh that it had poisoned her blood. The moment Arlyne entered her hospital room and gazed at the sad gray furrows lining her old friend's face, she knew that she did not have long to live.

Ethel turned to her and smiled. She was so weak, she could scarcely speak, but she beckoned Arlyne near. There were some things that Ethel wanted to get off her chest. She had always loved her children more than anything in the world, she said. Arlyne nodded. Now she was terribly worried about her daughter. She was a teenager—a pretty girl—and Tony Mirra had taken an interest in her. It was not necessary to say more. Tony was not the fatherly sort and there was only one possible reason for his paying attention to the girl.

"Look after your daughter," Ethel whispered. "The apple doesn't fall far from the tree."

After a night of soul searching, Arlyne knew what she must do. She got dressed up, as she always did at those moments when she had to make her shots count, and went to see her parents. She had not had a proper conversation with her father since she left Forest Hills to live with Luca. Now he listened impassively as she poured out her concerns. The painful irony of the situation did not escape Irving and Billie Weiss. After the years of heartache spent in trying to steer Arlyne onto the straight life, they had lived long enough to see her struggling to do the same with her own daughter. The one thing on which they all agreed was that Leslie must be removed from the Executive House and removed quickly.

The Weisses had already come up with a plan, which they had hoped to implement at the first reasonable opportunity. That was to send Leslie to a private academy, the Grier School in Tyrone, Pennsylvania. Arlyne agreed. She had never heard of the place but it sounded good to her. A girl's school for the horsey set. Leslie, after all, liked horses. It seemed distant, but that was for the best. If the apple was to fall, it was best for it to land as far as possible from the tree. Arlyne was now content it should land among the children of the respectable WASPs in the dappled hills of central Pennsylvania. It was not the life she had imagined for herself. But even a mob girl wants her child to be wonderful.

Arlyne's father, Irving Weiss (far right), at work in the family grocery store. Vain and indolent, he found racketeering more to his liking than honest labor.

Arlyne's mother, Sylvia Blum, at the age of fourteen. She joined the chorus line of the Manhattan Steppers and toured the country under the stage name "Billie Young." Upon her return, Billie rigged a raffle to win the love of Irving Weiss.

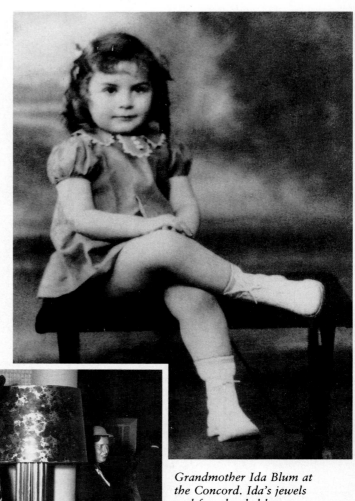

Little Arlyne, the darling of old East Broadway. She possessed a vitality that was disconcerting. By the age of four she had learned that the most important thing in the world was dressing well.

Grandmother Ida Blum at the Concord. Ida's jewels and furs dazzled her granddaughter. The grande dame's Lower East Side funeral parlor became the hangout for gamblers and union racketeers.

Billie, Ida, and Arlyne with "Uncle" Frankie Oxman, whose union connections led to the banishment of Ida's husband, Jake Blum. Frankie died in Ida's bed.

Arlyne and Irving Weiss during one of their winter idylls in Florida. Arlyne adored her father, who was "handsome as a movie star."

Shown here on vacation in the Catskills are Irving, in the driver's seat, with Billie beside him. The divine Ida Blum sits in back between two young chauffeurs. Early in his career, Arlyne's father rented touring cars to mobsters.

Tall and striking, Arlyne enjoyed showing off her tan.

The Weisses' twentieth wedding anniversary at the Latin Quarter. (From left) Arlyne's sister, Barbara; Billie; and Frankie Oxman. Across from Frankie sits Ida, then Irving and a glamorous Arlyne, age nineteen. Arlyne often accompanied her father to the races and fights. She sometimes fantasized that she was his date.

Virginia Hill in 1951 at the time of her appearance before the Kefauver Committee. In 1947 her lover Bugsy Siegel was gunned down at her house. Hailed as "the most successful woman in America," she was the quintessential mob girl and Arlyne's idol.

Arlyne Brickman showed up for her date with boxer Rocky Graziano wearing a fur coat—and nothing else.

Joe Colombo during an arrest in 1971. He was a buttonman and lieutenant of mob boss Joe Profaci when Arlyne Brickman met him. They had a brief "bed affair" at the St. Moritz. She found him cheap, and furthermore, he wore his boxer shorts unhemmed.

When Arlyne Brickman took up with Genovese wiseguy Tommy Luca, she dyed her hair black to look more Italian.

Carmine Persico, aka "Junior," aka "the Snake," reputedly killed his first man at the age of seventeen. As Joe Colombo's successor, he found himself and his capos the targets of a federal investigation. Operation Starquest would bring him down, with help from Arlyne Brickman.

Persico lieutenant Anthony "Scappy" Scarpati was believed to oversee the street-level operations of the Colombo Family's gambling and loansharking enterprises. His agents made a fateful loan to Tommy Luca and Arlyne Brickman. Scappy, shown here outside the candy store that served as the drop for vig, or interest, payments, conducts business under the government's watchful eye in this surveillance photo.

DiNotte's pizza parlor on Fifth Avenue in Brooklyn, site of Arlyne Brickman's proposed meeting with Scarpati. He got skittish, claiming the Avenue was too "hot."

An FBI surveillance photo shows Arlyne Brickman stepping out of her cherished white Lincoln to make an interest payment at Scarpati's candy store.

PART TWO

SIX

FORT LEE

Leslie Brickman almost made a clean getaway. Her mother, having taken a decisive step, found herself enjoying her new role, fussing over her daughter as conscientiously as if she were packing a little debutante off to Wellesley. The summer before enrollment, Irving had loaded the family into the corporate Caddy and driven to Tyrone, where they allowed themselves to be escorted with suitable deference around the grounds of the academy. Irving, Billie and Arlyne were delighted by the manicured lawns and plantationlike pretensions of the place. Leslie lagged behind, wearing a pout.

The girl's official position—one she had adopted even before this reconnaissance—was that she *hated* Tyrone and *hated* Grier and emphatically did not wish to leave Queens. The depth of her conviction was difficult to determine, however, since she appeared to dislike most everything. Leslie Brickman was feeling the effects of years of privileged neglect. There was a time when she would cry for her mother during the latter's frequent absences, but those yearnings had given way first to coldness, then to a self-destructive rage. Unlike Arlyne, whose mischief was a blatant bid for attention, Leslie was so disgusted by her elders that she had decided their attention wasn't worth having. What they loved, she abhorred. Whatever they wanted, she actively resisted.

In the matter of the Grier School, however, Irving did not solicit his granddaughter's opinion. Come fall, she was dispatched over her objections to Pennsylvania, where, during the first weeks of the semester, she was her nasty, sullen self. It was not long thereafter, however, that Miss Brickman began undergoing a rather remarkable transformation. Up to that point the happiest moments of her childhood had been spent riding ponies with her cousins on Long Island. Now at Grier, where equestrian pursuits were considered an integral part of a young woman's education, Leslie fell in love with riding. She rode three hours a day, in sunshine and in snow. This passion awakened her spirit and even gave rise to a nascent ambition. She had always been fond of animals, and had had a couple of dogs, which she declined to pamper as her mother and grandparents did. She felt that turning an animal into a baby showed a lack of respect for it. Accordingly, Leslie decided she might like to become a veterinarian. And even more remarkably, she began applying herself to her studies, doing two hours of homework a day.

Her rehabilitation was, of course, relative. Still susceptible to the call of the wild, Leslie and a couple of girlfriends would sneak out at night to meet boys in town, a habit that earned her a reputation as one of the fast girls on campus. Leslie would later insist that it was all "good clean fun," that all the time she was at Grier, she never did drugs, and that—had she been allowed to stay where she was flourishing—her life would have been different.

This was not to be. Leslie had not been away a full year when she received a call from her mother—hysterical and weeping—summoning her home.

During Leslie's absence, Arlyne's fortunes had deteriorated. Tommy was abusive as usual. But now he would disappear for days at a time without calling. The phone rang off the hook with creditors to whom he had given Arlyne's number. When Luca had dropped out of sight in the past, it had been his habit to return flush from some new score and for days thereafter it was like Christmas. Now he left broke and returned broke. On several occasions the two found themselves pooling their pennies to buy groceries. Arlyne was ashamed. She could put up with a hard life, but not a poor one.

It was during one of Luca's prolonged absences that Arlyne found herself forced once again to approach her parents like a beggar. The only consideration that ever induced Irving to loosen the purse strings was Leslie's welfare. This in mind, Arlyne formulated a plan. She would tell her parents that she was leaving Luca and that she wanted to bring Leslie back from school so that they could begin a new life. She was counting on her parents to bankroll a fresh start.

Arlyne's motives were, as usual, an alloy of self-interest and self-justification. She truly missed Leslie, whom she had always pressed into service as confidante during desperate times. With Tommy out of the picture, she was very lonely. She managed to convince herself that the girl was running with a bad crowd at Grier and that she should be brought home for her own sake.

It was more than Irving and Billie could possibly hope that their wayward daughter would finally take her responsibilities seriously. For the previous thirty-nine years, she had periodically professed contrition and gone through the motions of penitence, only to be caught red-handed in some new escapade. The Weisses would have suffered less if they could have summoned the courage to cut her off. But they did not find that possible. No matter how much pain a child causes, the history remains. Heartache becomes so entwined with tenderness that they are indistinguishable. So when Arlyne approached her parents with the announcement that she wanted to leave Tommy Luca and do right by her daughter, they played the role that fate had dealt them and agreed to help her out of one more mess.

Before opening his checkbook, however, Irving issued a proviso. Arlyne must leave Queens. No one knew better than Irving Weiss how attached a wiseguy like Luca becomes to his neighborhood. If Arlyne were to physically depart, he would be unlikely to try to follow her. Arlyne was not happy with this condition, but as she was in no position to dictate terms, she proposed taking Leslie to New Jersey. She had her eye on Fort Lee, a tiny bedroom community located just across the Hudson River at the foot of the George Washington Bridge. Given its proximity to Manhattan—only a five-minute drive across the bridge—it would not be like living in Kansas. Besides, Fort Lee was considered an up-and-coming place for professionals who wanted a New York–style penthouse at New Jersey prices. The high rises that were springing up among the ragged cliffs of the Palisades afforded a splendid view of the Manhattan skyline.

Arlyne and her mother were both excited by the prospect of luxury. They made daily forays across the river to look for apartments, finally finding one in a nine-story brick edifice on Hudson Terrace. Since the apartment at the Executive House had come furnished, Arlyne wanted her Fort Lee digs to bear the mark of her personal style. She and her mother proceeded to furnish the place "like newlyweds," installing expensive, if uncomfortable, white cane furniture in the bedrooms, with even pricier and more wretchedly uncomfortable yellow leather chairs in the living areas. The living area boasted a rather more inviting velvet couch, but it was off-limits to humans. When Arlyne and Billie finished, they had produced a stunning and virtually unlivable showcase.

Leslie, who had not been notified of the plans for her return until these were well advanced, was furious. The sullenness, which had been gradually lessening during her months at Grier, promptly returned. When her grandfather sent a car for her, she complied like a parolee returning to custody. Consequently, her homecoming was not the warm reunion for which Arlyne had hoped. Complicating matters was the fact the new apartment had only one bedroom, so Leslie found herself without privacy, once again playing girlfriends with a mother about whom she was deeply ambivalent. With time and patience, even this hurdle might have been overcome. But a few weeks after Leslie's return, something happened that would alienate her affections for good.

One night Sadie came to visit. Leslie rarely saw her old nursemaid. Sadie had followed Arlyne to the Executive House, but Tommy, suspecting that she was carrying tales back to Billie Weiss, insisted she be fired. Although this was not Arlyne's fault, Sadie apparently harbored a grudge. On the fateful night that she visited Fort Lee, she had been drinking. As she sat talking with Arlyne and Leslie in the kitchen—the only cozy nook in the place—her drunken talk turned hostile and she let it slip that Norman Brickman was still alive.

There were several moments of awful silence. Leslie appeared stricken. She turned to her mother, who, taken off guard, sputtered a stream of denials. Leslie stormed out of the apartment, slamming the door behind her. When she returned some hours later, her coldness was impenetrable. The only subject that she was prepared to discuss was that of her father. Several days thereafter, Arlyne dug out of the bottom drawer of her mother's dresser the one remaining photograph of Norman, the one taken on Barbara's wedding day, the one in which he had been included as an afterthought. Leslie stared at the photo and asked, "He knew where we lived; why didn't he ever come to visit?"

There was no good answer. If Arlyne left the impression that Norman hadn't cared enough to return, his daughter would feel abandoned. If, on the other hand, she broke ranks with the family and told the long-suppressed truth that Irving had paid his son-in-law to leave the family alone, Leslie would feel herself the victim of a conspiracy. In the end, Arlyne gave up the secret—not because it was the right thing to do, but because Leslie wore her down. The girl replied simply, "You should have told me. That way, if I wanted to find him, I could."

For a while, it looked as if the issue had been settled. There were no recriminations, none of the hysteria that usually accompanied Weiss family showdowns. But the calm was illusory. Although Leslie had been enrolled as a freshman at Fort Lee High, a good public school where it was expected she would continue her academic improvement, she began to cut classes. During afternoons, she could be found at the Junction, an old railway station that had been converted into a pizza parlor and X-rated movie house, hanging with a crowd of teenage derelicts. Years later, she would insist she hadn't gone looking for drugs, but if someone offered her something, she "wouldn't turn it down." At the Junction, Leslie discovered Quaaludes, which made her feel dreamy and peaceful. She hid them in her drawers where they were sure to be discovered by her mother.

When Arlyne came across the first pills, she felt sick. She quickly flushed them down the toilet, reasoning naively that this might be the end of it. But pills kept turning up in drawers, under the bed, sometimes lying right out in the open. Arlyne tried to talk to her daughter, but Leslie simply turned on her heel and walked away. Arlyne tailed her to the Junction and tried to bring her home, but Leslie wouldn't even let on to her street friends that she knew the woman beckoning to her frantically from a silver Chevrolet. On those evenings, Arlyne would return to her exquisitely furnished apartment with its view of the skyline—the promise of a new future—and suffer silently over the daughter who was slipping away.

Arlyne could never recall exactly what prompted her to telephone Tommy Luca. Perhaps it was a combination of loneliness and habit. When she could resist the urge no longer, she did the unforgivable and called him at home. He listened without comment as she described her fabulous new apartment across the river. Then she hung up and waited for the news to have its effect. New York, she heard, had become too hot for him. He was in trouble with serious shylocks and needed a place to hide out. Moreover, he was looking for "new blood"—new lenders, new scams, new scores.

Sure enough, a few days after she had dangled the bait, Tommy rang her buzzer. (She suspected he had been casing the place from a vantage point on the Palisades Parkway.) She let him in, and he glanced around approvingly and decided to stay.

Naturally, this reconciliation had to be kept quiet. The Weisses were paying their daughter's rent, a subsidy that was sure to end once they learned she had gone back with Luca. When Arlyne's mother dropped by every other day or so, Tommy stayed out of sight. There was a danger, of course, that Leslie would tell, but weeks passed and she remained silent. Since learning about her father, she was even angrier at her grandparents than she was at her mother.

Tommy divided his time between Fort Lee and Howard Beach,

using Arlyne's place as a base of operation. There he entertained a crew of "associates," who were always on the lookout for the big score, preferably one that was effortless, contained no risk and was, nonetheless, lucrative. Arlyne, sensing that one reason Tommy stayed with her was that she connected in circles he wanted to pillage, also kept her eyes peeled. In the fall of 1972, shortly after the move to Fort Lee, she stumbled across a beauty.

From the beginning of their relationship. Arlyne had strung Luca along with a number of pretensions, the most outrageous of which was that she was related to Meyer Lansky. Whenever Tommy had come up with a new scheme that needed a money man, Arlyne would suggest that perhaps "Uncle Meyer" might want a piece. If Tommy came home in a bad mood and landed a few punches on her arm, Arlyne invoked the dark specter of what Uncle Meyer might do to a man who abused his beloved niece.

The Uncle Meyer routine was not a total fabrication. Meyer Lansky had, in fact, grown up in the old neighborhood in close and familial proximity to other Eastern European Jews. The Lanskys, of course, knew the Laskers. Later in life, Meyer enjoyed business ties with the Blum and Oxman Funeral Home through his emissary Red Levine. Irving Weiss was on a first-name basis with Meyer, who had once come into Chester Motors browsing for automobiles. Irving tried to sell him a Cadillac but Meyer found it too flashy. When the Weisses stayed at the Fontainebleau Hotel during their winter sojourns in Miami, Irving was at liberty to wander over to the pool to chat with Lansky, who held court over a crew of bookies and union officials. Even Arlyne, then in her early twenties, could strut by in a swimsuit and expect a familial nod from the great man. For many years before she met Tommy, Arlyne had been dropping hints in influential places that she was Lansky's niece. Her references were never so specific that she could not disavow them if challenged. But she never was. And by the time Luca entered the picture, Arlyne had almost come to believe her own stories.

In November of 1972, Arlyne heard that Uncle Meyer was returning to America. For nearly two years, Lansky, now in his seventies, had been living in Israel, in flight from an advancing army of IRS agents. He had sought permanent asylum there, but the Israeli government, after lengthy debate, decided he was an undesirable and was preparing to ship him back to the United States. While the political subtleties of Meyer Lansky's exile were largely lost on Arlyne, she was aware of rumors concerning his return. Since moving in with Tommy, she had had infrequent contact with her parents. Her father, whose dislike of Luca had grown steadily since their first encounter at the beach club, scarcely spoke to her. Luca reciprocated the ill will, and Arlyne had to sneak out of the apartment on various pretenses whenever she wanted to see her mother. It was on one of these surreptitious visits to Forest Hills that Arlyne picked up a critical bit of intelligence. She was in the foyer, putting on her wrap, when she noticed her father and Uncle Sidney in the living room in hushed conversation. Moving closer to the door, she was able to catch the gist. Meyer, Irving said, was going to be coming back into the country within the next couple of weeks and he wanted $330,000 transferred quietly from New York to Miami. Irving had agreed to ferry the cash in the trunk of one of his Rolls-Royces.

Upon hearing this, Arlyne relayed the news immediately to Tommy, who became as excited as an eight-year-old. Three hundred thousand dollars was enough to clear out all his debts and get the shylocks off his back. Luca began formulating a plan to steal the cash. It should be done, he decided, while the car was still in the shop. To effect this plan he gathered together a crew with special expertise in breaking and entering, notably one Midge, a Genovese button man from Brooklyn, and two of his pals, named Davy and Paulie.

Once a week for three weeks Tommy, Midge, Davy, Paulie and Arlyne met at a luncheonette to plot the break-in. Arlyne had cased the shop and discovered that the Rolls was parked near the back of the store. It was decided that she would steal a key to the showroom and, at about 1:00 A.M. on the night of the proposed robbery, go in the front and unlock the door to the service entrance in the back. Midge and his pals would arrive half an hour later, roll up the door, break open the trunk and lift the cash. It sounded like a cinch. Because Midge, Davy and Paulie were taking most of the risk, they were to get 90 percent. Tommy, who had nothing more dangerous to do than watch the front door, was to get the remaining 10 percent, since he was the one who had brought them the score. Of his thirty thousand dollars or more, he would give Arlyne whatever he felt like giving her. This didn't seem quite fair to her, since she was the one who had actually turned up the job, cased the joint, stolen the key and stood to be arrested prowling through Chester Motors. But as it was clear she was being tolerated only as a necessary nuisance, she kept her mouth shut.

As the night of the robbery approached, Arlyne grew increasingly uneasy about Tommy. He would pick up and go suddenly without telling her where he was headed and get angry if she asked where he had been. She wondered if he were having an affair or, worse still, spending time with his wife. The fear of being abandoned kept Arlyne on edge. She sought constant assurances that he would not leave. But instead of reassuring her, Luca would taunt her with accusations that she couldn't "hold a man." Two nights before the proposed break-in, Tommy once again got up and left without warning. This time, Arlyne was determined to follow him.

Arlyne was at a strategic disadvantage at times like these because she did not own a car. Moreover, she had never bothered to get a driver's license—which did not prevent her from driving but did prevent her from renting a vehicle. This night, Arlyne called an old friend who owned a limousine service and had him send over a Cadillac and driver.

When the car arrived, she directed the chauffeur to Tommy's home in Howard Beach and, sure enough, as she pulled up the block, she spotted his blue Monte Carlo in the drive. Arlyne watched from a discreet distance until Luca came out the front door and got into his car. Then she instructed the driver to tail him. The driver, unfortunately, had no flair for cloak and dagger work and followed Luca too closely. As the two cars pulled onto Cross Bay Boulevard, Luca became suspicious. Without warning he slammed on his brakes, got out of the car carrying a baseball bat and bore down on the Cadillac in a fury. "You fuckin' whore," Luca shouted. "I'll kill the both of youse." Arlyne sat stunned as he rained blows on the windows and doors until the Cadillac was a tangle of broken glass and dented metal.

Arlyne screamed at the chauffeur to pull away, but by this time he was gasping and appeared to be having a heart attack. Even Luca had noticed the man's distress and had forgotten his own anger to help Arlyne soothe him. When the man had recovered sufficiently, Arlyne dismissed him, watching him crawl down the boulevard in his crippled Caddy. Without a word, she climbed into Luca's car and he drove her home, muttering, "I'm gonna break up with you. I can't take it no more."

But Arlyne achieved a small victory. Luca spent the night at her place. The next morning, however, her satisfaction was dashed. Midge called and wanted to meet them at the luncheonette. When Midge arrived, he looked grim. He wasn't as tall as Tommy, but he had an air of authority about him. What he said now was a shock to them both. Midge, who lived near Tommy in Howard Beach, had happened onto the boulevard the night before just in time to see Tommy pummeling the car with a baseball bat.

"You guys are crazy," he said, "and I don't want no part of you. I don't want no part of the deal."

This somehow didn't ring true to Arlyne, who suspected that Midge had simply gotten nervous about messing with Meyer Lansky's money and wanted a way out.

"What, are you afraid?" she asked.

Midge grew red. "Don't ever say 'afraid,' " he warned. "I'm not afraid of nothing." And with that he walked out.

This turn of events put Luca in such a foul temper that he began beating Arlyne on the sidewalk in front of the luncheonette. When she raised her arms to protect her face, the blows knocked off her false fingernails, tearing the skin beneath.

The following day, Arlyne learned that the Rolls with the $330,000 in its trunk had left Chester Motors as planned on its way to Miami. She was depressed for weeks. It wasn't because of Tommy's tantrums. She was becoming used to his abusive behavior. Nor was it because she had been lured by greed into betraying her own father. That should have bothered her, but the cold-blooded resolve with which she plotted the break-in of Chester Motors had come surprisingly easily. Human sentiment, she was learning, should never be allowed to interfere with business. She simply felt cheated.

In time, Midge recovered his good humor and he resumed his place with Tommy and the boys sitting around the kitchen table, plotting endlessly, and to no apparent purpose. Then one afternoon as Tommy, Midge and Paulie were drinking coffee, a friend of Leslie's dropped by.

The kid, who was around twenty-four, worked in the yard of one of the largest construction companies in Fort Lee. The youngster imagined himself a player, and he proposed a score for which he wanted a finder's fee. Every Friday, he said, a fifty-thousand-dollar payroll was delivered to the firm.

The proposed heist gave Tommy something with which to occupy himself. The job sounded simple and sweet. When the payroll arrived, Midge and Paulie would go into the office armed with shotguns and wearing ski masks. They would tie up the employees and loot the safe. Tommy, as usual, would serve as lookout. They would watch the delivery for a couple of weeks and observe the pattern. But the job, which was to take a maximum of three weeks, stretched on to seven, then ten, then eleven. Nothing went right. The truck never came on time. No pattern seemed to emerge.

Arlyne was not happy. To begin with, she was afraid that the kid who gave up the score might get into trouble. That, in turn, might put Leslie at risk. Also, since Midge and Paulie were going in armed, someone might be killed, and if it could be established that Arlyne had allowed her apartment to be used for the planning, she might somehow be involved in murder. Beyond that, the owners of the construction company were Italian and rumored to be connected to the mob in Jersey City. Tommy was so dazzled by the payroll, he was not considering possible consequences. What irritated Arlyne most was Tommy's asking her to take what seemed an enormous risk with no share of the profits. When she complained, he barked "Back off!"

On the day of the robbery, Arlyne stayed out of the way, confined to her kitchen as an observer. She saw Midge and Paulie leave. Then an hour or so later, they returned laughing like maniacs, gloating about how it had gone so smoothly they just took off their masks and walked back to the apartment. Not a cop in sight. It seemed to Arlyne, as she listened to the blow-by-blow, that things had not gone all that well. Although there had been two bags of bills, the robbers had gotten spooked and left one behind. So instead of fifty thousand dollars, they made off with only about twelve thousand dollars. This did not seem a cause for jubilation. Tommy, however, was full of himself and as weeks passed with no hint of retribution from either the law or the mob, he treated Arlyne with increasing contempt.

Where Tommy's moods were concerned, Arlyne had grown philosophical. When he was flush, he was a bigshot. When he needed money, he reverted to a panicky little boy. It was just a matter of time, Arlyne knew, before he would run through his cut of the stolen payroll and be once again desperate. And before long he was, indeed, out of money, beleaguered by shocks and in search of "new blood."

Arlyne had a connection that Tommy hoped to exploit. Over the years she had stayed in touch with her old friend Sophie—the red-headed terror of Forest Hills—who had since married a plump Jew named Sam Silverstein. Sam was a gofer for one Vince Lamattina, a major Genovese shylock whom Tommy wanted to hit up for a loan. Arlyne's friendship with Sophie had been off again, on again. (She had always suspected Sophie of blowing the whistle on her and Babe at the Forest Hills Inn.) Whenever there was money to be made, however, the two women put aside their differences in favor of business. Arlyne called Sophie to arrange a double date in Little Italy. The evening was unpleasant. Sam got drunk and yelled at his wife, who yelled back.

Arlyne managed to interrupt the feuding Silversteins only long enough to arrange an introduction to the loanshark. Soon thereafter, she was dispatched to Brooklyn to meet Vince Lamattina.

A few days before Christmas she showed up at Lamattina's vegetable store in a white fur coat and matching turban. (Arlyne's theatrical sense told her that this was one of those occasions that required her Virginia Hill routine.) When she first glimpsed Lamattina, a short, stocky man tending his arugula, her back arched and she was overtaken by the ancient impulse to seduce and conquer. Lamattina, however, had seen enough of aging mob girls to be impervious to their battle tactics. He knew how to put one in her place. He would give Tommy the loan, he said, but Arlyne would have to do him a little favor. At his instructions, Arlyne met him on Christmas day at a cheap motel and gave him a blow job. That evening Lamattina saw Tommy in a candy store in Rego Park and gave him the loan. He couldn't hang around and talk, he said, because he was hosting a big Christmas party.

Arlyne was insulted at not having been invited to that party. During her salad days, she would have made a circuit of four or five such galas in one night. What particularly galled Arlyne was that the fete was in honor of Vince's girlfriend—later wife—Gina, a short, dark Brooklyn broad who wore pancake makeup and looked as if she had just stepped off Delancey Street. That such a fuss should be made over a woman who didn't dress well showed there was no justice. Thereafter, Arlyne did her best to insinuate herself into Vince Lamattina's circle, but the only place she was welcome was at Sophie's apartment, where, if she was lucky, Vince would be visiting.

Tommy fared better with Lamattina. Gina seemed to like him and the two would spend a lot of time sitting in a corner discussing horseracing. At those times, Tommy acted as if he didn't even want Arlyne around. Luca also seemed to be getting tighter with Vince, who had introduced him to a friend of his named Tony, who, in turn, introduced him to a rising Gambino loanshark named John Gotti. Before taking Tommy to Gotti's hangout, a social club in Ozone Park, Tony warned Luca, "If you fuck up here, they'll kill you. You can't play games with these guys."

Tommy also seemed to be doing some kind of business of his own with Lamattina, but he was close-lipped about it. There were only two reasons for which Tommy seemed to want or need her, his nightly blow job and her services as workhorse for his new numbers business.

Soon after alighting in Fort Lee, Tommy had returned to bookmaking. It was technically a Brooklyn operation, but he ran it from the apartment on Hudson Terrace. Accordingly, Arlyne had installed two phone lines. On one, in the name of I. Weiss, she took calls from her mother. The other, which she established under the pseudonym Sophie Silverstein, was reserved for business. While Tommy spent his days at the races, Arlyne took bets called in from candy stores, a shoeshine shop and a luncheonette in Bedford-Stuyvesant. Each afternoon, the two would drive into Brooklyn to pick up the money and make the payoffs.

For about a year the business went smoothly. They never made a killing but at least managed to stay abreast of Tommy's debts. Then Luca began picking up bad vibes. Every so often he got the feeling they were being watched. Whenever they made their afternoon runs to Brooklyn, he drove evasively, speeding up, slowing down, darting up one-way streets. Arlyne was tempted to think he was crazy, but Tom, she had to admit, did have a sixth sense about some things.

It was just a week before Christmas 1974, a year after she had been snubbed by Vince Lamattina. Tommy was at home in Arlyne's kitchen drinking coffee. Arlyne, dressed—as was now her custom—in a billowing robe, had just finished decorating a small tree and was about to empty the trash. She opened the door to find a small army of police poised with a battering ram. Arlyne found herself staring down the barrel of a nickel-plated revolver, while a detective rousted Luca from the kitchen. She stood numbly as another detective explained the charges, "working for a lottery and conspiracy." Somewhere on the periphery of her consciousness, she realized that Leslie had come home. No words passed between them. The girl simply watched with her sullen, inscrutable stare as her mother and Tommy Luca were led from the apartment in handcuffs.

Tommy had been right, of course. They were being watched. Since early fall, he and Arlyne had been followed and their phone conversations monitored by the Fort Lee Police Department, which, it later seemed, had deployed an extraordinary amount of manpower to capture a pair of petty bookmakers. But this was all understandable in light of Fort Lee's obsession with mobsters.

For years before Arlyne and Tommy came along, the local police chief, Arthur Dalton, had cherished the idea of his little department working with federal agents on organized crime cases. Fort Lee was ideally situated for this role, since the luxury high rises that had drawn Arlyne Brickman and Tommy Luca were a magnet for high-living wiseguys on both sides of the river. In accordance with Chief Dalton's ambitions, Fort Lee became the first police department in the state to set up its own organized crime Intelligence Unit. The unit had been around for only a year or so before Luca and Brickman wandered into its sights. This happened largely by accident.

Arlyne had a habit of dumping her paperwork in a trash bin outside the apartment. About two months before the arrest, another resident of Hudson Terrace noticed a cascade of betting slips and called the police. The tip was passed on to the Intelligence Unit where it found its way to the desk of Lieutenant Joe Spina. The detective and his partner, George Diehl, studied the evidence. They were so new to the rackets that they were not familiar with all forms of betting. But the slips seemed to have been generated by a game called "bolita," also known as single action.

Spina and Diehl began checking around the building and, calling upon the help of an informant in the neighborhood, traced the slips to an apartment occupied by one Arlyne Brickman. From a surveillance point outside the apartment building, the detectives were able to observe that the suspect was a "white female approximately five feet, six inches, 150–155 pounds, with hazel eyes and black hair." She was often in the company of a white male, only a little taller than herself, weighing approximately 180 pounds, with "black-gray" hair and brown eyes. He drove a 1971 Cadillac. When the detectives ran a check on the two, Brickman turned up clean. Luca, however, was classified by the New York Police Department as a "known gambler" with a history of arrests dating back to 1961. Moreover, he was reputed to be an associate of the Genovese.

Spina and Diehl felt like wildcatters who had hit a gusher. They quickly obtained a wiretap order for the suspect Brickman's phone lines, one listed to I. Weiss and the other to Sophie Silverstein, and for a little over a week they heard Arlyne phone the shoeshine parlor and luncheonette to take bets. Every afternoon when the races were over they heard someone call her from Aqueduct or Belmont to tell her what it paid. And they listened as she told the Brooklyn lottery writers how she and Luca would drive in that evening to settle up.

Spina and Diehl made plans to tail the pair on one of their forays into New York. It is a matter of courtesy for one jurisdiction to ask permission to intrude upon another's turf. When Fort Lee notified New York of its intentions, the Brooklyn Public Morals Squad also wanted in on the act, and the proposed expedition assumed comical proportions. One Tuesday afternoon late in November, ten police officers, each in his own radio-equipped car, gathered in the vicinity of Hudson Terrace to watch and wait.

At around a quarter to six, Arlyne and Tommy left the building and got into Luca's Caddy. When they pulled out of the lot, all ten cars fell into quiet pursuit. At the George Washington Bridge, however, the convoy hit rush-hour traffic and only one of the cars managed to hang on Tommy's tail. The stragglers caught up with the lead car in Brooklyn, where the bookmakers, by this time, were making their appointed rounds. Luca was going through his standard evasive action, driving seventy, then slowing to a crawl. Infuriated at having temporarily lost sight of him, one member of the surveillance team drove off the road and up a sidewalk to catch up with the speeding Caddy. Spina was certain that the caravan had been spotted, but the following day as they listened in on Luca's conversations, the bookie gave no hint that he suspected anything.

The madcap chase did manage to confirm what the detectives had been hearing over the wires. This gave them enough evidence to seek a search warrant. On December 19, a superior court judge gave permission for them to search Arlyne's apartment for betting slips and other gambling paraphernalia. Armed with the writ, Joe Spina led a platoon of officers down the hall to 6P. No sooner had they hoisted the battering ram than the door opened, revealing Arlyne Brickman with a trash basket full of evidence.

Arlyne had never experienced the humiliation of an arrest. She could not pretend that she was Virginia Hill cutting a fashionable and romantic figure before popping flash bulbs. She was an overweight, middle-aged woman in a muu muu on her way to city jail. For the first time in her life, Arlyne felt like a bad guy, and she had inherited just enough of her parents' bourgeois pretensions to feel the shame of her condition. Her cuffs were removed so that she could be fingerprinted and mugged. Then she was handed over to a female officer who searched her for drugs. Although the probe of her intimate cavities was done with impersonal efficiency, Arlyne felt the same violation that she did every time she was penetrated. By the time she was taken down the hall for questioning, she was on the verge of hysteria.

The detectives had intended to pull a good cop–bad cop routine. Diehl, a large, good-natured man, usually assumed the ingratiating role while Spina, the more imposing of the two, played the heavy. The suspect Brickman, however, seemed too fragile for such a workover. The detectives decided to treat her more gently. She was not, after all, the target they were after. If they played their cards right, they reasoned privately, they might win her trust so that she would deliver the goods on Luca and his Genovese associates.

The detectives had good reason to believe that Arlyne might be turned. While listening in on her phone conversations, the detectives had intercepted a call to the New York State Police where she left a message for a Lieutenant Mike Minto. Naturally curious about what business a suspected bookmaker might have with a state police investigator, the detectives contacted Minto, who told them that a couple of years earlier, he had visited Brickman in Fort Lee. Acting on a tip that she was estranged from her boyfriend, he caught her in a talkative mood and she told him about Luca's bookmaking venture with Fritzy Giovanelli.

Confronted with this now, however, Arlyne would not give Luca up. This was not so much out of loyalty as because she simply did not know who to trust. Luca, himself, was not inspiring much confidence. On the way to the station house, he urged her to take the rap. They would go easy on a woman with no criminal record, he told her. He was also thinking of his own skin when it came time to arrange bail. It was impossible, he said, for him to call his wife or brother because it would be admitting to them that he had been with Arlyne. In the end, he persuaded her to reach out to her mother. Billie Weiss quickly summoned Sadie and sent her across the river to post her daughter's fifteen-thousand-dollar bail. (In the confusion of the moment, she also posted bond for Luca.)

As Sadie drove her home in the falling snow, Arlyne reflected upon her mother's parting words, "I'll never talk to you again. I'll never send you another penny."

Given their potential conflict of interest, Luca and Brickman decided it was best to get separate attorneys. As soon as Arlyne heard the wiretaps played back to her, she realized that Luca's constant references to "niggers" were likely to prejudice jurors against them both. Arlyne agreed to a plea bargain. As a first-time offender, she received a year's probation and a two-hundred-dollar fine. Luca was in a similarly reasonable mood. He pleaded guilty to a lesser charge and got six months in the county jail.

Since the chaotic night of her arrest, Arlyne had not spoken further with Spina and Diehl. The question of her offering testimony against Luca had not arisen during the course of the plea bargaining, but the detectives had left open the invitation for her to come in and talk. At first, Arlyne had rejected the notion out of hand. With Luca doing time, she found herself missing him. And when he asked her to help him get work release, she agreed. It required her only to romance a fat, unappetizing county employee over dinner and follow that up with a blow job. As a result, Tommy was released every morning, ostensibly to work as a day laborer in New York. Arlyne picked him up at five. They had breakfast and then she took him to Union City where he caught a bus across the river. In the evening, she met him at the same spot and they spent a few hours together before she returned him to captivity.

One evening as she was letting Tommy out in the jail lot, two men approached the car. One was a hulking goon, the other a short guy who resembled Paul Anka. Without warning, they grabbed Tommy, beat him with their fists and left him bleeding on the pavement. Arlyne was stunned. She ran to tend to Tommy, who, it turned out, looked in worse condition than he really was. His attackers, he told her, were Joey Scopo and Jackie Cavallo, collection men for John Gotti.

Gotti, as Vince Lamattina's friend Tony had once warned Luca, was not a man to be messed with. Tommy seemed to have taken this warning to heart, but his arrest and sentence had made it difficult for him to make his vig payments. The fact that he was doing time, however, did not excuse him. Joey and Jackie would wait for him outside the jail evenings as a reminder that they could reach him anywhere.

Arlyne could see that Tommy was scared. Once again, he was in desperate need of her help. Arlyne managed now and then to scrape together a few hundred dollars and take them to a place in Ozone Park that she knew only as "The Club." (Its full name, she would later learn, was the Bergin Hunt and Fish Club.) Usually, she'd give the envelope to Joey or Jackie. One day, she would later claim, she arrived to find the Gotti brothers standing outside. She handed the money to either John or Gene. Arlyne, however, did not have the means to make these payments indefinitely, and Tommy finally sent her to Vince Lamattina's vegetable store to pick up cash. She found the normally inhospitable shylock strangely accommodating. Arlyne naturally assumed that Tommy had arranged for a loan from Vince to pay Gotti, but as the weeks wore on and she picked up more and more envelopes from Lamattina, she began to suspect that something was amiss. Her suspicions were not unfounded. A few discreet inquiries to Sophie and others revealed that Tommy had gone into a partnership with Vince and was now in the shylocking business.

Arlyne was furious. There was a code of honor observed by otherwise dishonorable men of Luca's stripe. It held that if a man went to jail, his partners were obligated to take care of his dependents. By rights, Arlyne reasoned, Vince Lamattina should be taking care of her. Instead, she was ferrying cash from the enterprise to the shylock Gotti. The balance was being forwarded to Tommy's wife and family.

Arlyne seethed. Then she picked up the phone and called Joe Spina.

If you had asked Arlyne Brickman in the summer of 1975 if she was an "informant," she would have said "no." An informant was always someone else. He was the jerk who was too stupid to pull off a con and had to squeal to get himself out of a jam. Or he was some distant figure like "Uncle Meyer's" nemesis, Abie Reles. Arlyne did not think of herself in these terms. She was struggling to survive. There were occasions when cooperating with the law was useful. More than a decade earlier she had gotten her revenge upon Norman Brickman by delivering evidence against him. She did not think of herself as a snitch. Just a woman in search of justice.

Back in the fall of 1972 when Lieutenant Minto had shown up at her door, she had been angry at Tommy for favoring his wife. She invited him in for coffee. Whenever she got lonely and depressed, she tended to talk freely. She had liked the burly, affable investigator and soon had told him all about Tommy's dealings with Giovanelli. (She even gave him a copy of the numbers book she and Tommy had faked to fool Fritzy.) On occasions, she would even call Minto and arrange to meet him on West Street near his offices at the World Trade Center. There she would deliver some tidbit of gangland gossip. It made her feel important. It gave her some leverage over Tommy. But an "informant"? No, Arlyne Brickman was no snitch.

It was this same prodigious power of self-justification that allowed her now to make her first fateful call to Joe Spina. Tommy had screwed her. She was depressed and wanted to talk. Spina was happy to oblige. Throughout the summer and fall of 1975, he met her whenever she liked on the side streets of her neighborhood. She would climb into the front seat of his car and gossip. She told him about Fritzy, who was rumored to be expanding his enterprises to Fort Lee. She laid out the details of Tommy's business dealings with Vince Lamattina. She went through her entire litany of lovers from Nate Nelson through Tony Mirra. Spina did not recognize many of these names, as he was unfamiliar with New York's Lower East Side, but he relayed the information back to Diehl, who recorded it on scores of meticulous notecards.

In this early stage of their association with Arlyne Brickman, Spina and Diehl were not sure what they had. Arlyne threw out so many names and places that they were hard put to make sense of them, let alone verify them. They were excited, nonetheless, to have found such a voluble source. Spina wanted to bring her down to the station for a more complete debriefing, but Chief Dalton would have none of it. Despite his fascination with organized crime, the chief did not want his detectives tainted by association with someone he described as "a tramp for the Mafia." For almost a year, therefore, Spina and Diehl worked Arlyne informally. She would call Spina at one or two in the morning and he would listen to her never-ending stream of sorrows. He found himself becoming rather fond of her.

During the summer of 1976, it became clear to detectives Spina and Diehl that Arlyne was in some kind of trouble.

It was difficult to tell precisely what was wrong. Arlyne's distracted, stream-of-consciousness conversation rarely brought her straight to the point. Beyond that, she seemed reluctant to be specific. Spina suspected she was into loansharks and he urged her to come clean. If she owed money, he reminded her, the debt would be canceled if the lenders went to prison. She refused to discuss the matter until one day Spina received a call. "We've got to talk," she said urgently. "I'm afraid they're gonna kill me." Spina and Diehl agreed to meet her on a street behind her apartment. There—red-eyed and frantic—Arlyne explained her predicament.

As Spina had guessed, she was being hounded by sharks. While Tommy was in jail, she had been hard up for money. Cut off "once and for all" by her parents, she had had to support herself and Leslie through betting and borrowing. A year earlier she had gone to a Genovese shylock with whom Tommy had done business. He was a short mustachioed fellow whom she knew only as "Fish." Arlyne had gone to see him at his customary hangout, an Exxon station in Weehawken. The Fish loaned Arlyne one thousand dollars but, thereafter, turned her over to one of his goons named Billy David. Every week Arlyne met Billy and a gofer named Chickie at one of several restaurants around Hudson and Bergen counties to make a payment of $160 or so.

Arlyne did not tell her detective friends the entire truth, which was that she and Billy had been having an affair—of sorts. Billy was blond, good-looking and a sharp dresser and the moment she laid eyes on him, she decided she wanted him. Billy was basically a ne'er-do-well. An Irishman, he liked to imagine he was Italian, though his inappropriate ethnicity naturally limited his chances for advancement. He was much too fond of booze and women and Arlyne flattered herself that she could manipulate him. Some weeks when she went to make her payments she would end up with Billy in a motel room. Sometimes, she would later claim, he would take her out to dinner just because he liked her.

Because of their special relationship, Billy seemed inclined to go easy on her, letting her slide for weeks on end. Her original $1,000 loan, meanwhile, ballooned to $5,300, on which she was paying 3 percent a week. Finally, the Fish lost patience and told Billy to get tough or else. Since then—and this was the part Arlyne chose to share with Spina and Diehl—Billy had been visiting her on Hudson Terrace, yelling, waving his arms and telling her she was going to be visited by a bone-crusher named Frankie LaGuardia. He even insinuated that one of his thugs might rape Leslie.

Joe Spina ran a check on David, which showed him nominally to be a car salesman. He had had two arrests, one for gambling, the other for threatening to kill a possible loanshark victim in North Bergen. David's history lent Arlyne's version of events credence. This was the opening that the detectives had been waiting for. As a victim, Arlyne would be strategically placed to play out her connection with David, which might lead them to the mysterious Fish and perhaps even deeper into the labyrinthine world of the Genovese family.

August 25, 1976, was the day the world changed for Arlyne Brickman. Her name was entered into the records of the Fort Lee Police as an official informant. A file was opened on her and she was given a number: SCI 75-02. There was no discussion of payment. (Indeed, at that early stage of her work for law enforcement, Arlyne was not aware that informants were paid.) Instead, the arrangement was couched as a favor for a favor. Arlyne would provide intelligence, and they would go after her creditors.

Throughout the fall, Arlyne kept in constant touch with the detectives, giving them tips on the whereabouts of David and his crew. Often she was overwrought, calling Spina in the early hours of the morning to tell him that Billy was coming to beat her up. "Don't let them upstairs," Spina warned. "Meet them in the lobby." Then he would cruise by and watch from the end of the drive as Arlyne met Billy and Chickie in her huge glass foyer. Billy would wave his arms and scream, Arlyne would wring her hands and sob, each playing a part in a hysterical pantomime. After twenty minutes they would leave.

The Fish never came on those visits and his identity was still unknown. Then one day, Arlyne called to say that the elusive shark was scheduled to be at the Exxon station. Spina and Diehl showed up that night and waited until a man answering Arlyne's description arrived. They snapped photos and later identified him as a reputed Genovese associate named Robert Anthony Fischetti. Over the next few weeks, the detectives tailed Fischetti's brown Cadillac from the Exxon station along a circuit of restaurants that Arlyne described. SCI 75-02's file expanded rapidly with photos and intelligence reports. But Detectives Spina and Diehl were not quite sure how to proceed. The investigation was extending beyond Fort Lee's ability to handle it. Most of the loansharking activity seemed to be taking place not in Bergen but in nearby Hudson County and the detectives were not so familiar with that terrain. They needed outside help. Spina approached the Bergen County prosecutor but found his office too overloaded with cases to take on another. Then he went to the state police, which assigned an investigator, but for undisclosed reasons let the matter drop. There remained one last option. Since Billy David had allegedly made threats to make his collection, that constituted extortion. And extortion was a federal crime. Early in 1976, Detective Joe Spina called the FBI.

Spina, as it happened, was friendly with an agent assigned to the Newark field office. His name was Jeff Dossett and he was expertly acquainted with the cast of organized crime characters operating out of Hudson County. When Spina approached him with the news that he had a line on a shylock named Fischetti, Dossett recognized the name and crew. Fischetti, he said, answered to Tommy Principe, a soldier for the Genovese Family operating out of Jersey City. At the time of Spina's call, the FBI was not actively investigating the Fish, but now Dossett's interest was piqued. He asked the detective to arrange a meeting with his informant.

When Arlyne learned that she had an appointment with the Federal Bureau of Investigation, the full import escaped her. Arlyne, in fact, did not even know what the FBI was. A product of the Lower East Side, she had always thought of police as either beat cops or detectives operating out of local precincts. Her study of the career of Virginia Hill was directed to particular aspects of the mob girl's appearance and love affairs, and she was ignorant of the role of the federal government in her downfall. In conveying to Arlyne the significance of what was about to occur, Spina had simply described the FBI as "people who could help her."

On the night of her meeting with Agent Dossett, Joe picked her up

in front of her apartment and took her to a motel near the George
Washington Bridge. Spina had chosen the spot because he thought it
would be secure. He knocked on one of the doors, and the agent
answered.

Arlyne's nerves had been tingling in anticipation of meeting the
agent, whose position, she concluded, must make him dangerous. She
was surprised—and possibly a little disappointed—to find herself face to
face with an amiable, moon-faced man, who appeared as unassuming as
the corner druggist. Although he fell short of her expectations, she
decided she liked him. She also decided it might even be possible to
manipulate him. (His good-old-boy drawl reminded her a little of
Stamey's.) So, crossing her legs, she began reeling off the names of her
friends and lovers.

Dossett, who was a tougher sell than he appeared, found it unlikely
that Arlyne really knew all of these people. But, he concluded, if she
knew even *half* of them, she might be put to good use. And if she had
indeed been threatened by loansharks, then she was a victim. That gave
the government grounds to pursue Fischetti and his crew. Accordingly,
he put in a call to V. Grady O'Malley, a federal prosecutor assigned to
the Organized Crime Strike Force in Newark.

Arlyne's reputation preceded her. O'Malley had been alerted to the
fact that the "victim" was not some hapless merchant who had gotten in
over her head with loansharks, but an aging bombshell who ran and
often slept with the mob. If the government decided to prosecute and the
case came to trial, it would be difficult to make her appear sympathetic
to a jury. Moreover, there was the question of her own criminal history.
Her rap sheet showed only one conviction, but should a case against
Fischetti and associates come to trial, the defendants would have
knowledge of any other criminal activity in which Arlyne Brickman
might have been engaged and could utterly destroy her credibility. The
intelligence O'Malley had received on Arlyne indicated that she lived
from day to day, week to week, gambling and handling what was
possibly stolen merchandise, which she would either sell or pass on for
a finder's fee. (Arlyne later denied engaging in these activities.) As far as
O'Malley could discern, however, Arlyne had never been involved in
anything truly serious. He concluded that, while she talked a good game,
she did not have the savvy or intellectual stamina to carry through on a
deal. O'Malley told Dossett to see where the informant could take them.

At first, the deal offered by the government sounded good to Arlyne.
She would agree to go to meetings with the loansharks wearing a small

tape recorder under her blouse. In turn, the Feds would give her the
money for the vig payments. As she began to consider the consequences,
however, she realized that this could be very dangerous business.
Wiseguys were deathly afraid of wires and to be caught wearing one
could mean being hustled out of a restaurant to a vacant lot and
strangled. That she was a woman was not likely to save her.

Arlyne's fears seemed justified by events of the days to follow. With
O'Malley's approval, she taped a telephone conversation with Billy
David during which he made an unmistakable threat to Leslie. "Two
guys are sitting by your house," he warned. "If you don't come in, your
daughter will come in eventually." The following day, Billy and Chickie
muscled their way into the apartment, where they ransacked her drawers
and closets looking for valuables.

From the government's standpoint, these were encouraging developments, which essentially verified their victim's version of events and
established that she had not exaggerated the seriousness of the threats.
O'Malley and Dossett set in motion plans for the first wire, which was
scheduled for ten days hence, the date of Arlyne's next payment to Billy.

The rendezvous with David was to take place at the Waterfront
Lounge, a restaurant and bar in Edgewater. Beforehand, Arlyne met
Dossett and Spina at the motel near the bridge. There, she was
introduced to Agent Dewanna Stratton. It was mandatory when dealing
with a female informant for the Bureau to provide a female agent for
such functions as wiring. It was also Stratton's responsibility to hover on
the periphery during the actual meetings, not only to assure Arlyne's
safety but also to bear witness to the transaction. If the case went to trial
and Arlyne's character and veracity fell under siege, the agent could be
called in to bolster her testimony.

Arlyne took an instant dislike to Agent Stratton. Not that there was
anything conspicuously offensive about her. But Arlyne had a natural
suspicion of women and a horror of being touched by them. Her
hostility increased when Stratton directed her into the bathroom and
proceeded to make the mandatory check of Arlyne's internal cavities for
drugs. Arlyne removed her blouse as the agent produced a small tape
recorder called a Nagra. Stratton explained that it could be worn either
in front or behind. Arlyne chose the back. Agent Stratton held the Nagra
in place and secured it with broad strips of adhesive tape wound around
the chest. Then she threaded a small transmitter—which would allow
Agent Dossett to listen in from a remote location—up through the front
of Arlyne's brassiere. Although it was a warm spring night, Arlyne wore
a coat to conceal any tell-tale contours.

It was clear to Arlyne that she was involved in events over which she stood to have little control. That realization always caused her anxiety. By the time she reached the door of the Waterfront Lounge, she was trembling. The presence of Agent Stratton, a few paces behind, did little to allay her rising panic.

Just inside, Arlyne passed a couple of her friends at the bar, to whom she gave a nod. Then she spotted Billy, who was sitting at the bar with one of his other girlfriends, Valerie. Joining them Arlyne turned without ceremony to Billy's little friend and said, "Valerie . . . could you go to the ladies' room for a minute?" Then she turned to Billy.

"I don't know what's going on," she said. "You're moving too fast for me, Billy."

Billy replied, "I made a deal."

"I can't hear ya," Arlyne said, arranging her chest so that the transmitter was closer to him.

"I made an arrangement with you Saturday—gave you the break you asked for. Today's Monday and . . . you're supposed to do the right thing. If you did the right thing, we're the best of friends. If you didn't, we're going to be the worst of enemies."

"I want to ask you a question," said Arlyne. "You know I am in a world of trouble."

"Let me ask you a question before we start this," Billy interjected. "How much money do you owe?"

"Fifty-three hundred dollars."

"No, I don't mean that," he corrected. "How much money do you have to give me?"

"I have to give you nine hundred dollars."

"How much have you got there now?" he queried.

"Are you going to start a war?" Arlyne asked pointedly.

"It better not be less than five hundred dollars, cause there'll be a fuckin' war like you'll never see in your life . . ." Billy replied.

"All you do . . . all you keep doin' is threatening me," she pressed.

"I'm not threatening anyone," Billy replied. "I don't have to do that. I have people to do my slob work."

"What do you mean you have people to do your slob work?" she pressed further. "I don't understand you."

Billy would not be pushed off track. "I want to know how much money you have," he insisted.

"Well, I came tonight with three hundred dollars."

He was upset. "You promised me . . . on your daughter's life."

They haggled for a while over terms until Arlyne protested, "I can't think today, Billy. My head is poppin'."

"You better have a drink," he advised.

Arlyne knew this was not a very good idea. Drinking always got her in trouble, as it had the night so long ago when she got smashed at the Wagon Wheel with Sally Burns. But she could feel the Nagra pressing against her back and she thought a drink might calm her nerves.

"I'll take a Scotch," she said.

Valerie returned from the ladies' room and Billy, in a more congenial mood, asked Arlyne if she would like to stay for dinner. Having taken a few sips of whiskey, Arlyne felt her inhibitions falling away. The calmer and dreamier she felt, the more clearly she saw her task. And the more curiously aggressive she became.

"I can't believe he's so nice to me today," Arlyne said to Valerie. "Maybe because you're here . . . you had to see him Saturday . . . I was afraid to let him even touch my dog.

"You see, I like ya," she turned back to Billy. "I'd be nice to ya, you understand?"

"Three weeks I been chasin' ya," Billy bridled. "That's bein' nice to me?"

He asked her if she wanted a steak.

"No," she replied, "I'll take another drink. I might as well get bombed. Honey," she reminded Billy, "it's Leslie's birthday. If you get a chance send Leslie some flowers, for her birthday.

"I can't now," Billy protested. "It's after six."

"That kid was frightened Saturday," Arlyne insisted boozily. "She was . . ."

"It's your fault, it's not mine," Billy insisted.

"You're like in the days of Al Capone," she pressed.

"It'll be worse next time," he warned.

It was hot in the restaurant and it would have seemed natural for Arlyne to remove her coat. She was afraid the wires would show. Consequently, she had begun to sweat. She could feel the dampness under her armpits and the rivulets of perspiration trickling down her back. And then, to her horror, she realized that the adhesive strips were coming loose. The Nagra was slipping down her back.

For a second she contemplated excusing herself and beating a quick retreat to the ladies' room. But her instincts told her that the best defense was a good offense. She pressed on more aggressively.

"You know, I had Chickie bamboozled for a while," she boasted. "He's a doll."

"He's not cut out for this business," Billy groused. He had been drinking a little too much himself and he, too, was getting reckless. "But the next guy that comes up to your house, he's cut out for this."

"You mean Frankie?" Arlyne queried.

"Yeah."

"You want to make a bet I can have Frankie twisted around my little finger?"

"You know what Frankie would do to you if you came near him," Billy blustered. "He'd throw you right out of your window."

Arlyne knew that she had gotten what she came for. She disengaged herself from Billy with promises that she would try to scrape together a payment of $178. Then she tottered unsteadily out the door, took a deep breath and fled to the car where Agent Stratton recovered the dangling Nagra.

In the days thereafter, Arlyne was exultant. She had done a thing that terrified her and come through with flying colors. The FBI agents, even prosecutor O'Malley, were lavish in their praise. Arlyne had managed to elicit at least three distinct threats: Billy's assertion that he had people to do his "slob work," his contention that there would be "a war," and the warning that the goon, Frankie, would "throw her out her window."

O'Malley was particularly impressed with Arlyne's ability to ask the second or third question. If, for instance, Billy David warned that something might happen to her, Arlyne would follow up with "*What* will happen? *How* will it happen?" As it was dangerous for an informant wearing a wire to appear too inquisitive, this persistence on her part was admirable. It was also useful from a legal standpoint since specifics were helpful in convincing a jury that a victim had actually been threatened. Arlyne could play a role very well. But then, O'Malley concluded, she had been acting for years.

Even while she was basking in praise, however, Arlyne was maneuvering to alter the conditions of her employment. Now that she was—to her way of thinking—one of the team, she found it beneath her dignity to have to submit to any more drug searches. She was also furious that her wire had slipped. In the future, she told Agents Dossett and Stratton, she did not want the Nagra taped to her body. Her first complaint got nowhere. The search could not be waived under any circumstances. Sensing her aversion to being touched, however, the agents allowed that in the future, she could carry the recorder. Accordingly, they supplied an attractive brown handbag with two handles and a middle compartment wherein Arlyne stuck the Nagra. The mike

protruded slightly above the zipper and she covered it with a handkerchief. This meant that Arlyne could start and stop the tape herself, an
arrangement which left her feeling more in control. Control, she had
decided, was the name of the game. Control over the Feds, control over
her quarry, control over herself. She vowed that she would never again
drink while wearing a wire.

Two days after the Waterfront surveillance, Arlyne met Billy again,
this time at a restaurant in Union City. To her dismay, he eased up on the
threats. She tried to get him to elaborate on his menacing remarks about
Leslie but he insisted that he had "never mentioned the child." The only
thing she managed to elicit was that he had hit someone that day and
that the episode had left him "depressed."

Arlyne tried a seductive approach. "Supposing things went very bad
for me," she purred. "Would you have any pity?"

"Very little," Billy replied coldly.

Arlyne grew incensed. "I gave you three quick blow jobs—not
even—nothing from it. Not even a Christmas present. Not even a present
for Leslie's birthday."

Outside in the surveillance car, Agent Stratton shot a glance at Jeff
Dossett, who muttered to himself, "If this thing doesn't get a plea, we're
in trouble." Later, during debriefing, he admonished his informant to
"keep these conversations on business."

Nevertheless, over the next two months, Arlyne managed to draw
the noose tighter. Over the next two months she continued to meet Billy.
Once she arranged to have a payment delivered by Dewanna Stratton,
whom she had introduced to Billy as an airline stewardess. The
government did not want to be in the position of carrying Arlyne's debt
indefinitely. If O'Malley had been ready to seek an indictment that
spring, Arlyne could have been placed under witness protection until
trial. The prosecutor, however, was looking into the case of another
victim who was being threatened by the same crew and that investigation
promised to take some time. This necessitated leaving Arlyne in some
safe and solvent position until the case was ready to try.

There were other advantages in leaving Arlyne out on the street. She
had demonstrated that she had a valuable set of contacts, not only in
New Jersey but also in New York. O'Malley decided that she needed the
freedom to work without harassment. The government, therefore,
agreed to pay off the debt.

Disentangling oneself from a shylock loan, however, was not a simple
matter. Arlyne knew perfectly well that a shark prefers to keep the

principal outstanding and collect the vig forever. The negotiation of a paydown, as it was called, was a delicate issue and subject to rules of protocol. Accompanied by her "friend," the airline stewardess, Arlyne had paid Fischetti a visit to raise the subject. The loanshark indicated he might be willing to accept a twenty-five-hundred-dollar settlement, but the deal had to be concluded at a sit-down with Arlyne's "people." This raised a difficult problem since Arlyne's people at this juncture were FBI agents and a federal prosecutor.

It was Arlyne who came up with the idea to reach out for Tommy, who had apparently gone back to his wife.

As usually happened during her estrangements from Luca, she missed him. Whenever the excitement of the surveillances ebbed, she felt the emotional void created by his absence. She could never explain why he had this hold on her. Their relationship was not based on warmth or respect or even, in the strictest sense, love. The attraction was powerful, nonetheless, and based, she would later conclude, on a sick need. Tommy needed her for sex. He needed her to run errands. He needed her to earn. She, in turn, needed him for both excitement and security. The bottom line was that a mob girl must be attached to a man. And Luca—while no Joe Colombo or Tony Mirra—was connected. It was an irony—not lost on Arlyne—that even now, when she had gone over to "the other side," she still needed Luca to consummate a deal.

Arlyne found the twin prospects of using Tommy for her own ends while bringing him back into her personal orbit highly appealing. How to do this without telling him about the Feds, however, was another matter. It was not, strangely enough, that Luca objected to her working as an informant. Some time after she had struck up her relationship with Mike Minto, Arlyne had told him about it. According to her recollection of events, he had flown into a rage, beat her, called her a "stoolie," then calmly decided that her treachery might work to their mutual advantage. The information that Arlyne was feeding to Minto didn't seem to be bringing him any heat. And it was entirely possible that she might prevail upon her "friend" to do favors, such as go after his creditors.

The current situation, however, was different. Tommy no longer owed anything to Fischetti and so bore him no ill will. Furthermore, Luca would never consent to serving as her patron at the sit-down if he knew Arlyne would be wearing a wire. Tommy was savvy enough to know that showing up on tape made him a potential witness—or even defendant—if the case went to trial. Worse still, he would be revealed to be consorting with an informant. Arlyne chose to keep him in the dark.

There had been recent developments that would pave the way for an overture to Luca. Early in April, Tommy and Vince Lamattina had been arrested in Queens and charged with bookmaking, assault, loansharking and extortion. In the aftermath of the bust, old injuries were forgiven and Arlyne found herself impressed once again into service as intermediary, making bail and other arrangements. Relations with Tom remained cool but the lines were now open—as long as she did not call his house.

There were a couple of places Arlyne could now reach Luca. He and Vince had just opened a gambling club called Blackjacks in Queens. He was also hanging out a lot at a Forest Hills beauty salon of which Vince owned a piece. One afternoon she called him at the salon to ask his help. She needed to clear up this thing with the Fish, she said. A guy named "Chuck" was putting up the money, but she needed Tommy to go to the sit-down, pretend the money was his, and close the deal. Amazingly, he agreed.

Luca's own motives soon became clear. On the night of the sit-down Arlyne met the agents to receive her Nagra. They followed her to Union City. Arlyne spotted Luca outside the Four Star Diner. He got into her car to talk. He proposed "holding back" the money from the sharks. Arlyne, who realized that Tommy had intervened only so that he could make off with Chuck's twenty-five hundred dollars, pleaded with him until she got him into the diner. Neither Fischetti nor David had yet arrived.

As the waitress brought coffee, Tommy groused, "I wonder if it's going to rain before we get back to Brooklyn."

"I didn't . . . tell you you have to do anything with me," Arlyne replied defensively.

"Little lady," Tommy snapped, "speak when you're spoken to."

Billy arrived with a sidekick whom Arlyne knew only as Frumpy. Fischetti was nowhere to be seen.

"Bobby couldn't make it here on prompt time," Billy explained, but he was clearly empowered to begin the negotiations. He threw out a figure of four thousand dollars.

"That's the best he wants to do?" Tommy clarified.

"Would you like coffee, fellas?" asked the waitress.

"No." Billy paused. "Give me a Tab." He turned back to Tommy. "Take it. You can't beat it. A guy takes off more than a third what the thing is. It ain't for bad, you know."

Billy went on to complain how he had had on occasion to wait three weeks for a collection from Arlyne. Whereupon she countered, "[Don't] you wait sometimes for six . . . and seven weeks?"

Billy acknowledged that sometimes he did.

"Do you threaten their homes?" Arlyne pushed. "Do you threaten . . . the daughters?"

"That's gonna stop," Tommy insisted.

"Wait a minute," Billy protested, offended. "We're not threatening the daughters. Wait, here's Bobby now."

Bobby Fischetti had appeared at the door of the diner. He beckoned Luca outside.

This development threw Arlyne into a panic. The heavyweights at this sit-down were now out of hearing range. She had to maneuver herself back into their company without appearing obvious.

She turned to Frumpy. "Why did they call Tommy outside?"

"I don't know," he replied. "But I don't care."

"Well I care. It's my money. Look, whatever deals they make, they make in front of me."

She picked up her brown leather bag and marched outside. Fischetti was explaining how, though he could have turned out the money at five points, he had loaned it to Arlyne for three. Seeing her opening, Arlyne interjected, "But you originally said . . . that you were going to give it to me for two."

The three haggled for a while until Arlyne, seeing that Tommy was bringing the matter no closer to resolution, finally seized the initiative.

"You want me to tell you something, Bobby?" she asked.

"Go ahead," he replied.

"I brought Tommy . . . because . . . I figured he's with people and you know his people, you understand?"

"Right."

"And they like to do the right thing too."

"Go ahead."

"I been around, and I'm not stupid. I think . . . enough of this . . . the whole thing calls for three thousand, the most. Cash. One, two, three and walk away. . . . What do you think, Tom?" She turned to Luca for ratification.

"Look," Luca deferred. "I'll let Bobby's conscience be his guide. What can I say?"

In the end, they struck a bargain for three thousand dollars. Tommy handed over the twenty-five hundred—money that was supposed to be coming from him, but that he thought was coming from Chuckie, but that was really coming from the Feds. And he invited Bobby and Billy to Blackjacks the following Wednesday so that they could pick up the other five hundred dollars.

Luca didn't want to hang around. He cut out for Brooklyn, leaving Arlyne in front of the diner. Though abandoned, she felt exultant. Her secret knowledge gave her power over Tommy. What's more, there was a team of federal agents somewhere out there in the night hanging on her every word. For the first time in her life she felt like a success. Little Arlyne was the center of attention. Little Arlyne was one of the boys.

SEVEN

ATLANTIC
BEACH

All that spring, Arlyne had a fine time. She had picked up law enforcement lingo, which she used with gleeful, often impression-istic abandon. Each of her exploits with the Fischetti crew was a "surveillance." There were long afternoons when she and Dewanna would conduct surveillances—that is, wait—for Billy David in a motel parking lot near the Lincoln Tunnel. Arlyne sat bag in hand, Nagra in bag, poised for action. As the days grew warmer, the waiting became increasingly uncomfortable. Agent Stratton would roll down the win-dows to catch a breeze. Arlyne, who during her career as mob girl had tended to use automobiles as a reliable indicator of power, found it odd that the government could not afford air-conditioning.

Arlyne bore these discomforts with uncharacteristic equanimity, however, because she had been infected with esprit de corps. She was beginning to believe that she truly was a federal agent. Agent Dossett had been so impressed with Arlyne's contacts that he had passed her name along to one of his colleagues, Agent Greg Hendrickson, in the Brooklyn-Queens Office. Arlyne plied Hendrickson with tidbits of gossip on purported drug deals and heists. She had been waiting years to get back at her old antagonist Vince Lamattina, and carefully laid out the details of his shylocking operation. She provided details on the shady political contacts of her old flame, Walter Perlmutter, another scoundrel she figured deserved his comeuppance. She would happily have delivered whatever dirt she could on Sally Burns, but he had disappeared years earlier. His body, she had heard, had been found in a trunk.

Arlyne was actively courted not only by the FBI but also by the DEA. When Joe Spina had invited Agent Dossett into the Fischetti case, he had extended a similar invitation to a drug enforcement agent named Edward Magno. The initial lure was a report from Arlyne that the Fischetti outfit was looking to sell some five hundred pounds of marijuana. Ordinarily, the Drug Enforcement, as Arlyne preferred to call it, considered pot cases beneath its consideration. Agent Magno, however, thought it was possible to parlay this marijuana connection into a buy of coke or heroin. Acting on an introduction arranged by Arlyne, Magno met with Chickie Nardone at a Holiday Inn. The expedition turned up dry. It served, however, to pique Magno's, and the DEA's, interest in informant Brickman's ability to "effect undercover agent introduction."

As Arlyne reeled off her list of associates, Magno scribbled. Every so often, a name seemed to arouse his interest. One of these was John Gotti. After listening to Arlyne's account of Tommy Luca's indebtedness to the crew at the Bergin Hunt and Fish Club, Magno asked her to try to arrange a meeting between the Gambino captain and a young Italian kid who had gotten into a jam and had agreed to work undercover. Arlyne contacted Joey Scopo, saying she had a prospective borrower who wanted to meet with Johnny. But Gotti, who had only recently been released from prison, was apparently playing it cautious. Joey refused to take the proposal to his boss.

Agent Magno did not appear discouraged. Arlyne talked on; he scribbled. When she came to Joe Spione, he stopped her once again.

Spione, also known as Joe the Barber, was a bookmaker who worked out of a body shop in Queens. He also sold drugs. Arlyne had met Spione through Tommy and later, during one of her estrangements with Luca, she and Joe had enjoyed a brief fling. When the Drug Enforcement asked her to wear a wire, she agreed without hesitation, reasoning that she was not really doing a job on an old friend but helping to get information on a character in which the government had an even keener interest—Joe's brother-in-law, Tommy DeSimone. A hijacker allied with the Lucchese Family, DeSimone was also suspected of dealing heroin.

At Magno's request, Arlyne arranged for him to meet the Barber and his notorious brother-in-law on a side street near Hudson Terrace. She introduced Eddy as a "friend" and prospective buyer. Then she walked back to her apartment. Eddy never told her the outcome of that meeting. Agents, she was learning, never gave their informants any more than was absolutely necessary. Some months later, Eddy called her to say that Joe had disappeared. (One account published a decade thereafter would claim that Spione had run afoul of the Gottis and been dismembered in a back room of the Bergin Hunt and Fish Club.)

The short-lived surveillance of Joe the Barber, however, set off a chain reaction of minor investigations. While Arlyne was working on Spione, the DEA became interested in one of her neighbors at Hudson Terrace, a petite blond named Yvette. Arlyne was only slightly acquainted with Yvette, who appeared to be kept by her boyfriend Rusty, a wiseguy who owned a gourmet shop. He would bring Yvette bread and fine cuts of meat.

Arlyne had found Rusty a nice guy and enjoyed flirting with him. The Drug Enforcement's interest in this pair was that Rusty's brother-in-law was reputed to be a major heroin dealer. Agent Magno let Arlyne know that big things were expected of her. She should try to set up an undercover to make a heroin buy from Rusty. More important, she should try to trace the drugs to their source, which Rusty had indicated was somewhere in Europe. This might even necessitate her traveling abroad. Arlyne applied for a passport and waited, every nerve and fiber atingle with excitement.

At the height of her new importance, however, her confidence began to crumble. This loss of nerve was not due to any single event, but to a series of disquieting developments.

Throughout her hectic schedule of debriefings and surveillances with Hendrickson and Magno, Arlyne's main job remained the investigation of Fischetti, Nardone and Billy David. In that pursuit she stayed in regular contact with her case agent, Jeff Dossett, whose down-home manner calmed her nerves. In her loneliness Arlyne had come to enjoy and depend upon his attention. She had begun to think of him as her friend. One afternoon, Jeff asked her to meet him at a diner off the turnpike. There he broke the news that he was being transferred to an office in South Jersey. He would still be case agent, he explained, so she could always reach him by phone. Dewanna would still be around. Another agent in the Newark office would be designated to take her calls. But Dossett's assurances did not dispel Arlyne's suspicions that she was being abandoned.

With the departure of Jeff Dossett, Arlyne ran smack up against reality. In the excitement and intrigue of the surveillances, she had lost sight of the fact that she might be called to testify. The prospect now gave her the jitters. What could she have been thinking? It was one thing to gossip privately to an agent; quite another to tell the world. If Fischetti and company had been inclined to harm Leslie before, what would they do if she sent them to prison? More to the point, what would their friends do? Fischetti, she believed, had ties to the Gambinos, whose numbers included the vicious Bergin clique. "What happened here,"

Arlyne would recall matter-of-factly, "was I got scared . . . I mean, it was all playing fun and games and it was wonderful, but now I hadda testify against these guys who were killers."

Arlyne's anxiety increased the following spring, when she was called to the federal courthouse in Newark to testify before a grand jury. Although she was required to endure only the questioning of a sympathetic prosecutor, and this in relatively cloistered surroundings, it served to remind her of the day when she would be shoved into a more dangerous arena.

Grady O'Malley summoned Arlyne to Newark to confer with the federal marshals about entering the Witness Protection Program. It was not a congenial scene. To begin with, Arlyne had heard that entering the program was no guarantee against being killed. One had to place one's entire faith in the marshals, who—she had heard on the street—were susceptible to bribes. Leslie, of course, had no use for cops of any kind and had to be dragged, sullen and unkempt, to the Strike Force Office. There she slumped into a chair, expression set in stone, while the marshals explained how they would be moved to another part of the country where they would be given new lodging and fresh identities. They would not be allowed under any circumstances to contact old friends or even family. At one point Leslie jumped up and shouted, "C'mon, Ma. Let's get the hell outta here."

Arlyne did not have to be persuaded. She could not imagine living in a strange city. Fort Lee had been a stretch, but then all she had to do was look across the river and see New York with its promise of intrigue both legal and illicit. What would she do all day? She couldn't work for the government. Under the gaze of the marshals, she certainly couldn't run with wiseguys. She tried to imagine a world in which she couldn't call her mother. Unfamiliar terrors seemed more intimidating than the familiar ones. And Arlyne Brickman declined Witness Protection.

The question then became how to protect herself. When in early September of 1978, an indictment came down against Fischetti et al., Arlyne knew she had to make her move. She called her mother. "Ma," she laid it out bluntly, "I got a big problem . . . I've been working for the FBI."

There was a moment of stunned silence before Billie replied, "You've been ratting people out?"

Brushing aside the reproof, Arlyne pressed on. "I gotta get out of Fort Lee. They're looking for me. The cops, the wiseguys. If they find out that I did this, what am I going to do?"

"Well," Billie replied, "I'm gonna see what we can do here."

The logical thing would have been to go to Irving, whose intervention years ago had gotten his daughter free of her poisonous entanglement with Jimmy Doyle. But Irving and Arlyne had become so emotionally distant that he almost refused to acknowledge that she still lived. He certainly did not want to hear that she was in more trouble. It fell to Billie, therefore, to see what influence could be wielded on her daughter's behalf. For a good many years the Weisses had been friendly with a reputed henchman of Tommy Gambino, eldest son of the late Carlo Gambino. The fellow owed a favor to Irving, who had once given his auto a free paint job. Billie now implored him to intercede with the family. The henchman agreed. But weeks passed with no sign that the Weisses' emissary had made any contact. Arlyne finally realized that her father's old friend had exaggerated his influence.

In desperation, Arlyne turned to Tommy Luca.

Until now, Arlyne had withheld from Luca the knowledge of her work for the government. Now, a tactical confession seemed in order. Tommy was surprisingly calm. His main concern, it seemed, was that she not take the stand so that the Gambinos not learn that he had been hanging out, however unwittingly, with a snitch. She must get out of Fort Lee, beyond the reach of the Feds.

But where to run? Forest Hills was out. Every agent she had come in contact with knew that her parents lived there. Equally inappropriate was Miami, since it was widely known that the Weisses spent much of the year in Florida. Then she was seized by an inspiration. Atlantic Beach. What more unlikely hiding place than a beach resort in winter?

Arlyne arrived in Atlantic Beach on a drizzly gray afternoon, quite different from those hot golden days of Natie Nelson and Al Pennino when she had sunned among the cabanas at the Capri. With Tommy's help she found a summer rental in which the landlord had installed baseboard heating. It was a beautiful house with a large dining room and three bedrooms. Arlyne designated one of these for Leslie, who had insisted upon remaining a little longer in the apartment in Fort Lee. She and her daughter had bunked together long enough. Leslie deserved a room of her own. It was time, Arlyne decided, to try to be a mother.

Tommy also seemed charmed by the hideaway and without any special fanfare made it his base of operation. He had taken up with a new pair of running mates, Nick Paterno and his brother, Dom. From what Arlyne was able to gather, Tommy had met the Paternos two or three years earlier when they owned a dry-cleaning outfit in Brooklyn.

They were both slender and dark. Nick was the better looking of the two. Exactly what their business with Tommy was, Arlyne did not know—but hoped to find out. The brothers began coming out to the Island with some frequency; sometimes for dinner, sometimes to spend the night. So Arlyne's little household grew. There were Tommy, Nick and Dom. There was the expected arrival of Leslie. And then, of course, there was Shadow.

Shadow was a silver Keeshond whose beauty was a source of fierce pride to Arlyne. She had gotten him a little over a year earlier when her poodle, Candy, died of a respiratory infection. Arlyne had wept inconsolably. Leslie, with characteristic dispassion, announced that she wanted a sheepdog. This matter had to be cleared with Tommy, who did not like dogs in general, large dogs in particular. Once, while he and his family had been living in an apartment in Howard Beach, his wife had gotten into an argument with the people upstairs. When Tommy went up to settle it, the neighbors' Great Dane lunged and sank its teeth into his throat. Tommy reportedly grabbed a knife and killed the animal.

Leslie's insistence upon a dog became so annoying, however, that Tommy finally relented, even offering to pay for it if this would buy some peace. Arlyne took Leslie to a pet shop that advertised sheepdogs. One look at the animals, however, caused Arlyne to conclude that one would never be happy in an apartment. Leslie threw such a tantrum that the store owner finally drew Arlyne aside and asked if she wouldn't please take her daughter home. Just then, Arlyne spotted a little ball of fur that looked much like a gray angora kitten. "Gimme that," she instructed the storekeeper. And she made her getaway, Leslie and the ball of fluff in tow.

Shadow—so named because his fur ran a glorious range from silver to black—grew to be nearly as large as a sheepdog. And from the beginning it was clear that he was not quite right. He would be romping one moment, then stare off into space as though he had lapsed into catatonia. If genetic quirks caused this aberration, his condition was exacerbated by fright. Whenever Tommy went into one of his tirades, he made it a point to go after the dog. Shadow would take off and hide under a bed, quivering. Gradually, however, his temperament turned from cowering to vicious, as though he had assumed the traits of his tormentor. He refused to be held or petted. Every time Arlyne tried to attach a leash, he went for her arm. Still, he was so beautiful, she adored him. She doted upon him, referring to him as her "little boy." He never returned her affection. It was a little like loving a wiseguy.

Nevertheless, Arlyne, ensconced in Atlantic Beach with her transient lover and disturbed Keeshond, was content that she was out of harm's way. This illusion of security lasted several weeks. Then the doorbell rang and—as Arlyne later recalled it—she stood face to face with a pair of clean-cut, suited young men. They were FBI.

Tracking down Arlyne Brickman, as it turned out, had proved no difficult task. Although Leslie had steadfastly stonewalled the agents and Fort Lee cops who showed up at her door, Joe Spina simply procured a record of the toll calls from the apartment at Hudson Terrace. They showed one placed to a number in Atlantic Beach. He passed this intelligence along to the Bureau. Thus cornered, Arlyne was ordered to stay put until she was called to testify. Or be served with a subpoena.

This time, Arlyne stayed put, partly out of a new respect for the government's long reach, partly because she retained some of her old faith that fate would intervene to rescue her from the brink of disaster.

For the moment, life seemed good. Tommy was again flush. He was out of debt and that always sweetened his mood. He was now demonstrating the generous spirit that was companion to his violent side. He bought not only gifts for Arlyne but toys for the neighborhood children. Tommy had made friends with a neighbor, an ex-cop who was now into swag meats. That meant they could get any cuts they wanted. Their dinners were extravagant—filet mignon and lobster in rich sauces.

Nick and Dom were always around and Arlyne guessed they probably had something to do with this new affluence. The three men were careful not to discuss business around her but every once in a while someone would slip and mention "Billy." Late one winter evening Tommy received a call. Afterwards, he and Dom grabbed their coats and raced out the door. They had to help some guy whose car had broken down on the road. Arlyne waited for hours, then fell asleep. She was awakened by raucous laughter. Pulling on her coat and peering out the window she saw Tommy and Dom in the company of two other men. The elder appeared to be in his fifties and wore dark glasses even though it was night.

When Arlyne ran to meet them at the door, Tommy motioned her away, saying, "Go to sleep . . . it's none of your business." Arlyne held her ground. "No, no," said the man in sunglasses, indicating that she could stay. His voice was raspy and, Arlyne thought, sexy. Arlyne divined that this must be the mysterious Billy. He beckoned to the younger man hanging in the background. The latter came into the house carrying a shopping bag. Arlyne was stunned to see that it was filled with money. In the past, when Tommy had hit a number, she had seen enough bills to fill a shoebox, but never a shopping bag. There were bills in tight rolls secured by rubber bands. Among these were loose bills stuffed with seemingly little care. Arlyne had never before seen money in such plenitude. Instinctively, she felt the urge to seduce.

"Would you like a cup of coffee, Billy?" she cooed.

"Yeah. Make coffee. Make coffee," he bade her.

Arlyne not only made coffee but laid out a spread of leftover cake, freshly made broccoli rab sauteed in olive oil and garlic, and a couple of loaves of Italian bread. Billy attacked it with apparent relish. He told about breaking down and getting towed to the State Police barracks. Everyone seemed to think that was a fine joke.

"Gee, this is nice." Billy observed. "Whadda we gotta hang out in Brooklyn in a nigger's house for? Let's hang out here."

After polishing off the crumbs, Billy and his crew headed out to the car and returned with several gunny sacks, which Tommy instructed them to put in an empty bedroom upstairs.

By now, it was clear to Arlyne that Tommy and his new friend were dealing heavily in weed. As she watched the sacks being hauled into her house, she asked Billy, "What happens to me?"

"Don't worry about it," he assured her. "You live good and everything will be happy for you."

And that was how Arlyne made the acquaintance of Billy Ricchiutti.

Billy lived in Plainview not far from Atlantic Beach. He had four sons. The eldest, Frank, had been with him the night he first met Arlyne. The Ricchiuttis enjoyed the distinction of being—as one drug enforcement agent expressed it—one of the "pioneers of reefer" on Long Island. They were periodically busted, but when they got out they went right back to the family business. The boys' mother, Arlyne heard, was an upright church-going woman who either did not know about, or turned a blind eye to, the goings-on around her. This must have taken an impressive feat of mental gymnastics, since Nassau County Police who raided the Ricchiutti home one Christmas season found that the "gifts" they exchanged were envelopes stuffed with money. Billy loved women—fat, thin, plain, pretty—it didn't matter. He had lots of girlfriends. His favorite was a nude bodybuilder. The boys could see their father was a whoremaster, but they worshiped him just the same.

The Ricchiuttis, it turned out, needed not just a place to hang but a repackaging and redistribution point for marijuana being shipped in from out of state. Billy had two planes that ferried the stuff from Colombia to the Florida Keys. He also rented a fleet of cars, which made the trip from Florida to New York carrying anywhere from two to three hundred pounds of smoke in the trunk. Sometimes these runs were made by Billy's sons. Often, however, Ricchiutti *pere* would take out ads in a Florida paper reading "Car going to New York. Driver wanted." Ricchiutti's hiring preference ran to attractive young women, who, he thought, would not arouse the suspicion of state police. If, perchance, they were stopped and a patrolman found pot in the trunk, they would say, "What are you, crazy, mister? I just answered an ad." That way, they eluded prosecution.

The grass arrived at the beach house in pillows or cartons, there to be parceled out for a varied clientele. There were "people" from Albany and Saratoga who bought gold. But the real money, Arlyne learned, lay in wholesaling to the blacks in Brooklyn. Bed-Stuy was thickly dotted with tiny smoke shops, which traded over the counter in such innocent commodities as gum and cigarettes, while conducting a thriving under-the-counter business in nickel-and-dime—that is five- and ten-dollar—bags of marijuana. In some neighborhoods these stores were run by the Chinese. In others, by the Dreads of Jamaica. Billy Ricchiutti sold to a crew of Dutch Guianans on Fulton and Bedford streets. His chief contacts were a pair who went by the street names Lazro and Linton. Together they owned about thirty shops.

From time to time, Arlyne was allowed to accompany Tommy, Billy and Frankie on a smoke run into Brooklyn. They would take one of the flashier cars, a large white Lincoln or yellow Cougar, since Luca felt this would impress the Guianans. Arlyne felt that it was rather stupid for white people to drive into a black neighborhood in a flashy car, since it was an invitation for cops to search the trunk. But the crew's luck held and they were never picked up.

They would arrive at Fulton Street close to midnight, meeting Lazro or Linton in front of a store. Although Tommy complained in private about those "fucking niggers," he was all smiles if there was money to be made. "Hello, my man," he would boom. "The Lord loves a cheerful giver." There was the obligatory haggling. Lazro complained the pot was seedy and Ricchiutti complained they were being short-changed. But these disagreements always got resolved with Billy giving the signal for Tommy and Frankie to start hauling the one-pound bags to the back of the shop.

While Ricchiutti and crew never hung out with the Guianans socially, they would sometimes make deliveries to their apartments, which smelled of cooked okra and rice. There were never any children around so Arlyne concluded no one actually lived there. They were just places to hang out. The rooms, while shabby, were furnished with large televisions and stereos. The closets were full of clothes. Lazro and Linton always wore sports jackets.

Lazro was partial to Arlyne. He saw Luca raise his hands to her one day and whispered in her ear, "You be my woman. I'll never hit you." He even offered to take her home to Dutch Guiana. Lazro was handsome and never had a body odor, but to Arlyne the idea of sleeping with a black man was out of the question. One thought that tormented her constantly was that Tommy might be sleeping with a black girl. She had no proof of this. But her suspicion had been aroused one evening when she and Luca had been invited to a party in Brooklyn thrown by one of Ricchiutti's associates known as Terry the Stasher. Terry was a small American black in his late thirties whose apartment was plastered with photos of light-skinned nudes. (Billy had used this place as a hangout before moving his headquarters to Atlantic Beach.) Terry not only dreamed of silky-skinned, caramel-colored women, he managed to attract an impressive number of them to his parties. Arlyne attended one bash with Tommy. Terry served up plenty of coke and women. In some rooms the guests were freebasing; in others, getting laid. Arlyne, whose idea of an elegant evening derived from the soirees of Ethel Becher, did not consider this class. She watched Luca for his reaction. Tommy never did drugs, but she thought she detected an admiring interest in Terry's women.

After that she did not give Tommy any peace. She pestered him with accusations that he was sleeping with niggers, which he, of course, denied. But the thought consumed her. When she could contain herself no longer, she called Terry's main woman and asked if Tommy was going out with one of her friends. The girl replied tersely, "Look in your own back yard."

Years later, Arlyne would insist she could never get into drugs or the scene that surrounded them. The sight of black men coked up and fighting, she claimed, disgusted her. For the most part, cocaine and heroin were abstractions. Pot seemed more familiar, probably because her guest bedrooms were full of it. She would later insist that the first time she toked—this was after moving to Atlantic Beach—she "got crazy" and started throwing dinner plates. After that, she claimed, she never tried it again.

Her professed aversion to drugs, however, in no way diminished her enthusiasm for the drug business. Tommy and Billy were making so much money that they were literally throwing it at her. "Go shopping," they told her. "Go do this. Go do that." To Arlyne, this all seemed strangely innocent. Surely, under the Ricchiuttis' expert tutelage, she had learned how to weigh and package the pot. On one occasion, she had driven a car to Florida carrying $348,000. But it wasn't like she was a *dealer*. She developed several lines of reasoning that allowed her to rationalize this position. First of all, she wasn't being paid. Not really. She preferred to think of the consideration she received as "house money." When queried about these transgressions later on, she would insist that she had been involved only "to a certain extent." Furthermore, whatever she did with Tommy Luca seemed beyond moral accountability. What "I" did might be personal. But what "we" did was business. And in business, profit bathed everything in virtue. Lastly, Arlyne would argue—and perhaps even succeeded in convincing herself—that whatever drug activities she engaged in were with the knowledge, if not the express permission, of the DEA or FBI. It was a position she would never abandon. Documents obtained from the government, however, indicate that for at least the first six months or so of her association with the Ricchiuttis, Arlyne did not bother to inform anyone in officialdom about the enterprise flourishing beneath her roof.

Her most elaborate rationalizations, however, still centered on Leslie.

As the weather warmed, Leslie finally agreed to join her mother in Atlantic Beach. Arlyne worried whenever her daughter stood to be brought into a living situation with Tommy Luca. At the back of her mind still lingered the scene at Ethel Becher's deathbed when she confided in Arlyne her fears that her own daughter was being exploited by Tony Mirra. Had Tommy ever made such a move on Leslie? Surely, Arlyne reasoned, Leslie would have told her. Besides, Arlyne reasoned more aggressively, it was good for Leslie to be around Tommy. He was, after all, a father figure.

A few days after Leslie pulled up in a little red Mustang convertible, a gift from her ever-doting grandfather, Arlyne realized she had new problems. Leslie, who spent most of her time in the side yard tanning in a skimpy two-piece, had caught the eye of Billy Ricchiutti. Arlyne, who had told Billy very little about her daughter, was now distressed to see him pulling her aside to talk, cozying up to her as if she were just another bimbo. It was apparently during one of these furtive conversations that Billy recruited Leslie to make the Florida run. Leslie presented it to her mother as a fait accompli, leaving her no graceful opening to object. Arguably, a good mother—a better mother—might have stepped in to say, "It's time to stop. We're getting out of here."

But, Arlyne reasoned, Leslie was headstrong and would do what she would do. Besides, it was only pot. If Leslie were caught, she probably wouldn't do any time. At the bottom of these self-serving delusions lay the fact that to cross Billy would be bad for business. So she remained silent.

Leslie, as it turned out, didn't do any driving. She just rode as a companion whenever Billy wanted to make it look as if the travelers were a young couple on vacation. Sometimes she went with Billy's sons, other times with a strange fellow who dealt as a sideline in exotic birds. Whenever he acquired one of these creatures, he insisted upon making the trip back from Florida with the windows rolled up and no air-conditioning so that his acquisitions, beating their wings against the back seat, would not catch a chill.

Occasionally, she rode with Billy. On one of these trips, they stopped for the night at a motel near Washington, D.C. She woke up to find him in her bed. She screamed, "Get outta here, will ya!" He did not bother her again.

Leslie was making a lot of money, which put her in a good mood. Tommy was not being pestered by shylocks, which left him in a good mood. Arlyne was spending "house money" hand over fist, which left her in a very good mood, indeed. It seemed that life just couldn't get any better. That summer Arlyne and her extended household moved into a beautiful new rental right on the bay. It boasted a boat dock, where Billy could receive deliveries by water, and there was a huge cellar for storing shipments. Tommy was feeling expansive and commanded the place be redecorated top to bottom. The dining room was furnished with a huge antique table with four chairs on either side and one at each end, so that it could easily accommodate the Ricchiutti clan, Tommy, Arlyne, Leslie and a couple of visiting drivers, boat captains or pilots in Billy's employ.

They had been there only three weeks when there was a knock on the door. Arlyne opened it to find a "colored girl" whom the landlord had sent over in the event that his new tenants needed domestic help. Beatrice, Arlyne suspected, "wasn't exactly pure." In fact, she would later learn that the woman had just gotten off probation for attacking her husband. Nevertheless, she had a tribe of children to support and she struck Arlyne as a "poor soul."

"Can you cook?"

"Yeah."

"Can you clean?"

"Yeah."

After that cursory interview, Beatrice was hired. Arlyne was delighted to discover that her new maid had a zest for high living that rivaled Sadie's and a larcenous streak that matched her own. Putting their heads together, they devised ever more inventive ways of padding grocery bills and other expenses to increase the flow of "house money." Arlyne, of course, saw that Beatrice got a generous cut. In her role of benevolent employer, Arlyne turned a blind eye as Beatrice filched grass from the cellar and took it to the black neighborhoods where she sold it to pick up extra cash. Arlyne did not have many friends, and while she did not fully trust Beatrice, she came to rely upon her as confidante.

Even Shadow enjoyed periods of relative contentment. He claimed for himself a seat in the large windows overlooking the water and rarely strayed. That was why Arlyne was so disturbed one warm summer night to find him missing. She looked in the dining room, the living room, all the bedrooms and the cellar. No Shadow.

She panicked. Dressed only in a nightgown, she began running through the house, then out onto the lawn, calling his name. As she was conducting her frantic search, Tommy, Billy and the crew were hauling into the house a shipment of weed. They were expecting the momentary arrival of "the guys from Syracuse" who would make a bid on it. For Arlyne, however, all considerations of business and house money were blotted out in her concern for her little boy. She called the police.

By the time the cops arrived, the weed was safely stowed in the basement. Tommy and Billy were nonetheless confounded to see a cruiser pull up to the curb. They began chattering madly in Italian as Arlyne greeted the officers and offered them coffee. The patrolman lost no time in locating Shadow, who was cowering upstairs under a bed. Only after the cruiser pulled away and she was enduring a torrent of abuse from her aggrieved associates did Arlyne realize that the house was filled with the pungent aroma of gold.

Could it be possible that the cops had not smelled it? That seemed unlikely. Moreover, passing patrols could not have failed to notice the succession of Lincolns and Oldsmobiles and Cadillacs pulling into the drive. Nonetheless, when two weeks or so passed without an arrest,

Arlyne began to believe that cops were duller fools than she had thought. And then there was a knock on the door. She opened it to find a pair of officers from the Rackets Bureau of the Nassau County Police. "You're coming down for questioning," they informed her.

Arlyne would later claim she told the pair nothing of consequence in that initial interrogation, which took place at the Rackets Bureau in Plainview. Her interrogators were, however, sufficiently convinced of her ties to the notorious Ricchiutti Family to pass her along to a pair of colleagues, Edward Lindberg and Louis Isnardi, county narcotics detectives who worked closely with the DEA's Long Island office in Melville. As Arlyne later recalled that incident, Isnardi, who was the sterner of the two, threatened to have her arrested if she didn't tell them what was going on. To which she replied, "You can't arrest me . . . I work for the Drug Enforcement."

Startled, the two detectives set about checking it out. Arlyne, meanwhile, made a call of her own. Experience had taught her that if you were on the spot, the thing to do was to cause havoc. If possible, turn your antagonists against one another (she called it "steaming them up"), and once they fell to fighting, you could slip away unnoticed. As Lindberg and Isnardi were on the line with the DEA in Melville, Arlyne called the DEA office in New York City and appealed for help. Apparently jealous of its prerogatives, New York dispatched an agent to the Island to reclaim its property. Squabbles over informants happen more frequently than the government would care to admit. This one ended in an acrimonious encounter where the New York agent was forced to concede that Ms. Brickman was technically inactive. Whereupon, the DEA in Melville formally registered her as an informant.

Having failed to free herself from this entanglement, Arlyne was now forced to make her best deal. As Arlyne recalled that agreement, it required her to maintain a show of normalcy at the beach house, all the while providing intelligence on the comings and goings of the Ricchiuttis. In exchange, she would enjoy immunity from prosecution. Arlyne would later insist that she was promised any cash taken in the bust.

There was one more thing. Although she had been warned to keep silent about her arrangement with the government, Arlyne could not resist the temptation to tell Tommy. Apparently realizing the jig was up, Luca urged her to make a deal for him as well. Working through Louis and Eddie, Arlyne was able to obtain from the Nassau County District Attorney's Office tentative assurances that Tommy would not be prosecuted.

Having come back into the good graces of the DEA, Arlyne now sought to cover herself with the FBI. Early in September, she met with Agent Hendrickson, giving him detailed information on the drug operations of Billy Ricchiutti. Not only was he importing up to eighteen hundred pounds of pot a week, he was now getting into Quaaludes, bringing in fifty thousand to one hundred thousand a week, most of it going to a customer in Staten Island.

Billy Ricchiutti, as he was emerging from the intelligence of Arlyne Brickman, was no small-timer. He was even rumored to be hooked up with a couple of powerful Colombo capos. The DEA and the FBI both wanted a crack at him. Late that month, both agencies sent representatives to the offices of Special Attorney Joel Cohen in New York's Eastern District, asking him to mediate this jurisdictional dispute. The prosecutor ruled that in this instance, Arlyne Brickman properly belonged to the DEA.

Against the backdrop of this bureaucratic dance, the atmosphere at the beach house, not surprisingly, had grown tense. Faced with a cut-off of revenue from the Ricchiutti connection, Tommy began sneaking around behind Billy's back, making deals with other suppliers. Arlyne and Tommy managed to keep their secret to themselves, but it did not draw them closer. More often now Luca's temper erupted without warning and he would strike her. Billy, whatever his other flaws, loved women and it bothered him to see them hurt. He warned Luca to cool it. Tommy appeared unfazed and proceeded to beat Arlyne with the viciousness of the old days. Billy and his son Frankie came home one day to find her bloody and too sick to move. Disgusted, the Ricchiuttis moved out.

Arlyne was home alone one night when Billy showed up to collect the trunks. This placed her in an awkward situation. Not many days before, she had turned these over to the DEA as evidence. "Billy," she lied, "we thought you were never showing up again, so Beatrice and I took the trunks and we threw them into the water." Billy seemed to accept this ludicrous explanation. So they sat around talking, having a few drinks. As Arlyne scrutinized Billy across the antique dining-room table, she was reminded again that he was a pretty good-looking guy, even if he did have a pot belly. That evening she ended up giving him a blow job. It was an affectionate gesture, appropriate, she thought, for the circumstances. It did not trouble her that she was in the process of doing him in.

*   *   *

The stream of intelligence that Arlyne had been feeding Lindberg and Isnardi provided the basis for a thirty-day wiretap order on Billy's house on Roundtree Drive in Plainview. The Ricchiuttis had been at their game long enough to avoid talking business on the phone. The detectives had to resort to more innovative means of surveillance. Incredibly, Billy and his sons carried on their activities within a stone's throw of the Rackets Bureau. If you went to the top of the building, you could, in fact, observe Roundtree Drive. The Nassau police mounted a camera on the roof to record the Ricchiuttis' comings and goings. This initiative too ended in disappointment. The surveillance equipment, supplied by the DEA, did not produce good images. (Nassau police always groused that the Feds gave them junk and kept the best stuff for themselves.)

So the Nassau cops turned their attention to Frankie, who lived in nearby Stony Brook. Frankie, too, was apparently wary of talking on his home phone. He would, instead, go across the street to a synagogue where he used a phone in the foyer. A detective posing as an habitué of the temple got close enough to Frank to hear his conversations, the substance of which provided enough grist for search warrants. On January 10, 1980, police launched simultaneous raids on Roundtree Drive and Sycamore Drive where they seized quantities of marijuana, hashish and methaqualone with an estimated street value of three hundred thousand dollars, and a loaded .25 caliber handgun. In the sweep they arrested Frankie, two of his brothers and their mother. Tommy and Billy were picked up later.

These arrests did not bring Arlyne all the satisfaction she had hoped. For one thing, there had been between sixty-five and eighty thousand dollars in cash confiscated in those raids. She expected to receive at least a percentage of this windfall. As the weeks wore on, however, it became clear that the DEA was not going to give her a penny. What's more, she had been under the impression that Tommy Luca would escape arrest. He was not only arrested, but prosecuted and convicted. Whatever leniency Arlyne's intervention had been able to win him showed up in the sentencing. Tommy got probation while Billy got jail time.

Even as Arlyne continued to work on his behalf, Luca stepped up his attacks. Perhaps, Arlyne later reasoned, he resented this demonstration of her power. Whatever the cause, he could not seem to control his rage. One night, shortly after New Year's, he exploded and took a ball bat to Arlyne's rented Cobra, breaking every window. After that, he stormed home to his wife.

Emptied of the Ricchiuttis and now Luca, the beach house seemed desolate. If Arlyne had counted upon Leslie to elevate the mood of the place, she was to be disappointed. As soon as it became clear that the high times were over, the girl loaded up her little Mustang and headed for New York City.

After the defection of her daughter, Arlyne wandered about the empty rooms all day in her nightgown, distracted only by Beatrice and the increasingly irascible Shadow. She was irritated by the realization that the show was passing her by. In truth, there was nothing holding her in Atlantic Beach. Several months earlier, Fischetti et al. had copped pleas so she was no longer obligated to testify. Neither was she obligated to stay put. She simply had nowhere else to go, and no money to get there.

Then, almost miraculously, as though some invisible jailer had turned the key, the door to Arlyne's cell swung open. Her parents, she learned, were moving to Florida, this time for good. Irving planned to open a luxury car showroom in Palm Beach. That meant that the Weisses' fabulously appointed apartment would be vacant. Circumventing her father, who was still maintaining his silence, Arlyne approached her mother about renting the place on favorable terms. A return to Queens, she argued, would allow her to keep a closer eye on Leslie. Reasoning, no doubt, that this arrangement would allow her to keep an eye on—if not control over—her own daughter, Billie once again gave in to the pleading.

Arlyne closed the beach house and headed out of exile, into the action.

EIGHT

FOREST HILLS

Over a quarter of a century had passed since Billie Weiss had taken the family to Queens in search of a better moral climate for her daughters. In all that time, the apartment in Forest Hills had exerted an irresistible pull, like a gravity field Arlyne could not escape. As a young wife, then young mother, and always the eternal mob girl, she had run home only to storm out in anger—only to run home again broke and down on her luck. Now, as Arlyne turned the key in the lock and pushed open the heavy green door, she felt she had reclaimed her rightful domain. There was the same huge chandelier with its tiers of crystal balls as well as the antique clock with its mother-of-pearl face. Above the piano hung a familiar oil painting of the Weiss girls: Barbara as a plump preadolescent; Arlyne, at sixteen, sporting vermilion nails, her long auburn hair framing an expression of waning innocence.

Arlyne had lured Beatrice to Forest Hills with the promise that she would share in whatever scores her mistress turned up. The two women celebrated their new condition with Chinese take-out. Shadow, deprived of his customary window seat, sulked. Arlyne had always assumed that the animal's bad temper was the result of Tommy's abuse. She had every reason to hope that with Luca gone things would improve. They did not. At walk time, when she tried to attach the leash, Shadow would growl, fangs bared. Still, she never really believed he would harm her until one afternoon he lunged for her arm.

When she recounted this attack to her parents, Irving Weiss—in an extraordinary move—temporarily broke his silence to advise her to have the dog put to sleep. But every time Arlyne looked at Shadow, his fur glinting silver, eyes glowing with malice, she thought he was the most beautiful creature she had ever seen. She could not bring herself to destroy him. Instead, she took him to the family veterinarian, who, after examining the dog, couldn't suggest treatment by any conventional means. He gave her the name of an "animal behaviorist" who reputedly specialized in personality disorders.

Dr. Bouchard, the behaviorist, made house calls, for which, he said, the fee was fifty dollars. Arlyne arranged with him to visit the apartment one afternoon to observe Shadow in his natural habitat. Beatrice had laid out a generous spread of lox and bagels and Dr. Bouchard, a thin little man in his thirties, seemed pleased by the hospitality. Arlyne invited him to take a seat by her on the couch where she regaled him at length with Shadow's symptoms. The dog dozed on the carpet unaware that he was the subject of analysis. For nearly four hours, Arlyne and the doctor drank coffee and chatted. Their conversation ranged beyond Shadow's mysterious malady to Arlyne's sex life and her troubles with Tommy. She was flattered that he seemed to enjoy her company. Finally, he announced that it was time for him to go and she handed him fifty dollars.

"That was fifty dollars an hour," he corrected. "You owe me two hundred dollars."

For this fat fee, the doctor offered no diagnosis but laid out at least two prospective courses of treatment. The first involved conditioning. He provided Arlyne with a whistle and instructed her to blow it loudly whenever Shadow came at her. She tried this for a few days, and amazingly, the dog stopped midattack, cocking his head with a mixture of confusion and curiosity. This treatment might have worked, but Arlyne couldn't resist blowing the whistle at odd moments just to see Shadow startle. That, of course, undid all her good work. Shadow ignored the whistle altogether, and his mistress was forced to resort to treatment two, which was to have him neutered.

All the attention Arlyne lavished upon Shadow served to obscure for a while the larger issue of why she had ostensibly returned to Queens— which was to keep an eye on Leslie. Not that she loved her daughter less than her dog, but worrying about the dog was easier. Shadow was a dumb beast who for all his savagery was still under her control. Leslie was at large. Arlyne simply did not know how to regain charge of a wild and reckless child.

To date, every attempt Leslie had made to take control over her life only seemed to steer her more inexorably toward destruction. Even while nominally living in Atlantic Beach, she had spent three or four nights each week in the city working as a cocktail waitress at Max's Kansas City, a seedy club that catered to an artsy crowd. It was the hangout of early punk groups like the Sex Pistols, New York Dolls and Siouxie and the Banshees. Arlyne, who had frequented a good many nightspots in her day, had no familiarity with a place like Max's or the punk scene and so could not tell if it had any class. Leslie had taken to shopping in the vintage clothing warehouses of SoHo, which was supposedly very chic. Arlyne thought it looked shabby. Leslie, furthermore, never wore makeup, insisting she couldn't stand the feel of it on her face. Yet she assured her mother that the tips were good and that she was hanging out with celebrities. Sometimes she came around with her boyfriend, a thin blond boy named Richard, who, Leslie said, was trying to put together a band of his own. He was filthy and insolent. For these, and for other reasons she could not quite put her finger on, Arlyne did not like him.

It was Beatrice who saw the needle marks on Leslie's arm.

There remained about Arlyne Brickman a curious naïveté in regard to drugs. Despite her association with Joe Spione, Rusty and other big-time dealers, heroin seems to have remained an imponderable. She had, she would later claim, never seen anyone shoot smack. She had no idea what it did to people. It was simply a commodity. When Beatrice confided her suspicion that Leslie was doing heroin, Arlyne shut her ears. To acknowledge that painful truth would mean having to act. It was better to pretend that nothing was happening.

Had Arlyne summoned the courage to ask her daughter exactly what *was* happening in the spring of 1980, she might have confirmed what she suspected: Leslie's new friends were hard-core heroin addicts. When she had first started work at Max's, Leslie would recall years later, she was still a relative virgin doing mostly Quaaludes. But in that fast company she moved quickly to cocaine, which did not suite her taste as it left her feeling jumpy. She began snorting heroin. Then one day she was watching another hanger-on at Max's shooting up and she was overcome by curiosity.

"Lemme see how that feels," she demanded. "Lemme see if it hurts as much as a doctor's shot."

As the needle slid into her vein, Leslie experienced no pain. Just a "very down, mellow, nodding out kind of feeling," a sensation that left her at peace with herself.

After that, Leslie's entire day revolved around recovering that radiant oblivion. Although Richard was her "boyfriend," their relationship was essentially platonic. "We didn't have sex or anything," she would later explain. "When you do heroin, you don't have sex. It just becomes a dead feeling. Your main concern is getting . . . high."

Her days assumed a dull and desperate pattern. "You wake up in the morning. You're sick. You gotta go and cop. Then by the time you come back, that's like a half a day wasted. Then you get high and you just sit around and it's like okay."

But things were not okay. That much was apparent to her mother. Although Leslie split with Richard and left her job at Max's, she spent the day shooting up with friends at a welfare hotel. To support her habit she got a job dancing topless at a joint near Canal Street run by Matty "the Horse" Ianniello. (It was Ianniello who had reputedly owned the Wagon Wheel Bar.) At the back of her mind was the suspicion that her daughter, if sufficiently desperate, might turn to prostitution.

Prostitution, unlike heroin addiction, was something Arlyne Brickman could understand. After all, she herself had been one of Ethel Becher's party girls, trading sex for cases of whiskey and packages of frozen vegetables. But that was nothing to be ashamed of, Arlyne told herself. Ethel had class. The specter that haunted her was that of Leslie walking the streets, hopping into cars and turning tricks in alleys. So horrible was this prospect to her that she insisted upon driving Leslie to work at the strip joint. (As a concession to her employers, Leslie wore mascara, but she steadfastly refused to wear base makeup.) Then Arlyne would sit outside and wait for her, closing her eyes against the insidious ripples of neon. She could never bring herself to go inside.

Shortly after Arlyne returned to Forest Hills, she received a visit from Nassau County detectives Lindberg and Isnardi. They had no particular business to conduct, they said. They were just in the neighborhood and thought they'd drop by. Arlyne thought this a little odd—not because the cops were, in fact, confined to any jurisdiction. Their working relationship with the DEA gave them license to wander Long Island and the boroughs. What Arlyne found strange was this friendly overture in light of the hard feelings generated by the Ricchiutti case. But the detectives seemed content to let bygones be bygones and, in fact, began dropping by more often for drinks and Chinese food.

Arlyne found herself increasingly attracted to Eddie Lindberg, who was the muscular, clean-cut type. She thought the feeling might be mutual and if left alone they might "do a little hoochie coochie." But she never got a chance to test this theory, since he was always in the company of Isnardi, whom she considered an uptight little wop. Isnardi and Lindberg were so close she began calling them Strelka and Belka after a pair of dogs the Soviets shot into space. The detectives, in turn, called her "Auntie."

Louie and Eddie, it became clear to Arlyne, were not dropping by simply because they enjoyed the company, but because they still hoped to cultivate her underworld connections. Since establishing her head-quarters in Queens, Arlyne had been making the rounds, letting old friends know she was back in town. They called her day and night with prospective scores. "That was a cookin' phone of hers," Lindberg would later recall with amusement. "I don't think there was ever a conversation on that phone that was legal."

Arlyne issued her own challenge to Lindberg and Isnardi. Set her up in a dummy apartment and she would have every wiseguy in the world floating in with stolen property. Together they could engineer a large-scale sting operation. The detectives did not take her up on the offer, for reasons never explained, but probably because Arlyne, over the long haul, would prove a very tough operative to control. Instead, they encouraged her to pass along any interesting tips. One of these came from Tilly Palladino.

Tilly lived on the Island. Shortly after the move to Atlantic Beach, Luca had struck up an acquaintance with her and she had loaned him money. Tilly's husband was reputedly a small-time loanshark or book-maker who ran with the Corona mob. He had disappeared or been killed, and she had several boyfriends.

Arlyne liked Tilly's style. She was a thin, attractive blond who possessed undeniable animal magnetism. Although she wore designer clothes, these were always rumpled, suggesting she had slept in them. No matter how casually she dressed, Tilly always wore hats. Cloches, hats with brims, straw hats, felt hats. She never felt completely dressed without one. And she always carried guns. Tilly boasted that she was a hit woman (for whom, she didn't say). Her signature, she insisted, was to "hit 'em in the kneecaps." Since Tilly did a lot of freebasing, Arlyne tended to take these claims with a grain of salt.

Tilly's social life cut a wide swath. One of her boyfriends was a sergeant with the Nassau County cops so she attended a lot of police parties. At these blowouts she strutted around in her eccentric hats, now and then sidling up to a reveler and whispering something dirty in his ear. Cops loved that. At these parties, Tilly picked up a lot of information that she stored away, apparently planning to get the goods on someone. She made the mistake of confiding this to Arlyne Brickman.

One day Tilly dropped by the house and happened to mention that her boyfriend, the police sergeant, had suffered some insult at the hands of an inspector. Now, he was going to pay. She revealed the details of how, at a retirement party, she had taken certain "embarrassing pictures." Arlyne, who liked but felt no particular loyalty toward Tilly, cheerfully passed this along to Strelka and Belka, who greeted the news with astonishment. The inspector in question was their boss.

The news of Tilly's alleged snapshots created consternation at headquarters. Lindberg and Isnardi were charged with persuading the informant Brickman to wear a wire on Tilly, who would, they hoped, outline her plan for the record. Arlyne balked. Tilly Palladino had certain peculiarities that left Arlyne feeling uneasy. Whenever she had been freebasing, Tilly claimed that vibrations came off her fingertips giving her clairvoyant powers. Arlyne was skeptical until one time she touched Tilly's hands and found they were "burning." This incident convinced her that Tilly was a witch. And if this were the case, she would certainly know if Arlyne were wearing a wire. The thought made her kneecaps tingle.

Rather than confront Tilly in the flesh, Arlyne placed a telephone call in which she got the self-proclaimed hit woman talking about what she was going to do with the inspector. Nassau's tape was rolling. Tilly Palladino, it was decided, must be neutralized. Once again, Arlyne was pressed into service, this time to arrange an introduction between Tilly and a sergeant in Eddie and Louie's division who arranged to buy from her about an ounce of cocaine. She was busted and, presented with her options, turned informant. Arlyne never heard from her again. Either Tilly did not realize who had turned her in—which was unlikely—or as a fellow informant, she had been warned to respect Arlyne's distance.

Arlyne stayed in touch with Lindberg and Isnardi. They dropped by her apartment for drinks; she passed along tips gleaned from her day-to-day contacts. Arlyne Brickman's day-to-day contacts, as always, ran to the exotic, and often, larcenous. Once a week she went to a shop in Brooklyn to have her hair done. There she struck up a friendship with a little hairdresser named Charo. The girl was a talker and as she dyed Arlyne's hair Italian black, she boasted that the ten-carat diamond she was wearing was a gift from her boyfriend, a Cuban named Gamez. Arlyne passed the name to Eddie and Louie who recognized him immediately as a "real bad ass" and reputed multi-kilo cocaine dealer. Eddie and Louie were anxious for a bust.

During the course of her weekly visits with Charo, Arlyne had let it be known that she possessed some impressive drug connections of her own and now, at the detectives' behest, Arlyne suggested to Charo that she might introduce Gamez to some friends interested in about twenty keys. (The whole deal, Arlyne figured, was worth about $1 million, of which, she would later claim, she had been promised forty thousand dollars.) Charo went for the bait.

On the night of the proposed buy, Arlyne picked up Charo from her apartment. She was in the company of a short, thin man who wore his shirtsleeves rolled. This was not Gamez, Charo explained, but his righthand man. He did not speak English, so Charo translated. During their ride down the Long Island Expressway, the man remained largely silent while Arlyne and Charo discussed amounts and percentages. Charo had also been promised a piece of the action.

As Arlyne and associates were in transit, around eight drug agents had gathered at the task force headquarters. Eddie Lindberg wanted to take his Trans Am, which was clean of radios and wires. The sergeant in charge, inexplicably, insisted the detectives take his Cadillac, which had a DEA radio transmitter in the trunk.

By the time Arlyne, Charo, and the Righthand Man pulled into the lot of the Holiday Inn—a site chosen for its proximity to the task force headquarters—Detectives Lindberg and Isnardi and their backups had already arrived. As Arlyne walked into the bar, she could see the Righthand Man stiffen. He had sensed that the place was filled with agents. (This was not a difficult conclusion, Arlyne later observed, since Feds have a peculiar way of staring.) The tension was not relieved when she introduced the Cubans to her friends, who were sitting at a table near the bar. Eddie was wearing white dungarees because, he explained, he had just come off his "yacht." He kept jumping up nervously to plug quarters in the juke box. Arlyne could tell he was coming on too strong.

The man turned to Charo and she translated. "Let me see your car." The detectives found this unusual but they took the Cuban out to the Cadillac and opened the door. He shook his head and pointed to the trunk. Lindberg and Isnardi were confounded. No one ever asked to look in a trunk. Now they were in a tight spot. They could not, of course, open it, since the DEA transmitter was sitting in plain sight. Refusing to accede to the Cuban's wishes, however, would confirm his suspicions. Lindberg broke the impasse. There were fifty thousand dollars in the trunk, he said. He wasn't going to open it in front of someone they didn't know. The Cuban beckoned to the two women and sped away, leaving the detectives and their surveillance team in the dust.

At the Holiday Inn there was general dejection, made deeper by the fact that the Cuban had been identified not as the supposed Righthand Man, but as Gamez himself. Thanks to a small blunder, a big fish had slipped through the net. To ease their disappointment, Lindberg and Isnardi repaired to the bar and ordered martinis. What appeared to have been forgotten amidst all the grousing was that "Auntie" was traveling up the expressway in the company of a dangerous man.

During the standoff at the trunk, Arlyne had been too far away to tell what was going on. She just sensed there was some kind of trouble. Now, during the ride home, Charo and her friend argued furiously in Spanish. As far as Arlyne could tell, Charo was still defending her, insisting she was her friend and could be trusted. She dropped the two off at Charo's apartment with not a word of farewell. If it hadn't been for the little hairdresser's intervention, Arlyne knew, she probably would have been killed.

Arlyne's first response at having been released so suddenly from the grip of danger was smug satisfaction. Fate had once again affirmed that she was one of its favorites. Almost immediately, however, that bravado gave way to terror as she realized how narrow had been her escape. That night or the day after, she read Eddie and Louie the riot act for leaving her so exposed. But they did not appear to think it was any big deal. It seemed to Arlyne that drug enforcement types were rather casual about the safety of their informants. She was, furthermore, wary of the DEA office in Melville, which, she suspected, had carelessly revealed her identity after the Ricchiutti bust.

The FBI, Arlyne concluded, had much more class. During the early months of 1980 after her return to Forest Hills, Arlyne had resumed work with Agent Hendrickson, who also hoped to be the recipient of the tips from her "cookin' phone." She had always liked Hendrickson, whose mild, innocuous looks reminded her of a schoolteacher's. He was always polite. At the time she had cut out unannounced for Atlantic Beach, Arlyne had been feeding him intelligence on Vince Lamattina. Now she picked up where she had left off. Vince, she said, was dealing heavy drugs. He was throwing his weight around and getting in scrapes with other wiseguys. What's more, he was becoming increasingly paranoid. At one point he made a comment to Arlyne that suggested that he knew she was an informant. She placed a panicked call to Hendrickson to see how this might be, and he said he didn't know.

Around the first week in May, Arlyne received a call from Vivian, an aging mob girl who worked as hostess at Blackjacks. She was also an old lover and confidante of Vince Lamattina's. Vivian was frantic. She had heard that Vince had been grabbed outside his apartment building, pushed into his car and driven off by strangers.

To all appearances, Vince had been abducted. He had left behind his beloved wire-haired terrier. As callous as he could be toward humans, he loved his dog and Arlyne could not believe he would leave the animal voluntarily. Still, she could not shake an inexplicable feeling that Vince was alive, an impression reinforced by the discovery that he had cleaned out all the money he had kept in a vault. Perhaps he had staged the kidnapping to throw his creditors off the track. Perhaps he had turned informant and been whisked off into Witness Protection. There was a rumor on the street that police had found an FBI squad code scribbled on a piece of paper near his bed. (The Bureau later refused comment.)

Shortly after his disappearance, the missing man's car was found abandoned in the Bronx. Whatever Arlyne's private qualms about the official story, this development brought an end to her surveillance of Vince Lamattina.

Even as Vince fluttered into the dead file, Arlyne passed along to Hendrickson at least three other promising leads. One concerned a Brooklyn numbers man named Nathan Pincus, who allegedly had burned his auto parts store for the insurance money. Pincus, it turned out, was also being investigated by the IRS and had reputedly tried to bribe an agent. When Arlyne conveyed this to Hendrickson, he suggested trying to set Pincus up with a former IRS supervisor suspected of corruption, hoping that Pincus would try to buy the bureaucrat's influence in an attempt to get his case fixed, thus allowing the Bureau to nab two birds with one sting.

The second lead involved John Gotti. During her conversations with Hendrickson, Arlyne had told how, when Luca was serving out his bookmaking conviction in Jersey, she would take vig payments to Ozone Park. She seemed to recall handing the payments "once or twice" directly to John Gotti or his brother Gene, who, she insisted, just happened to be standing on the curb outside the club. As far as Arlyne knew, Tommy still owed the Gambinos around thirty thousand dollars. The FBI was eager for any intelligence it could get on the Gottis, and Hendrickson instructed Arlyne to contact her old friends Joey Scopo and Jackie Cavallo and dangle the prospect of a substantial payment in hopes of setting up a meeting with "Johnny."

The third tip came to Arlyne directly from the lips of Tommy Luca. After his furious departure from Atlantic Beach, Tommy had gone home to his wife. They argued so bitterly over money that he stormed off to live with his mother. This he found too confining, so he arranged to be put up temporarily by a friend who was a driver for the New York *Daily*

News and also into swag and shylocking. When Tommy, rootless as a nomad, learned that Arlyne had come into possession of her parents' apartment, he came knocking, flashing his shameless grin.

Just why Arlyne took him back was, as usual, unclear. It wasn't because of flowery promises. He had left his wife for good, he said, leaving open the prospect that he would be free. At this point in her life she had lost all hope of marriage. But she was bonded to Tom by an insidious adhesive of obsession, habit and, not least of all, greed. They were a good team: Tommy with his contacts on the street; she with her "friends the Feds." Together, they could play both sides—and earn.

And Tommy handed her a score. He had been hanging out at a diner in Jamaica, Queens, where some guys were planning a cash robbery from American Airlines at Kennedy International Airport. Luca was deliberately vague about who the plotters were. All she could learn was that they were Italians and one had a girlfriend who worked for American and had touted them onto the score. On other details, Luca was quite specific. He described a room, located near a staircase, to which more than one million dollars in cash was delivered by armored car every Friday morning. One guard remained in the truck while two others carried in the money. The conspirators apparently planned to wait until the cash had been deposited in the charge of one old man who looked after the room. Then they would enter using a security code leaked to them by their contact at the airline and lift the cash at machine-gun point.

Luca's own involvement in this proposed heist was murky to say the least. Arlyne thought perhaps he had been in league with the guys from Jamaica but had fallen out with them over terms. Whatever the case, he now wanted her to take this information to her friends the Feds. He expected it would be worth about $10,000.

Agent Hendrickson, of course, was very happy to receive this tip and promptly informed American of the threat to its security. Tommy's grandiose assessment notwithstanding, the Bureau estimated the worth of this information at only $1,000. Hendrickson met Arlyne on a side street near her apartment to make a payment of $700. She was stunned.

"Why," she asked, "are you giving me so little money for this?"

"That's all it's worth to the FBI," he replied.

She hastily pocketed $400 of this—figuring it was her due—and prepared herself to walk upstairs to explain to Luca the $9,000-odd shortfall.

A decision to tape Tommy appears to have been made on the spot, although years later neither Arlyne nor Hendrickson could remember the reason for it. Arlyne seemed to recall that the government wanted to hear Tommy acknowledge that he was the source of the tip and that he was receiving money for it. Agent Hendrickson seemed to recall that Arlyne wore that wire "probably for her own safety." But there was clearly a more specific reason. Hendrickson wanted Arlyne to continue needling Tommy for the identities of the would-be robbers, and to ascertain if Luca himself were part of the conspiracy. He wanted that conversation on the record.

The Luca Tape, as it came to be known in the subterranean channels of law enforcement, was a remarkable document that froze and preserved the circular treachery of Arlyne Brickman's world. Listening to it, one hears an informant wearing a wire for the government on her lover, a known criminal who is providing information through her to the government that is supplying the wire. It demonstrates how Arlyne had jerry-built her existence so haphazardly and so opportunistically on such conflicting alliances, that whatever move she made she was likely to betray someone. The greater moral questions, however, were not on Arlyne Brickman's mind as she entered the elevator and ascended, Nagra rolling, for what promised to be a stormy confrontation with Tommy Luca.

When she turned the key in the lock, Shadow began to bark. Neutering had not improved his disposition.

"Hi, Shadow. Hi, sweet little boy," she soothed him.

Tommy was now sleeping on the couch in the den.

"You better get up," she said, "because there's a . . . little problem . . . I went to Greg. He had the guy from American Airlines there, okay? They gave me exactly—and I'm not bullshitting you, $300. I went to OTB and I made a bet for you, okay? . . . I kept $10 for myself. . . . I swear on my father, he should die, the only money I took out of that is $10."

Luca was at first uncomprehending. Then the magnitude of what Arlyne was saying sank in.

"Three hundred dollars," he sneered. "You're supposed to tell him, 'Listen, you fuckin' pimp, $300. Stick it up your fuckin' ass.' That's what you should've told him. But you don't know how to talk to people. You think you know everything. You know shit."

If the information was so worthless, he then asked her, then why did Hendrickson give her the $300?

Arlyne thought quickly. "Because he knows I need the money. He doesn't know I'm coming back here to give it to you . . ."

Luca, she knew, had a big vig installment due and had been counting on payment for the airline tip.

"You've gotta get the $1200 today, don't ya?" she pressed. "All right now," she proposed. "I can get $10,000 if you'll tell me exactly how you got all that information. . . . It isn't like the DEA. . . . Greg's word is his bond, you know that."

"Too late for that," Tommy growled. "I don't know what you're talking about. . . . Now, just forget it. . . . They got some fuckin' nerve . . ." he groused. "Three hundred fuckin' dollars . . . I need $1200 in three hours."

Luca did some anxious figuring. "How much have I got here, right now, without the horses?" The payment minus Arlyne's "cut" and OTB came to only about $100.

"I need $1100," he observed dejectedly.

"Yeah." Arlyne readied for another assault. "We could have it if you'll tell me how you got this information."

But Tommy's thoughts were clicking along another track. He wanted Arlyne to pawn a diamond ring. It was one of the few pieces she had left. The suggestion made her frantic.

"You better think of another way because I will not do it. I'll do anything for you [but] I will not hock my ring."

"I says you'll have it ten in the morning," Luca insisted. "One day . . . twenty-four hours. At ten in the morning, I'll give it back to you."

Arlyne was growing hysterical.

"I don't wanna do it! I don't wanna—I wanna have a little something. You don't mind, do ya?"

"I'll kiss your fuckin' ass in Macy's window if I don't produce the money you take out for the ring at ten in the morning! . . . No, I'll do one thing better. You know what I'll do? I'll get a fuckin' divorce tomorrow and marry you!"

"I don't want you—no way."

Tommy was disconsolate. "Now, I have no way, unless a miracle happens and this horse stands up. . . . Then I'm in action. Or else I'm dead at seven [o'clock] with Hook Crook, bee bop boop . . ."

"You have a miracle," Arlyne insisted. "All I gotta do is—"

"Stop askin' me," Tommy cut her off. "It's a dead issue."

The Nagra was running. Downstairs Agent Hendrickson, sitting in his car, could hear the entire conversation over a transmitter. There were certain things Arlyne wanted to get into the record.

"Lemme ask you a question, Tommy," she probed. "What did you tell me about Pincus?"

Luca was wary, as if he seemed to suspect that his words might be overheard.

"To do something . . ."

"I wanna learn about a lot of things, Tommy. I would like to ask you a question, all right? We don't have no money, is that right?"

"Right."

"I keep telling this to Greg that I don't have no money. . . . The only way that I survive with Greg is by helping him with certain things, which I've done quite a lot of things—"

"What do you want? Come to the point."

"I gotta get outta this house. . . . I'm living from today 'til tomorrow, okay? Half of the times I don't care what I do anymore, okay? I feel I'm good only here for about another year, another two years in New York. I mean nothing's happening between you and . . ."

"What are you trying to say?"

"We've discussed a lot of things. We've discussed Nathan Pincus with Greg, okay?"

"What are you trying to say?"

"I'm gonna ask you a question now. Why can't I go over and pay the Gottis for you?"

At the mention of the name, Tommy's face assumed a terrible expression.

"No." Arlyne could see what was coming. "Don't get mad! Okay."

"If I ever hear you mention that fuckin' name again, I'll put a bullet in your fuckin' mouth, you tramp!"

He began to punch her.

"No," Arlyne protested, shielding herself from the blows. "The dog, you're getting the dog. . . ."

The beating stopped, but Luca's fury did not subside.

"I told you forty times don't mention that to me. Keep your mouth shut. You're threading [sic] on thin ice. The FBI can't protect ya. They can't. They'll take your fuckin' mother and put a needle through her throat and make the blood drain out of her slowly. You're dealing with a sick guy. You fuck him up, he'll go right to the source and kill everybody, because that's the way he operates, and that's the way he's supposed to operate. Now, if those fuckin' fag Feds want him, then let them go get him without a slut like you."

"I'm walkin' the dog," Arlyne announced. "C'mon, Shadow. Come with me, sweetheart."

By the time she reached Hendrickson's car, her face was swollen from the punches. She returned the Nagra and the agent—Arlyne would later recall—gave her another three hundred dollars for her pains.

Tommy got his miracle. The horse came in, which got him off the hook with his creditors. For days he basked in that security, unaware that Arlyne was surreptitiously undermining his happiness and security by attempting the forbidden overture to John Gotti.

At the FBI's instruction, Arlyne called Joey Scopo where he hung out at an auto shop near the Bergin Hunt and Fish Club. Jackie and Joey had been looking for Tommy "high and low" and agreed, Arlyne would later insist, to set up a meeting with Johnny. About a week later, Arlyne set out, Nagra rolling, to meet Jackie and Joey at a luncheonette across from the Club. That sit-down was brief and disappointing. The two goons, it became clear, still had no intention of letting Arlyne talk to their boss, whom they insisted was not around. As she left the restaurant, Arlyne thought she saw John Gotti on the curb getting into a gray Lincoln.

Arlyne stewed in frustration. The Gotti surveillance had struck a wall. She could make no progress on discovering the identities of the conspirators in the airline heist. She fared somewhat better on the Pincus case, arranging a meeting with the former IRS supervisor, a thin little man with round glasses, who, after insisting that he would participate in nothing illegal, announced he had contacted an agent connected with Nathan's case and thought they could "make a score for six figures." But this investigation, too, for reasons Arlyne could not fathom, entered a holding pattern. Work on all of them came to an abrupt halt when Greg Hendrickson announced that he was being transferred to Tampa.

Unlike the transfer of Jeff Dossett, which had struck Arlyne as a personal betrayal, the departure of Agent Hendrickson seemed business as usual. In the almost six years since she had been registered as an informant she had grown philosophical, distilling her feelings in a sardonic aphorism: You must never like agents; they move away on you. It was part of becoming a professional.

And if there was one thing Arlyne had come to consider herself, it was a professional.

By the spring of 1980, her fame as an informant for hire had spread through an impressive network of local, state and federal law enforcement agencies. Her credits included work for not only New York State, but the Fort Lee police, the Nassau County police, the DEA, the FBI and most recently the New York City police, whose Intelligence Division had begun using her as a resource. Arlyne was never paid a lot. She received, rather, a few hundred dollars here and there, save for the occasional big job that brought in one thousand to two thousand dollars. And, of course, the government repaid her loans.

Her eccentricities were unmistakable. Investigators could tell instantly if a surveillance tape was Arlyne's because of certain signature phrases that popped up throughout—notably "Can I ask you a question?" and "read my lips"—both rendered in an ingratiating whine. Her sexual bravado was equally legendary. A story circulated among the New York City police of how, when two investigators went to her apartment to debrief her, she slammed a bottle of Scotch on the table and declaimed, "anyone want a blow job?" She played up the role of the foul-mouthed, streetwise moll, largely because she felt cops expected it. But her professional persona had considerable range. Depending upon what circumstances demanded, she could play the scatterbrain, the fussing Jewish mother or the poor soul playing on the sympathies of her prospective victims. The informant Brickman was often unorthodox, often unpleasant, but she often got results.

Arlyne took a great deal of pride in her work, boasting in later years, "My reputation exceeded itself." She was not, she was fond of reminding one, your run-of-the-mill street rat working off a crime. She disliked the term "informant," preferring the more flattering designation "cooperating individual." She disdained "cheap money," that is, fees bartered for phony or useless information. She felt it was beneath her dignity to engage in the common informant-to-cop haggling that went, "I saw Frankie with Tommy. Don't I deserve one hundred dollars for that? Don't I deserve fifty dollars for that? Don't I deserve . . . etc., etc."

As to her essential status, however, Arlyne had no delusions. She knew the contempt with which police officers and agents viewed informants. No matter how close you became to them, they would never fully trust you. No matter how friendly they appeared, you must never respond too familiarly. No matter how stupid they were, you must never appear smarter. "I was being used by these various agencies," she later reflected. "But while they were using me, I loved it because it was dangerous. It was getting out there. It was working."

Working gave Arlyne a rush more satisfying than any she had found in drugs or alcohol or sex. There was the tension that would build before a surveillance, culminating in a tremendous climax of relief and self-esteem made all the sweeter by the camaraderie she enjoyed with the agents afterward. Arlyne reached again and again for that release, the pursuit of which obliterated what remained of her old loyalties. In the beginning, she had turned over creditors like Bobby Fischetti or old enemies like Vince Lamattina. Now, in the heat of the campaign, she turned, quite effortlessly, on old friends.

In recent years, Arlyne had not heard much from Tony Mirra. This was not surprising considering Tony spent nearly half his life in prison. In 1980, however, Arlyne learned that her old flame was back in action. This news excited Tommy Luca, who urged Arlyne to contact Mirra in hopes of borrowing money or perhaps even getting in on his drug business. Arlyne had passed all of these developments along to Hendrickson, who saw an opportunity to gather intelligence on certain of Mirra's Bonanno associates, in particular one Nicky Marangello, with whom Tony owned a club in Chinatown.

Tony, who had been moved from Riker's Island Prison to the West Street Jail in Manhattan, put Arlyne's name on a visitors list. When she showed up, wearing tight pants and top, his motive became clear. He was on some kind of work release at a construction side on Park Avenue South. This relative liberty allowed him to bribe guards and bring up broads to get laid. He was recruiting Arlyne for service. The coldness of the proposition hurt her. She held off his advances, saying she had a business deal that might appeal to him. Tony, however, had no interest in doing business with Luca, whom he had correctly pegged as a screw-up.

Arlyne persisted, visiting Mirra twice after that. One meeting occurred at a Chinese vegetable market next to the club. He insisted upon this site, she assumed, because their conversation could not be overheard in the general hubbub. And he was right, because the tape Arlyne made on that occasion was too muddy to be deciphered. He could not, at any rate, be lured into discussing Marangello or anything else of value. Arlyne took another shot, this time at a luncheonette on Madison Street. This time, Tony took her for a ride in his maroon Mercedes to the bridge at South Street and forced her to give him a blow job.

During the entire time she was wearing a wire on Tony, Arlyne felt no remorse. (Tony himself had not been the target, after all. She had only used him to get dirt on his friends.) Had she needed a reason to justify her coldness, she could have found one. Tony had been rough. He only wanted her for sex. But then, Tony had always been an animal. His crude behavior did not negate the fact that she had once been under his protection. He had beaten up her husband for her, a favor that should have ensured a lifetime of loyalty. Nonetheless, Tony Mirra became a casualty of Arlyne's enthusiasm.

So, too, did Paulie Messina.

Over the years, Arlyne had kept better track of her Uncle Paulie, who, she heard, had been convicted of trafficking in heroin. He was out on parole when she happened to run into him at Kennedy Airport as he was picking up his aging mother off a flight from Florida. Their exchange, as Arlyne later recalled it, went like this.

"Paulie. I need a good score. I need some money. I've gotta make some money."

To which he purportedly replied, "The only thing I got is Quaalude powder."

Paulie was a good-hearted man—far better than Tony Mirra—who had done many favors for her and her family. His parole could be revoked at the first misstep. Simple decency would have dictated letting him be. But the spirit of the hunt had already been roused and Arlyne passed along her conversation with Paulie to Lindberg and Isnardi. After that, Arlyne's poor unsuspecting uncle was drawn into deeper trouble with each passing day.

At the detectives' insistence, Arlyne later claimed, she introduced Paulie to another of her marks, a Brooklyn hood who had gotten Luca into peddling poppers. Tommy found himself in debt to his connection, and so instructed Arlyne to neutralize him. Accordingly, she had set the supplier up with an undercover agent from the DEA in hopes of inducing him to sell heroin. With that drama in progress, she suggested to the target that he might want to buy Paulie's Quaalude powder. As the result of that introduction, the two men agreed they could do some business. Arlyne monitored the progress of this marriage by visiting the Manhattan construction site where Paulie was working to satisfy the terms of his parole. She went wired, and on the tapes of one of those encounters happened to mention a "Matthew Burton." At this, the Nassau County detectives pricked up their ears. Burton had apparently offended a Nassau cop, who, thereafter, had it in for him. Arlyne recalls being asked if she could do "a little favor" for "the guys from Nassau" and try to arrange to buy from Burton an ounce or two of crystal meth.

It was a quick job. Arlyne, introducing herself as a friend of Paulie's, contacted Burton and arranged to meet him at a bar he owned far out on the Island. She drove out one night—a string of cops on her tail—and entering the bar was shown to Burton's office, a tiny room outfitted only with desk and file cabinets. The proprietor resembled a weight lifter, with huge shoulders and tapering torso. Few words passed between them. He took the crystal meth out of his pocket and she handed him a little less than two thousand dollars. The main thing, Eddie and Louie had told her, was to get out in a hurry. And she did.

Within hours of Arlyne's buy, all hell broke loose. A team of DEA agents and Nassau cops swooped down upon Burton and others Arlyne had drawn into this web of intrigue, making a raft of arrests. Arlyne, at her own request, was busted along with them. Picked up at her apartment in Queens, she allowed herself to be driven to Nassau County where she went through the motions of being photographed and fingerprinted. Then she was hauled up the back stairs of the courthouse in handcuffs. During her arraignment she acted like a "punk broad." Safely out of sight of the other prisoners, Arlyne shed her cuffs. The police made out an arrest record, but this was for show and was later sent back to her in the mail.

The charade fooled no one. Word reached her that Paulie Messina knew, or had at least guessed, who set him up. While Arlyne did not actually believe that Paulie would harm her, she was less certain of Matthew Burton, who, she knew, was a tough character. A DEA agent assigned to her case argued to his superiors that based on the "types of persons" arrested as a result of the informant's cooperation, "there is a very real danger that [she] will be eliminated unless immediately relocated." Once again, Arlyne was offered the Witness Protection Program. Once again, she declined, accepting instead an unusually generous payment of six thousand dollars to relocate herself.

Cash in hand, Arlyne pushed Beatrice and Shadow into her car, and headed for Florida. They got as far as Dillon, South Carolina, where they took a room in a motel called South of the Border. The motel, lying midway between New York and Miami, was a familiar stopover for Arlyne. She usually rented a room and caught a few winks before driving the remaining eleven hours to Florida. Now she lingered. One day. Then two. She and her household remained in that shabby room for a week until she could decide what to do.

When she took the relocation money, she had really intended to set up housekeeping in some safe haven. Now, however, as she pondered the consequences of permanent banishment, her resolve weakened. Leaving New York would mean that she would never again be part of the game. No more rush. No more action. That was unthinkable. Arlyne Brickman turned the car around and headed back to the city. If you had done something really bad, she reasoned, no one would figure that you would go back home. According to that logic, her apartment made the perfect hideout. Sneaking back in under cover of night, Arlyne and Beatrice spent several days tiptoeing about and whispering to one another. Shadow did not feel similarly constrained. Whenever anyone passed the door, he would bark loudly.

After a couple of weeks, the tension eased. Arlyne took her relocation money and went out shopping for jewelry. She invited Tommy Luca back over to share in the riches. One night as she and Tommy were crossing the street to the apartment building, a car cut them off. It was Paulie Messina.

"I want to talk to you," he said without emotion. The three of them went silently upstairs, Paulie bringing up the rear. As the apartment door closed behind them, Paulie pulled out a handgun.

"Paulie, please," Arlyne pleaded, "I'll be quiet."

Tommy was looking from one to the other as if he were puzzled. "Paulie," he entreated, "how do I know what she did? Do I know anything?"

"Scum," Arlyne thought.

Paulie took a chair by the piano and waited a moment. Then he asked softly, "Why did you do it to me?"

Arlyne knew Paulie had a soft heart and was susceptible to a lie. "I'll have to tell you what happened," she began hesitantly. "You'll understand, Paulie. Leslie was taken on a drug charge. She's gonna go to jail unless I cooperate. They knew that we were friends. I don't know how they knew it. It was either you or Leslie who was going to jail."

Paulie put away his gun. "Eileen," he said (Paulie was one of those who could never pronounce "Arlyne"), "I never want to see you ever again. I don't want nobody to ever call me up. And I never want to hear your name." And he walked out the door.

Arlyne was giddy with relief. At the time all she could think of was how funny it was that she had put one over on Paulie. It was only years later, when the ghosts of friends betrayed began intoning their plaints in her dreams, that she would recall the incident as "pitiful."

Arlyne stayed on in New York, resting in the illusory assurance that the best way to avoid harm was to place herself squarely in its path. She remained on the informant rosters of the DEA and the FBI, all the while engaging—"to a certain extent"—in shady business with Tommy Luca.

The Ricchiutti bust had interrupted Tommy's pot trade only briefly.

He quickly found other suppliers and continued wholesaling to the smoke shops. Dom Paterno was no longer in the picture. He had run afoul of some bad Sicilians who held him for ransom in the back of an espresso shop. His brother paid the money—because he was, after all, family—but after that Tommy and Nick decided Dom was so dumb he was a liability and kicked him out of the crew.

By now, Luca had overcome his qualms about hard drugs and moved down the line to cocaine and heroin. He was deliberately closemouthed about his new contacts, but Arlyne knew from snippets of overheard conversations that he had fallen in with a character named Pete the Beeper. She could learn little about Pete, except that he did business out of Brooklyn near Staten Island and he was always on the lookout for new suppliers. Tommy and Nick were his scouts.

For the first time, Luca began wearing a beeper. He would not give Arlyne the number, which infuriated her. It was only when he was shorthanded that he would ask her for help. This happened fairly often since Nick, who enjoyed renown as a world-class coke cutter, was also a cokehead and was frequently incapacitated by his habit. On one such night, Tommy was scheduled to make a delivery of coke to the Guianan, Lazro, in exchange for ten thousand dollars. Nick, who had originally set up the deal, didn't show. Luca and Lazro had had a falling out. So Tommy pressed Arlyne into service as a courier. Taking Beatrice for moral support, Arlyne drove to Brooklyn, where she spotted Lazro on the street and exchanged her brown parcel for an envelope of bills. She did not insult him by counting them. Lazro was no beat artist. About five hours later, he called the apartment, babbling furiously that the heroin Tommy had given him had been hit so many times it was "junk." Luca just laughed. He enjoyed getting the best of the niggers.

There was one other incident, notable not so much for its importance at the moment as for its importance to Arlyne's future dealings with her friends the Feds. Again, Nick had failed to show, this time to hold about three hundred thousand dollars that Luca intended to exchange for a shipment of heroin up on Avenue O. Once again, Arlyne was recruited as stand-in. Late that evening, she and Luca went to meet a guy named Petey (not to be confused with the Beeper), who had brokered the deal with some Sicilian suppliers. Tommy double-parked in front of Petey's apartment, an unimposing two-family walkup, and handed Arlyne a shopping bag. Its heft told her that it was full of bills. The close proximity of money always caused Arlyne to tremble with something akin to sensual delight. Good sense now told her not to look into the bag. She went along without complaint as Tommy escorted her up the stairs into Petey's kitchen.

It was a surprisingly domestic scene. There were Petey and his partner—a pair of Italians in their thirties—and Petey's wife, a short, nasty blond with a baby in her arms and a toddler at her feet. Petey pointed Arlyne to a club chair in the kitchen. She parked herself there, keeping the shopping bag close beside her. Tommy left to pick up the goods.

Arlyne sat for what seemed like hours, making light conversation. Nothing about drugs, naturally, since Petey's wife and kids were there. Arlyne noticed two handguns: one on top of the table, the other above the refrigerator. At last, the phone rang. Petey handed her the receiver. It was Tommy, who told her, "Give this guy who's comin' up the money. Everything's okay."

Soon the doorbell rang. It was a middle-aged Italian wearing a checked suit and a baseball cap. Petey nodded at her to give him the money. "Where's Tommy?" she asked him. The man in the suit didn't reply. He just took the bag and left. Tommy didn't show up until 3:00 A.M. By then Petey's wife and kids had gone to sleep, leaving the men free to talk about where they could get smoke.

On the drive home, Arlyne and Tommy had another row. She tried to get out of the car; he pulled her back in. In the days thereafter they made up. Arlyne would later claim she never received a cent for that night's work, which in her mind rendered her blameless. Christmas was coming, however, and Tommy gave her a little over one thousand dollars and told her to go out and get herself something. She bought a dining-room set, the centerpiece of which was a large, octagonal table with a glass top.

It didn't take a genius to see that Luca's excursions into hard drugs were creating an unwholesome domestic situation. Although Leslie Brickman was not living at home, she dropped in every now and then. With Leslie and her friends shooting heroin and Tommy selling it, it was only a question of time before they got together. Leslie introduced Tommy to her new boyfriend, a young Puerto Rican known as Willie.

Arlyne couldn't find out much about this so-called boyfriend. Every time she asked her daughter a question, Leslie started screaming. Knowing, however, that the girl sometimes confided in Beatrice, Arlyne slipped her housekeeper a few dollars to get information. Leslie, she learned, had met Willie when she had gone down to make a buy on the

Lower East Side. He was a heroin dealer on Allen Street and credited with being "one of the smartest spics around."

The lovers were living together in a project. Arlyne tried to phone Leslie but the phone was disconnected, so she dropped by unannounced. She was slightly reassured to see that the apartment was clean. Peering into the gloom, however, she could see cowry shells and candles in glass cylinders. Willie practiced voodoo. He also owned a large pitbull named Midnight, which he was training to fight. None of this made sense to Arlyne. However cold her daughter might be in some respects, she had always been humane toward animals. It did not seem in character for her to condone the slaughter of chickens or the torment and destruction of a dog. What seemed even more peculiar was her demeanor toward Willie, who was perhaps a year or two her junior. She indulged him like a child. Arlyne, who had always liked her men masterful, could not see the attraction.

Yet if there was any question of who controlled whom, it was dispelled in the weeks following her visit to the projects. Thereafter, whenever Arlyne wanted to see Leslie, she had to go down to Allen Street. There on the corner she would see pretty little girls as well as the burnouts prostituting themselves for heroin. Leslie was rarely out in the tiny square. She was, more often, inside a forlorn tenement. Arlyne would have to persuade someone to give Leslie the message to come out. Sometimes Leslie responded; sometimes she was "busy." In her heart, Arlyne knew that she was turning tricks for Willie.

Arlyne would later ask herself why, at a time when her daughter needed help so badly, she was overwhelmed by inertia. Part of it, no doubt, was that she did not have the emotional fortitude to confront the fact that her daughter was a junkie whore. Doing so would have meant acknowledging that she was, at least in part, responsible. And that, in turn, would have meant acknowledging that Tommy was no good for either of them. She still clung to the fiction that Leslie needed a father figure.

Years later, Leslie's assessment of her mother and her so-called father figure was spare and damning. "I used to buy my coke and heroin from him, so how much could he really care? Him and my mother only cared that if they needed money, they could borrow it from me. Well, not borrow it, you know, ask me for it. And I'd give it to them. I used to have to pay them up front if I wanted to buy anything. Tommy never gave me a discount or anything."

Arlyne would maintain to the end that it was Tommy, not she, who sold Leslie heroin. But one fact seems clear. Throughout most of 1981 and 1982, she knew about this unholy alliance and—out of fear of losing Tommy and her "house money"—she did not lift a finger to stop it.

There was a tacit conspiracy among members of the Weiss family not to tell Irving about his granddaughter. The truth, it was felt, would have killed him. Irving's car dealership in Palm Beach had done very well, but Billie, who was sensitive to the fact the locals were not partial to Jews, insisted her husband close up shop. They moved to a seaside high rise further down the Gold Coast where Irving enjoyed a gentleman's retirement, smoking Chesterfields and playing gin with his cronies by the pool. As a practical matter, Arlyne had no contact with her father. She spoke regularly with her mother, however, in whom she confided everything. The years had imparted to Billie some maturity and she bore the secrets with a dignity and tranquillity worthy of Ida Blum.

One afternoon Arlyne received a call from her mother. Billie was hesitant and her voice quivered as she broke the news. Irving had cancer.

Arlyne offered to fly down immediately but was persuaded to wait a few weeks until after the doctors removed a portion of his lung. When she finally arrived at his bedside at Hollywood Memorial, Irving wouldn't look at her. Her mother said it was the medication.

The operation was not an unqualified success and it would be necessary, the doctors said, for the patient to take radiation treatments. But Irving continued to deteriorate. Arlyne made several trips back to Florida to help her mother and Barbara care for him. But Irving did not want her to touch him. He insisted she smelled. Arlyne, who was obsessively scrupulous about body odor, realized that her father's olfactory hallucination sprang from memories of her affairs and abortions and lies. She went to bed crying.

After her return to Forest Hills, Arlyne tried to explain to Leslie what was happening to her Poppy, but the girl was preoccupied with her own problems. Willie had run out on her and she was having trouble making the rent. Seeing the opportunity to regain control, Arlyne rented her daughter a small apartment behind her own, furnishing it expensively. Leslie sold the furniture for two hundred dollars and bought drugs. Arlyne then persuaded Leslie to come live with her, at least for a while.

Leslie had tried to get straight. She had checked herself into a clinic near Beth Israel Hospital, where she stayed for three weeks. As a result, she had gotten on a Methadone program, which meant Arlyne had to drive her every day to 125th Street to get her medication. She was distressed to learn that Willie and Leslie were then selling the Methadone. After they split, however, Leslie seemed more sincere about recovery.

Having the opportunity to observe her daughter at close range, Arlyne was worried by what she saw. In the period of a few months, Leslie's round body had grown thin. She suffered from hepatitis, ran fevers and slept a lot. But convalescence was nearly impossible in that chaotic household where the phone and doorbell rang round the clock with Luca's angry creditors. The most persistent of these collectors was a young Colombian named Edgar Morales, a friend of Willie's and a coke dealer in his own right. Before splitting, Willie had introduced Tommy to Morales, who had given him part of a key on consignment. When it came time to collect the seventy-five hundred dollars, Luca was nowhere to be found. In exasperation, Morales showed up outside Arlyne's door, ringing the bell and yelling, "Mama, where's your man?"

Whenever Tommy deigned to come around, Arlyne would nag him to get Morales off her back. But he had grown used to tuning her out. Nowadays Tommy seemed preoccupied and suspicious. It could never have been far from Tommy's thoughts that Arlyne was capable of turning him in to the DEA. In fact, on any number of occasions she had been tempted to rat him out only to pull back when things seemed to be going better between them. It was Arlyne's habit to feed her friends the Feds only enough information to cover herself if Tommy or his friends were busted—but not enough to disrupt the flow of house money. Luca simply had to trust that she was protecting his interests. And as his interests took him into heavier drugs, his confidence apparently began to wane.

Fully aware of this mounting tension, Arlyne could not resist undertaking little jobs for the Feds. One afternoon, she was out trying to arrange a buy of quinine for the DEA when Tommy dropped by the apartment. Arlyne returned home to find Luca dressing to go out. He was buttoning a black shirt she had never seen before. "Only a woman would buy you a shirt like that," she charged.

"What were you doing today?" he shot back. "Ratting me out on the Beeper?" He brought his fist down on the glass tabletop, breaking it neatly in half. Then he stormed out the door.

The incident seemed to confirm for Arlyne that Tommy had a lover. She became obsessed with finding out who it was. She had once spotted his car at a motel near the airport and had cruised the parking lots of all

the hostelries in the vicinity. She caught him one night in the lot of a
hotel on Conduit Boulevard. There was a woman in the passenger's seat
but, as it was dark, Arlyne couldn't see her face. From the back, she
looked like a "little spic."

Arlyne had to know the truth. She was on generally good terms
with Nick, who, though Tommy's partner, had always been straight
with her. She called him.

"Nick," she asked bluntly, "what's going on here with Tommy?"

"Don't you know who he's seeing?" Nick asked.

"No, I don't know what's going on," she admitted.

"He's seeing Gina."

"Vince's wife?" she asked incredulously.

"Yeah. He's been seeing her for quite some time."

The words "quite some time" rattled hollowly in her brain. So
everyone knew, even Terry's girlfriend, who had warned her to "look in
her own back yard." Arlyne Brickman, who could find out anything
from anybody, couldn't see what was happening right under her nose. It
was an awful humiliation. Tossing caution to the wind, she called Gina
and demanded, "What's going on here?"

Gina professed surprise at Arlyne's distress. Tommy, she said,
had told her that he and Arlyne were never lovers, only business
partners.

It took Tommy less than an hour to realize that Arlyne had phoned
Gina. His response was rage. As Arlyne got into her rented Capri to take
Leslie on an errand, she saw Tommy speeding directly toward her. His
left fender rammed into the side of her car. Arlyne put on the gas to
make a getaway but he followed in hot pursuit. When she stopped at a
light, he got out of his own car, raised a gun and fired two shots. Neither
hit its mark, and apparently realizing he was in serious trouble, Tommy
fled the scene.

It was Arlyne's turn to be outraged. She filed a criminal complaint
and the arresting police had no trouble locating Luca hiding out at
Gina's. But there were complications. Luca would probably tell his
attorney that Arlyne was an informant and, if the case came to trial, the
exposure and publicity might blow her cover. She was still doing work
for the government as well as the New York Police Department. Arlyne
dismally contemplated her options—and finally dropped charges.

Arlyne decided that if she was to have justice, she must take matters
into her own hands.

Exactly when Arlyne told federal authorities about the Nigerian is
still a matter of dispute. To this day she insists she had mentioned him

before Luca took a shot at her in early February 1983. Detective
Lindberg recalls that it was not until after the breakup. (Indeed, the
documents detailing Arlyne's work on this case are all dated February
and beyond.) Quibbles over timing notwithstanding, the information
she passed along was this: Luca and Nick Paterno had been having
coffee in her kitchen one morning when they came across an item in the
morning paper that upset them. A Nigerian named Komolafe had been
arrested by Customs at Kennedy Airport with several pounds of heroin
in his possession. Tommy jumped up and ran down to a pay phone on
the corner. She surmised that he was talking to someone named
"Charles," who had called the apartment a lot in recent weeks. This
Charles spoke with an accent she could not identify.

Lindberg passed the tips along to Customs, which instructed Arlyne
to do some more digging into the identity of Luca's unidentified contact.
Arlyne approached Nick, who was feeling talkative because he and
Tommy were feuding. (Luca, he discovered, had been cheating him and
keeping two sets of books. He found the originals stuck in the sun visor
of Tommy's car.) Arlyne was able to learn that he and Tommy had been
doing business with Komolafe through an introduction arranged by one
Charles Anifalaje, also known as Anif. Nick did not know if he was also
Nigerian. They had apparently lost some money when the courier
Komolafe was busted. Charles had further screwed them by delivering a
package of inferior brown heroin. Now Tommy wouldn't return
Charles's calls.

Arlyne telephoned the mystery man at a number left on one of these
messages and asked him to meet her at the Floridian Diner in Brooklyn.
She was able, she told him, to get him back in Tommy's good graces.
Eddie and the Feds hoped she could learn enough to implicate Luca and
Paterno and, secondarily, arrange to make a buy.

It was a freezing February day when Arlyne arrived at the diner for
the rendezvous. Charles was late. She called his house and got no answer.
Then she saw him, an imposing black man wearing an expensive suit and
a Gucci bracelet.

"How've you been, sweetheart?" she greeted him.

Charles ordered a Heineken; Arlyne, a Bloody Mary. They sat
studying each other over untouched drinks.

"Charles," she said. "Let me ask you a question. You know Nick
was in the house when I called you the other night. He put me up to
calling you."

"Why he did this?" Charles asked. He was staring at her intently. It
made her self-conscious.

"[Why] do you keep looking at me—I know I'm heavy—I'll lose weight—I've been on a very strict diet . . ."

Charles got down to his complaints.

"Tommy's a nice guy [but] he has a temper."

"Tommy's got a temper," Arlyne commiserated. "You should see what he did to my car. . . . Let me tell you what went wrong. . . . They couldn't trust you. You gave them the brown stuff. Remember the brown stuff?"

"I let them know," Charles countered, "that it's not good—as in the past."

Arlyne turned the conversation to discovering Tommy's relationship with Komolafe.

"Charles, I'll tell you one thing. [They were] mad at you the day that, that guy got caught. If they could have killed you, they were gonna kill you . . ."

"Okay, what did they do?" he protested. "They didn't do nothing yet . . ."

"They gave you money up front . . . Charles."

"That's true—but you see—look—what I was talking to them about was—we all know that thing can cost two hundred and fifty thousand dollars—right."

"How much?" she probed for the record.

"Two fifty thousand," he repeated.

(Later in the conversation, Charles seemed to insist that there was no front money and Arlyne was at a loss to figure out why Tommy was so upset at the courier's arrest. Arlyne did manage to learn that a month earlier, Tommy had stopped by Charles's house to pick up a sample of heroin and the two haggled over price. But then, Luca hit the number and, relieved of the financial necessity to make a deal, did not get back with an offer.)

Arlyne boasted that it was she who was actually the brains behind Tommy's operation. "Okay, now if I make a buy—" (she slipped but quickly corrected herself) "—or no, excuse me—if I make a sale, it's always me that they know—like Tommy always sits behind me—you understand." Perhaps she and Charles could do business whenever he had "volume." His keys were gone now, he explained, but there were more coming.

"If it's on the market," she boasted, "I'll give you the money right there and then."

Charles was wary but intrigued.

Arlyne looked at her watch. She had to get going in order to pick up her daughter. "I will talk to you whenever you call me."

"I'll talk to you on Sunday," Charles promised.

It was over three weeks before Arlyne saw Anifalaje again. This time, he came up to the apartment ready to conduct business. In the interim, the Feds' game plan had changed. Arlyne herself would not make the buy, but would instead introduce him to an undercover agent—in this case, Louie Isnardi posing as her friend "Aldo." Arlyne did not let Charles know that she would be having a guest that evening as she felt it might scare him away.

Arlyne answered the door.

"I told you we live nice," she greeted him. "What do you think?"

"Uh, huh," he crooned admiringly.

She got him a Scotch.

"There's only three blacks that come to my house now," she told him. "You—Linton—and Lazro."

That clumsy admission was intended not only to flatter him but to see if he recognized the names of the Guianans from the smoke shops. He showed no signs of recognition. Charles, it turned out, was neither Guianan nor Nigerian, but a native of Ghana.

Shadow, who had been crouched in a posture of semireadiness on the carpet, growled at Charles, who glanced at him uneasily. From the bedroom, Leslie called out to her mother. "Okay, honey," Arlyne replied, too occupied to see what the girl wanted. Leslie was in fact sick and running a fever of 104. "I've got a good girl," Arlyne boasted. "She drives . . . to Florida in cars—you know what I mean? . . . We all work . . . we all make a living."

Arlyne got down to business. "I got to make some money—I got a very big problem here. Tommy . . . has left me with a lot of debts."

Charles produced a glass vial.

"What is that?" she asked disingenuously.

"That's coke," Charles replied.

"That's coke? What, are you going to snort a little?"

"Yeah."

"Lemme see what it is. Is it any good?"

Arlyne sniffed the white powder.

"Is it not good?" Charles asked her.

"Oh, God," she exclaimed. "That woke me up. That's good, Charles.

"All right then," Arlyne urged. "Let's start a rapport. . . . We don't

have to start big. . . . I've got a man that's got more [money] than
God. . . . Been waiting for this bastard to call me all goddamn night. He
was to show up and give me some money."

The phone rang. It was Aldo.

"Can he come up?" Arlyne asked Charles. "Or do you want to meet
him another time?"

Charles did not seem happy about this turn of affairs. All evening
Arlyne had felt him looking at her body. He seemed to like big women.
Now he began propositioning her in whispers.

"How can we have privacy? My kid—is here," she protested.

Charles at last agreed that Aldo could come, on the provision that
he would leave quickly.

"No," Arlyne insisted. "He's gonna stay . . . he's gotta stay . . . we
got to go over figures. . . . There'll be plenty of nights, Charles. Let me
get thinner."

"Okay," Charles relented. "Let him."

Arlyne told Isnardi to come up.

"Hi, puppy. Hi, puppy," the detective greeted Shadow.

"Hi, Charles," Isnardi said, turning to the guest of honor. "Pleased
to meet you." Isnardi took a drink offered by his hostess.

"She's been telling [me] a lot about you," he continued. "I've been
very eager to sit down with you—to see if we can do something."

"Right," Charles replied noncommittally.

"I don't want any consignment, okay. . . . Cash. COD . . . which
should make us very—very good friends."

Aldo claimed he could move a kilo at a time with five days' notice,
except for Fridays, which were out of the question.

Arlyne, who had been called away to the phone, rejoined the men.
"Aldo," she said, "guess who that was. Lazro—looking for Tommy. For
that money."

"I don't want to hear about Tommy," Aldo said flatly.

This struck a chord in Charles, who chimed in, "You see . . .
Tommy and Nick . . . they owe to me." He went on to explain how he
had known Nick for some twenty years, but this bad debt was now
destroying their friendship.

"I understand," Aldo commiserated. "That's why I do it differently.
Okay?"

Out of natural reluctance, perhaps, to discuss such sensitive matters
with a stranger, Charles's voice had gotten so low it could not be heard
by the surveillance team listening to the transmitter. Eddie Lindberg
phoned the apartment to ask Arlyne to do something.

"Excuse me," she said to Aldo, with the phone still in her hand. "Can you hear him? Maybe I'm crazy—I think I'm losing my hearing every time I'm around him."

"Okay," Charles replied, "the reason I . . . don't talk too loud is [this] is not the business to talk loud about."

"Okay," Aldo resumed the beat, "cash on the line. . . . If I want tan? If I want white? I tell you in advance."

Charles mumbled a reply and once again Arlyne lit into him. "I can't hear you," she badgered. "Would you repeat that?"

Clearly worried that she was coming on too strong, Aldo suggested, "Why don't you take the dog for a walk?"

His voice now loud enough to be caught on tape, Anifalaje told Aldo that he had a shipment coming in next week and that he would call him then. They would be doing business in the neighborhood of two hundred thousand dollars. The detective gave him his "son's" number in Hempstead where he was to ask for Aldo senior, not junior. (The line was being manned by drug agents.)

"I'll take care of her. Okay," concluded Aldo, indicating he would give Arlyne her cut.

Contrary to Arlyne's promise, there were not "plenty of nights." She never saw Charles again. After the introduction in her apartment, Anif did business strictly with Isnardi, entrusting the undercover agent with damning confidences. He was part of an organization that smuggled narcotics into the country by courier, one of whom was the Nigerian Komolafe. He, himself, had brought in two kilograms. Anif even invited Aldo to accompany him to India, Nigeria and Pakistan so that he could introduce him to his connections.

As the noose tightened on Anif, Arlyne entertained with satisfaction the prospect of watching Tommy dangle along with him.

Throughout the Anifalaje affair, Edgar Morales was making himself a constant pest. The first few times he had stood outside her door screaming, "Mama! Mama! You gotta pay," Arlyne had been more annoyed than alarmed. Edgar was not the brightest kid on the street—a baby, really—and she considered him harmless. Eddie Lindberg was not so sure. One night when the detective dropped by the apartment to discuss the details of a surveillance, the doorbell rang. Arlyne beckoned Lindberg to look through the peephole, where he saw Edgar waving a gun and shouting, "Mama, I'm going to kill you." Eddie and Arlyne remained quiet. Finally Edgar gave up and went home.

Arlyne scraped up small payments of four hundred or five hundred dollars to throw Edgar's way. That would quiet him temporarily, but a week later he would be back at her door or on the phone making threats. The hostilities escalated early in April when the persistent Colombian came for a payment and found Arlyne packing. Her father was very sick, she told him. She had to go to Florida, but she would pay him when she got back. To Edgar Morales it must have appeared that she was running out on the debt, and he decided to act quickly. The date he chose was April 12, 1983.

It was the day after Leslie's birthday. Arlyne, back from Florida, had been too preoccupied to make much of a fuss, so the girl had been wandering around the apartment a little forlorn. She was still thin, and occasionally feverish, but Arlyne was pleased to see that she was sticking with the Methadone. Privately, Arlyne acknowledged that her daughter was struggling to get herself straight so that she could qualify for welfare and get an apartment of her own. Leslie was obviously desperate to be out of her mother's clutches.

At about one o'clock that afternoon, Edgar Morales showed up at the door, this time without his usual belligerence. He wanted, he said, to take Leslie out to lunch for her birthday. Arlyne was suspicious, but Leslie, who knew Edgar from her days with Willie, seemed eager to go. She brushed out the door over her mother's warnings. Arlyne saw her get into a two-tone Chrysler Cordoba with Morales and two others.

The afternoon passed without word from Leslie. At a little before six the phone rang. It was Edgar. He was rambling but Arlyne caught the amount, eighteen hundred dollars, and the word "kidnap."

"Edgar," she snapped, "stop being crazy. Stop playing around."

Edgar said he would call back in an hour. Then he hung up.

It was as if Arlyne had been hit in the stomach with a hard fist. She struggled to breathe but felt paralyzed. When, after a few seconds, she recovered sufficiently to lift her arms, she reached for the phone and began dialing every cop she knew.

Eddie Lindberg was among those who responded to her frantic summons. Hurrying to her apartment, he was taken aback to find a mob scene. There were at least twenty officers, mostly aging, overweight inspectors from the Queens hostage squad. The dining area had been turned into a sort of situation room. In the middle of all this confusion was a screaming, weeping Arlyne.

The phone rang and everyone fell quiet. Arlyne answered it. It was Edgar. He had now upped his demand from eighteen hundred to two thousand dollars to cover the "added expense" of collecting the debt. As ransom went, it was a laughably small amount. In retrospect it seems incredible that no one seemed to have it on hand. The New York police were willing to produce the flash money, but only if the Feds guaranteed it in the event it was lost or stolen. Lindberg volunteered to pass this proposal along to the DEA. The Queens cops, Lindberg would later observe, hated Feds and had contempt for what they apparently perceived as a rube from Nassau County. But they agreed to accept the offer of assistance. Lindberg placed the call as promised, but Drug Enforcement would not guarantee the money.

The hysteria escalated. Someone had leaked the story to the round-the-clock news station 1010 WINS and there were cryptic, hourly reports about a bizarre kidnapping in Queens. The calls from Edgar were coming about every half hour. He was sounding increasingly strung out. The hostage squad determined that Morales was not calling from a single location but from various pay phones in Brooklyn. That meant he had left Leslie somewhere and was keeping on the move; or he was hauling his hostage around with him. The calls showed no pattern, however, and the cops could not anticipate his next overture.

Once again, the phone rang. Arlyne and the cops agreed it was time to act boldly. She picked up the receiver and told Edgar that she had the money. He should come up to the apartment to get it. But he must, she insisted, bring Leslie with him. Edgar, who was sounding desperate and eager to get this over with, agreed.

Eddie Lindberg was directed to sit in the surveillance van parked outside Arlyne's apartment. Of all the officers assembled for the rescue of Leslie Brickman, only he knew what her abductor looked like. All he had, however, was a fleeting recollection of Edgar's face through a peephole.

When a young Hispanic male wandered into the sights of the surveillance cameras, Lindberg waivered for a second. By the time he got out the words "There he is," Morales had made a sudden turn onto a side street and disappeared.

When the detectives above heard that the van had lost the suspect, they ran into the streets huffing and puffing in hot pursuit. That left Arlyne in the apartment alone. Her doorbell rang. She opened it to find Edgar Morales waiting for his money. There was no transmitter in the apartment so she had no way of signaling cops that Morales had found his way up the back way. Arlyne knew she had to get Edgar downstairs.

"Beatrice went down to get the money," she told him. "Let's go down and get Beatrice and we'll get the money."

When the two of them reached the street, Arlyne saw Eddie by the van. Lindberg, however, was forbidden by jurisdictional protocol from moving in on Morales and had to radio the Queens detectives, now running helter-skelter throughout the neighborhood, to move in for the pick-up.

Edgar was nabbed before he knew what hit him and quickly gave up the location of his hostage, who was sitting in the Cordoba a couple of blocks away. The only thing that seemed to be detaining her was the presence of Edgar's two friends, later identified as Stanley Gonsalves and Barbara Belquaglio, who were also placed under arrest. The hostage appeared to be in fine condition.

The detectives took Leslie to the precinct house. Arlyne's relief at recovering her was soon supplanted by outrage. It was clear, as she watched the offhand way in which the detectives questioned her daughter, that they did not believe that she had been in any real danger. The basis of their suspicions was one phone call in which they could hear Leslie in the background discussing with Edgar's friends which restaurant they should eat at. Maybe she had even taken a hand in planning her own abduction, they suggested. "Why didn't you run?" they asked her contemptuously.

"What was I supposed to do?" she shot back.

Arlyne would have given full vent to her indignation if there had not been lingering in the back of her own mind the suspicion that Leslie was perhaps involved. Having watched her daughter carry off the Methadone scam back in her days with Willie, she realized that the girl possessed cunning. Leslie had made no secret of the fact that she was looking for the first opportunity to break free.

On the ride back from the station, Arlyne confronted her. "Look," she said, "the cops have asked me . . . Leslie, were you part of this thing?"

"Do you think I would subject myself to this if I wanted money?" she replied icily. "I could ask you and get it."

Over succeeding weeks Arlyne managed to worm more details out of her. She had, Leslie insisted, been abducted in earnest. When Edgar tendered his offer of lunch, he had also promised to get her high. They did some drugs, then he took her into the basement of a friend's house and said, "You're kidnapped." Leslie did not believe that Edgar had the nerve to kill her outright. He didn't seem to be armed. But as he and his friends were smoking angel dust, she was afraid they might just wander off, leaving her there to die. She decided to "play along," she said, telling

Edgar, "If she's going to give you money, let's go to a restaurant." The ploy worked. Edgar moved her from the basement to the back of the car and drove around for what seemed like hours. When they finally pulled up to the curb near the apartment, Edgar turned to her and said, "Just stay calm. Your mother will give me the money and you'll be released." She saw no reason to run.

Arlyne thought this through. Why, after all, would Leslie have bothered with this charade? She had been a Brickman long enough to know that all she had to do was make a fuss and someone would give her money. At the police station, she had given Edgar up and was prepared to testify against him. No, Arlyne concluded. It didn't make any sense. She decided to believe her daughter.

After the incident, Leslie had assumed that Tommy would call to see how she was. But a couple of days passed and she heard nothing. This seemed to send her into a depression. Arlyne was surprised. Leslie did not often betray neediness. Her coldness set up an impenetrable screen to her feelings. To see her now hanging around the phone for a call that would never come was pathetic. It seemed that Leslie was hoping the kidnapping would serve as a broadcast for help, and now she was awaiting a reply from someone lost. Her father, perhaps. Any father.

Tommy did not call. About two weeks after the incident, however, Billie phoned with the news that Irving had passed away. There was no need to come to Florida, she said. She would be bringing the body north for burial.

When Arlyne told Leslie that her grandfather was dead, the girl showed no emotion. The only observable change in her demeanor occurred on the morning Irving was to be buried. She was pacing, smoking one cigarette after another. Leslie and Arlyne walked without speaking to the funeral home. There was a large turnout, including a fair number of elderly car dealers wanting to pay the good man their respects. Billie was thin, pale and composed. Barbara was thin, pale and dignified. Her children stood next to her, solemn and impeccably groomed.

Leslie had seemed calm, but as she approached the casket, open to reveal the kindly, disease-worn face of her grandfather, the girl stopped dead still. A tremor passed through her body, then increased in its intensity until her shoulders and body shook. She let out a terrible gasp. Her natural father had abandoned her. Tommy Luca had betrayed her. The one man whose love was constant—whose devotion she had held in such contempt—was dead. Leslie Brickman started to scream.

Arlyne took the girl to a restroom and bathed her face with cool water to quiet her. She managed to make it through the rest of the funeral without hysterics. Billie and the others planned to sit shiva at Barbara's. Arlyne decided it was best if she and Leslie kept the vigil alone. By the time they reached the apartment, however, Leslie's expression was, once again, stone cold. She had to go out, she said. Then she disappeared into the city, looking, her mother suspected, for Willie.

For several hours Arlyne sat alone trying to remember her father in his white suit and touring car, handsome as a movie star. His life was like a fable. Had he written it for himself? Or had she written it for him? The effect was the same. She had spent her years trying to be like him. He was a racketeer. She was a mob girl. She loved what she saw in him, and he hated what he saw in her. Himself. In some strange way, Arlyne envied Leslie her noisy, uncontrollable grief. Leslie, at least, was still one of the living. Try as she might, Arlyne could not bring herself to cry. When she thought of her father, she felt completely numb.

NINE

SWEETIE
PIE

Throughout the spring of 1983 the only emotion Arlyne could muster was jealousy. She hectored Eddie and Louie for information about Tommy, who was now living with Gina Lamattina in an apartment in Brooklyn. The detectives, seemingly amused by Arlyne's hysteria, baited her by observing how good her rival was looking.

The beneficiary of Arlyne Brickman's obsession was the government. Having worn a wire on Anifalaje, she was now obligated to testify in open court. The last time this prospect had presented itself, she had gone on the lam. Now she welcomed it as a path to revenge. Throughout her periodic conversations with Thomas Roche, an assistant U.S. attorney from the Eastern District, she made no secret of her motives. "Hell hath no fury like a woman scorned," she would intone slyly. This made Roche nervous, and he warned her never to say that in a courtroom.

Arlyne threw herself into the work with gusto. In her eagerness to see Luca convicted, she told Roche about Tommy's three-hundred-thousand-dollar heroin deal. In doing so she made herself look bad. She didn't care. All that mattered was hurting the man who had hurt her.

That June, Anif was arrested outside a diner where he had come from a meeting with Aldo. Nick Paterno was the next to be picked up. Arlyne waited to hear the sweet news of Tommy's arrest. But it never came. While Anifalaje and Paterno pleaded guilty, no charges were ever filed against Luca. Arlyne was dumbfounded. All that Roche would tell her was that there was not sufficient evidence.

Arlyne was not sure what this meant. She heard through the grapevine that Roche thought she would be a bad witness. Bad how? Did he think she had lied about Tommy? Did he think she would fall apart on the stand? Was he afraid she would blurt her views of "women scorned"? The longer Arlyne stewed, the stronger became her conviction that Tommy had cut some kind of a deal for himself. Luca had, after all, benefited over the years from her own coziness with law enforcement. "Go to your friends," he would say. "Talk to your friends the Feds." Was it so difficult to imagine that he had cultivated some friends of his own? If a deal had gone down, she would have no way of finding out. Arlyne had no choice but to lie low waiting for her next shot.

Arlyne's disappointment over the outcome of the Anifalaje case was made more bitter by the realization that Luca's departure had left her a devalued commodity. When she was with Tommy, she had belonged to a crew. Tommy was not a button and he might have been a screw-up, but he was Italian, and he was male. When she was with him, she had standing to deal. As greedy as wiseguys were, they were now suspicious of doing business with an unaffiliated Jew broad. What struck Arlyne as particularly unfair was that the same guys who shunned her as a business partner continued to hold her responsible for Tommy's debts. Among the loansharks pounding on her door were a pair from the Brooklyn crew, which had come in recent years to be called the Colombo Family.

Arlyne and the Colombos went back a ways, back to her brief and distasteful involvement with Joe Colombo at the St. Moritz. At the time, Funzie Mosca had taken pains to instruct her that Colombo was a soldier rising quickly in the organization of Joe Profaci. As Old Man Profaci grew increasingly feeble, his lieutenants, including Colombo, Carmine Persico and "Crazy Joe" Gallo, jockeyed for a place in the line of succession. The hostilities erupted into the Gallo-Profaci Wars, during which Colombo reputedly blew away so many of his rivals that he was promoted with honor to capo. After Profaci died of natural causes, Colombo eventually succeeded as head of the family, which thereafter bore his name.

While Arlyne would recall Colombo as a philandering cheap suitor, he projected the public image of an upright family man seen more often in church than in social clubs. Posing as a real estate salesman, Colombo transformed Profaci's gang of street hoodlums into a corporation of crime, opening offices in Manhattan, Queens and Long Island. Try as they might, federal prosecutors could never catch Colombo doing anything illegal. Had he been content to maintain a facade of quiet respectability, he might have been left to rule his subterranean empire unmolested. But he had a fatal fascination with the limelight.

Angered by an FBI investigation of his son, Colombo declared war on Hoover and, in the spring of 1970, led a protest march on the Bureau's New York headquarters. On the heels of that offensive, Colombo formed the American Italian Anti-Defamation League (later to become the Italian-American Civil Rights League) and in June of 1970 led a rally of fifty thousand supporters at Columbus Circle to protest government "harassment." Colombo's theatrics reputedly angered not only the government, but his supposed friend and one-time mentor Carlo Gambino. The following year when he arrived to speak at the league's second annual rally, an unidentified black man approached him and shot him three times in the head and neck. Colombo sank into a coma from which he never recovered. The leadership of his family passed to Carmine Persico.

Tommy Luca had been at the rally where Colombo was cut down. That afternoon he returned to the Executive House with Pete the Plumber. They were visibly upset. "Joey was shot," he told Arlyne. "Some nigger" had done it. Tommy and Pete then went off to a meeting at a bar in Brooklyn. Over the next few months there were a lot of threats and sabre rattling, but no one ever figured out who ordered the hit on Joe. Arlyne tried to remember what Colombo looked like when she left him, standing in his unhemmed boxer shorts. It would be appropriate, she thought, to feel some regret. But she could feel nothing at all.

It was not until the late seventies that Arlyne had moved back into the Colombo circle. In his continuing quest for cash, Luca persuaded his driver friend from the New York *Daily News* to introduce him to the people on Third Avenue in Brooklyn. "The Avenue," as it was known, was strictly a Colombo domain. Third Avenue and its immediate vicinity was the home of the Brooklyn Chapter of the Italian-American Civil Rights League as well as two prominent social clubs: the Diplomat, which was the headquarters of a Colombo underboss named Gennaro Langella, and the Nestor, haven and hangout for an influential capo named Anthony Scarpati.

When Tommy first began going to the Avenue, Arlyne had hoped to follow on his coattails. But he let her accompany him only now and then. On one of these occasions, she had looked across the street to see a stout, graying man who appeared to be scowling at her. She asked Tommy who he was and Luca reportedly replied, "That's Scappy," referring to Anthony Scarpati. "You know, we got to watch ourselves here because when you borrow from them, you're in trouble."

Scarpati, Arlyne would learn, was a close friend of Carmine Persico and his brother, Allie Boy. Since he had been made in 1976, his career had been on a steady ascent. First, he had been assigned to oversee the street-level operations of the family's gambling and loansharking business. Two years later, he made capo. When Carmine went to prison, Scarpati became one of the Colombo ruling elite. Arlyne could learn little else. Scappy was notoriously secretive and maintained an aloof posture on the Avenue, allowing loans and collections to be made by underlings. The factotum with whom Tommy dealt was one Vincent Manzo.

Vinnie was a short, dapper fellow who was generally well-liked on the Avenue. While he had never been made, he enjoyed special status as Allie Boy Persico's one-time bodyguard. Vinnie, in fact, so idolized his patron that he named one of his own sons Alphonse. A married man, Vinnie had nonetheless an attractive blond mistress named Madeline Calvaruso. Madeline's chief assets were a shapely pair of legs, which she showed off to best advantage in heels and short shorts, and a good head for business. Wherever Vinnie went, Madeline usually followed a few deferential steps behind. When it came time to close a deal, she stepped in to work out the details. She managed all this without injuring Vinnie's pride because she loved him and was ambitious for him. In time, Manzo's attachment to Madeline cost him status. Vinnie's wife, Arlyne heard, was a close relative of Gennaro Langella, and "Jerry Lang," as he was known, undertook to punish Manzo by trying to squeeze him off the Avenue. Manzo's stock sank even lower when he made some bad loans, most notably to Tommy Luca.

Taking advantage of Manzo's good nature, Tommy ran up a debt of twelve thousand dollars. For a time, he financed the vig payments with drug money from Billy Ricchiutti. When Billy was busted in January of 1980, Tommy lay low for about a year until desperation drove him to the Avenue to beg more money off Vinnie. He confided little in Arlyne and she once again resorted to tailing him to find out what he was up to. One afternoon in June 1981—it was the day of the Belmont Stakes—Arlyne tailed Tommy on the expressway. This time, instead of taking after her with a baseball bat, he motioned for her to follow him. And she did. To the Avenue. Arlyne parked and remained in the car, waiting to see what Tommy had in mind. Soon he approached her with another man whom he introduced as Manzo. Tommy, in turn, introduced Arlyne to Vinnie as a "very rich woman" who owned a clothing boutique in Queens. The game, Arlyne surmised, was to set her up as a potential borrower. So she kept her mouth shut and played along. That afternoon, she gave Vinnie fifty dollars to bet on a horse named Summing. It came in, paying a few hundred. When Manzo called her a few days later, she played the big shot and told him to apply her winnings against Tommy's vig.

Several days later Arlyne invited Vinnie to lunch at a restaurant on Flatbush Avenue. She wore all her jewelry, mixing the real stuff in with the imitations for better effect. Vinnie, who wore a lot of jewelry himself, seemed impressed. Arlyne asked Manzo for a loan of five thousand dollars. She needed it, she said, to buy inventory. "No problem," he said. And she had it the following day.

Arlyne took the money home, broke the bills, mixed them with fresh money and returned it to Vinnie two days later, with an extra thousand dollars for interest.

"How'm I doing with you, kid?" she asked Vinnie. He assured her that her credit was excellent. After that, Arlyne had no trouble getting loans. The money, of course, all went to Tommy. Luca found this association with a "rich woman" so profitable that he told Vinnie that she was now his girlfriend. It all became so cozy that Tommy and Arlyne and Vinnie and Madeline began to double date.

The advent of another mob girl usually aroused Arlyne's competitive instincts, but she took an instant liking to Madeline, whose brassy strut and tough talk reminded her of her own youth. Though she was seen sometimes in the company of Allie Boy's mistress, Madeline seemed to have few friends. She was also secretive, revealing little of her private life. Arlyne knew that Madeline worked during the day in the estate planning department of an insurance brokerage firm. Doing what, she did not know. For the sake of appearances, Madeline professed to be living at home with her parents, but in fact she stayed with Vinnie in a tiny basement apartment they called "the Dollhouse." Arlyne sometimes visited them there, entering through a laundry room, which opened onto a little kitchen. Beyond that lay the living room, which was absurdly decorated with *capo di monte,* expensive Italian figurines that had apparently come off a truck.

The Dollhouse reminded Arlyne of a cute little brothel. She later heard that it was used sometimes as a safe house as well as a storage place for loansharking records. Here, Vinnie and Madeline played at homemaking. This struck Arlyne as a little sad. It was a bad scene when a girl pinned her hopes on a married man. Arlyne knew from firsthand experience that a wiseguy rarely leaves his wife.

For the next few months, Arlyne saw a lot of the Quinella, as she called Vinnie and Madeline. She and Madeline talked about clothes and men. Arlyne even confided that she found Anthony Scarpati attractive. During that time she brought Vinnie prospective borrowers, including a friend and sometime lover of her old friend, Sweet Rose. Whenever she heard about jewelry scores she passed them along. Once she got a line on a rich widow whose late husband's brother was contesting her inheritance. Arlyne introduced her to Vinnie on the chance that a visit from an emissary of the Colombo Family might jolt some sense into the in-law. Arlyne was then shocked to learn that the widow wanted the man murdered. She scrambled to stop the wheels she had set into motion, but that proved unnecessary. The plot failed when Vinnie demanded a weekly salary and the widow didn't want him on the payroll.

Whatever goodwill Arlyne managed to build up with Vinnie and Madeline, however, was dispelled by Tommy's continued delinquency. His vig had now reached $550 a week and he couldn't come up with the payments. Vinnie and Madeline haunted the accesses to Arlyne's apartment. One night they were hiding in the stairwell when Tommy arrived. Vinnie leaped out and beat him with his fists. Then they all went up to Arlyne's for Chinese food, just to show there were no hard feelings.

When, in the fall of 1981, Vinnie turned up the heat, Tommy and Arlyne came up with another scam. They enticed Manzo into a "sports betting business," promising to produce six well-heeled clients. Manzo would use the winnings to defray interest on Tommy's debts. But there were no clients. Luca was the only bettor. At first, it looked like the ruse might work. It was football season and Tommy was on a hot streak thanks to Tilly Palladino, the self-proclaimed hit woman, who called one night.

"Now listen," she told Arlyne urgently, "my hands are hot. I feel burning . . . and I'm going to tell you something."

"What is it, Tilly?" Arlyne asked. "What is it?"

"The home team always wins at home on a Monday night," she announced portentously.

Arlyne frankly thought Tilly was nuts from freebasing, but they put an extra hundred dollars on the home team. For the next few Mondays, they beat the odds, racking up winnings of $5,000 to $10,000 a week. But then Tommy, feeling expansive, began betting basketball and their luck turned rotten. By the end of the month, they were into Vinnie for another $20,000, bringing Tommy's total debt—counting vigorish—to a startling $90,000.

Arlyne knew that they were in serious trouble. It was one thing to jerk around Vinnie Manzo, but a debt of this magnitude would surely draw down the wrath of the elusive Scappy. His back against the wall, Tommy played his ace.

"Why don't you go to your FBI friends," Arlyne would later recall him saying, "and let's do a job on Vinnie."

Thanks to her work with Greg Hendrickson, Arlyne still knew people in the Queens field office. One December morning, she showed up there and was passed along to an Agent Ward, who listened as she described the entanglements with Vinnie Manzo.

Arlyne's arrival was fortuitous. Queens had been conducting a limited investigation of the Colombos and was receptive to Arlyne's offer to help infiltrate the family's loansharking operation. She agreed to wear a wire on Vinnie. A little over a week after her visit to the FBI, Arlyne set off—Nagra in purse—to a rendezvous with Manzo on Grand Street near the Jewelry Exchange. When Vinnie climbed into her car, she asked him point-blank, "How much do I have to straighten out to make . . . me look good over there again?" They dickered over figures before Vinnie finally gave in to exasperation. "I don't even know anymore, Arlyne," he complained. "You've got me confused."

It was rotten luck, Arlyne concluded, to have gotten Vinnie in such a listless mood. As a result, she couldn't elicit a plausible threat. The Queens agents decided to drop pursuit and the tape was consigned to FBI archives where it was promptly forgotten.

For over a year, Tommy and Arlyne took pains to stay out of Manzo's way. Vinnie made a few ineffectual stabs at collection, but he proved easy to elude. And that was where matters stood on that February day when Tommy smashed into the Lincoln and walked out of her life.

Shortly after the split with Tommy, Arlyne called Manzo with the intent of learning whether she would be held liable for his ninety-five-thousand-dollar debt. Manzo gave her encouraging news. Tommy, he said, was with a new crew who had agreed to make good on his debts. There was to be a meeting soon between Scarpati and Tommy's people to work out the details.

It came as no surprise to Arlyne that Tommy had found new blood. But that these people were willing to bail him out of so sizeable a debt was remarkable. Throughout the summer, she made discreet inquiries among her circle of contacts to find out who Tommy's people were and when this meeting was to take place. She could learn nothing of substance. In September, she talked once again to Vinnie, who assured

her that the news was good. Tommy had arrived at the meet in the
company of "heavy hitters" who agreed to pay off the entire ninety-five
thousand dollars. If Scarpati had not recognized Tommy's new patron,
Vinnie hinted, he would have killed them both.

"So, in other words, I am off the hook?" she asked.

"So far," Manzo replied, "you're off the hook."

These were the words Arlyne had been waiting to hear. For
insurance, she had taped the conversation and now passed it along to her
friends at the NYPD Intelligence Division. It was filed away and
apparently forgotten.

The apparent resolution of her loansharking debts did not, however,
ease her day-to-day distress. Since the death of Irving Weiss, Leslie had
been out of control, demanding more and more cash. Arlyne knew
perfectly well that it was going to drugs, but felt helpless to stop it.
Arlyne was mortified by the prospect of her daughter walking Allen
Street, prostituting herself for a fix. The short-term solution was to give
her the money and ask no questions.

In addition to Leslie's demands, Arlyne had to come up with an
extra $850 a month to make the lease payment on her white Lincoln.
The pressure could have been eased by renting a more modest vehicle,
but Arlyne felt an irrational attachment to that car. Since the Lincoln
had originally been intended for Tommy, it gave her satisfaction to hang
on to it. And so on the first of every month, Arlyne found herself
scraping together the cash to make the payments.

She was desperate for any work she could find. That spring of 1984,
she was recruited by the NYPD and FBI to set up a sale of cocaine to the
leader of a Chinatown gang called the Gray Ghosts. The deal fell
through when the target refused to meet with a woman. While knocking
around the Lower East Side, however, she developed a line on another
of the NYPD's perennial suspects, Herbert Kaminski.

Since the old days, Arlyne had been on speaking terms with
Kaminski, a bespectacled goon who went by the nickname "Lonigan."
He belonged to the old Williamsburg crew to which Irving Weiss had
once belonged. Herbie, Arlyne learned, was currently working in the
Garment District waylaying loads of cashmere coats. He was always in
the market for scores. At the request of the Intelligence Division, Arlyne
went to Kaminski with a business proposition. They would set themselves up on the jewelry exchange as wholesalers, take gems on
consignment, sell them and disappear with the money. Herbie rose to the
bait and they formed a partnership called Brick Gems.

Every morning, Arlyne would cross the Queensboro Bridge and meet the cops on a quiet side street for briefing. Then she headed off for the exchange. There, with the blessing of the Intelligence Division, she finagled gems from hapless wholesalers, which Herbie sold to a jewelry fence. Whenever there was a sale, she and Herbie divvied up the spoils. Every evening, she was compelled to turn her take over to the NYPD. Arlyne was not happy seeing all this cash flowing so temptingly through her hands, particularly since all she received for her efforts was a paltry twenty-two dollars a day. Twenty of that went for parking. She was not even covering expenses. But even as Herbie Kaminski was busted and charged with grand larceny late that June, Arlyne found a new and potentially more lucrative score.

Now the U.S. attorney in the Eastern District was looking to bring indictments against members of the Gambino Family, including Ethel Becher's old flame Aniello Dellacroce as well as John Gotti. In trying to make the loansharking aspect of the case, federal prosecutors had found themselves short on witnesses. Arlyne's work on Jackie Cavallo and Joey Scopo seemed a gem waiting to be mined from a mountain of records.

That June a DEA agent familiar with Arlyne's perpetual financial turmoil called her with a proposition. As Arlyne later recalled the deal, it called for her to testify for "three minutes" before a grand jury. In return, she would receive enough cash to cover her next car payment.

Through her long association with Tommy, Arlyne had been infected by his uncontrollable fear of the Gotti brothers. Her qualms, however, were overwhelmed by a desire to keep the Lincoln. Accordingly, she agreed to a clandestine meeting with Assistant U.S. Attorney Diane Giacalone in a car in Brooklyn. The two women took an instant dislike to each other. Arlyne found Giacalone cold. Giacalone reportedly found Arlyne "undisciplined." Although the prosecutor had serious doubts about whether Arlyne's tapes were good enough to surmount the inevitable attacks on her credibility, she was nonetheless persuaded to bring her before the grand jury. Arlyne acquitted herself well, although she appeared to be having trouble with her vision that morning and had to struggle to identify the surveillance photos. Afterward, Arlyne counted her bills and drove off in the white Lincoln, which had received another month's reprieve.

Since she had appeared before the grand jury, there was a very good chance that Arlyne would have to testify in open court, a prospect she preferred not to acknowledge. Still, the case was not likely to come to trial for months, and something might happen to render her testimony unnecessary. Time, she had learned, had a way of resolving things. And indeed it did. Shortly after her appearance before the Gambino jury, Arlyne had been drawn into another slipstream of investigation, one which would have historic consequences.

Until the summer of 1984, Arlyne's chief usefulness to the government was as a mercenary hired ad hoc to bring down isolated targets. And given those limited objectives, she had done extremely well. Among her victories, she counted Fischetti and crew and Ricchiutti and crew, not to mention Anifalaje. As an informant of fairly minor rank, however, Arlyne Brickman had no comprehension of the government's overall war on organized crime. The June day that Arlyne testified in the Eastern District, federal prosecutors in the Southern District across the river in Manhattan were poised to seek a set of unprecedented indictments, which they hoped would bring down the leadership of the Colombo Family.

Until the early 1980s, such a sweeping attack on the mob would have been unthinkable. Throughout his fifty-year career, FBI Director J. Edgar Hoover refused to acknowledge the existence of organized crime. Attorney General John Mitchell followed the director's lead by forbidding any employee of the Justice Department to utter the word "Mafia." Federal prosecutors were limited to charging major mobsters with isolated and often insignificant crimes, ignoring the full scope of their syndicate activity.

The death of Hoover in 1972 freed the FBI to think in more coherent terms about organized crime. Moreover, the passage of the Racketeering-Influenced Corrupt Organizations Act gave federal prosecutors the ammunition they needed to attack organized crime at its roots. RICO, as it was known, made the mere act of belonging to a criminal organization a distinct and punishable crime.

RICO, unfortunately, was a complicated statute. Prosecutors did not understand it and were reluctant to use it until the late seventies when incoming FBI Director William Webster elevated organized crime to the top of his list of priorities. In New York City, home of five major crime families, the Bureau formed organized crime family squads, which were later expanded into task forces fortified with detectives from the NYPD. The job of each unit was to verify the existence and document the activities of the Gambinos, the Luccheses, the Genoveses, the Bonannos and the Colombos. It was hoped that one of these burgeoning dossiers would produce enough evidence to allow the Justice Department to bring a RICO prosecution against an entire family.

The first, it appeared, would be the Bonannos. Early in 1981, one Victor DiPenta, the protégé of a capo named Sonny Red Indelicato, fell behind in his loansharking collections and turned to the FBI for help. The Bureau set DiPenta up in a phony pasta importing company where he could entertain Sonny Red and his associates in the presence of hidden cameras.

These hopes were dashed when, on the day Sonny Red was to make his appearance, he and two other buttons were gunned down in an ambush. Victor DiPenta would have been put out of business had he not come to the attention of one Frankie "the Beast" Falanga, who, perceiving a vacuum left by Sonny Red, moved to take over the pasta business. Frankie, as it turned out, was an associate of the Colombo Family, and he proceeded to lead his new "partner," DiPenta, and unwittingly, the FBI into the heart of the family's criminal dominion.

For the next three years Operation Starquest recorded the history of what one agent called "the Neanderthals of crime." Agents documented the Colombos' infiltration of the construction industry and restaurant unions, its narcotics trafficking and its brazen bribery of government officials to get Boss Carmine Persico preferential treatment in the federal prison system. As the government was winding down its investigation in the summer of 1984, only one major figure threatened to elude indictment—Anthony Scarpati.

FBI agents who tailed Scarpati from his home in Bensonhurst to the Nestor Social Club found him a contradictory and enigmatic figure. Although a reputed ladies' man, he lived with his mother. While projecting a gentlemanly exterior, he was certifiably dangerous, having served eighteen years for manslaughter. While reputedly in charge of the family's street operations, he was far from a common thug. He had been picked up on tape once discussing the nuances of the RICO statute. Scarpati was cautious, never saying enough to implicate himself. During the course of the investigation, the FBI had turned up a loansharking victim from Staten Island who had reputedly been threatened by Scarpati. To satisfy the requirements of RICO, however, the government would have to prove that he had committed at least one more illegal act. It was at this juncture that someone recalled a tape made by an informant named Arlyne Brickman.

About a year earlier, Arlyne had come to the attention of Sergeant Philly Buckles, who was then a detective in the NYPD's Organized Crime Control Bureau. At that time Buckles and his partner, Billy Vormittag, were investigating a loansharking operation in Brooklyn when they came across a number of Colombo associates, one of whom was a frequent visitor to a club run by Vincent Manzo. In checking around the department, they learned that the Intelligence Division was working an informant who had some dealings with Vinnie. Philly and Billy paid a visit to Arlyne, who was in a loquacious mood that day and told them about the taped conversation in which Vinnie had assured her she was "off the hook."

At the time, Buckles's conversation with Arlyne led nowhere, but after he and Vormittag were transferred to the Colombo task force in January of 1984, he heard the name Scarpati and it rang a bell. Sergeant Buckles brought this to the attention of Squad Leader Damon Taylor, who dispatched a special agent named Oliver Halle to pay Arlyne a call. Arlyne, who had been alerted to this visit, answered the door wearing a billowing house dress and an enormous grin.

"Oliver," she simpered, "I hope you have a looot of money for me."

Arlyne took an instant liking to Agent Halle. He didn't dress like an FBI man. Although he carried the ubiquitous briefcase, he wore a safari shirt. She found his thin, intense face "intelligent." But most important, she found him respectful. In her years of working with federal agents she had learned that beneath their charade of goodwill, most considered informants dirt beneath their feet. Realizing that she was alert for signs of condescension, Agent Halle was careful to be courteous. Taking the chair offered him at her kitchen table, he explained that the government now needed a conversation establishing beyond any doubt that Manzo worked for Scarpati and that the loan money came from the capo himself. They would need her to wear a wire and if it panned out, she would be required to testify. The unspoken subtext of this proposition was the possibility of having to take the stand and deliver—in full view of Carmine Persico—the coup de grace to one of his most trusted lieutenants.

In her ten years as an informant, Arlyne had dealt with some dangerous characters. Tony Mirra had been a reputed enforcer for the Bonannos. She had seen Jimmy Doyle's bloody handiwork firsthand in the corpse of Natie Nelson. Her grand jury testimony concerning Jackie Cavallo and Joey Scopo had placed her at considerable personal risk from John Gotti. But never had she run afoul of such a powerful and violent figure as the boss of the Colombos.

Carmine Persico came from Brooklyn, where his father, Carmine Senior, was reputed to have been a soldier in the Genovese Family. "Junior," as he was known on the street, followed in the old man's footsteps, becoming leader of a gang called the Garfield Boys. He displayed deadly skill with a gun and pipe, and, according to government documents, had killed his first man by the age of seventeen. Junior was spared prison when his brother, Allie Boy, took the rap. Over the course of his criminal career, federal prosecutors alleged, Carmine Persico committed a dozen murders, boasting to one confidant that he was one of the masked assassins who gunned down Albert Anastasia as he was having a shave at the Park Sheraton Hotel. During the Gallo Wars at least nine of Crazy Joe's crew were killed either by Persico or at his direction. Carmine harbored a special hatred for cops. He kicked and beat policemen who raided one of his after-hours joints and shot another in the face. On balance, however, Junior was not lucky in eluding the law. Of his first thirteen years as boss of the Colombo Family, he spent ten in the federal penitentiary. Still, he never lost his grip and continued to direct family affairs from prison, first through Acting Boss Thomas DiBella, then through Gennaro Langella. Through most of the Starquest investigation, in fact, Carmine was serving time for parole violation and bribery. He was released in the spring of 1984, just as the government was winding up the operation that threatened to place him back behind bars for a very long time. To protect his freedom, he was likely to be ruthless.

This was the man Arlyne Brickman stood to cross. But on the day she was visited by Agent Halle, Arlyne was flush with confidence. To his proposition, she replied, "If anybody's going to get Scappy, it's going to be me."

Oliver Halle knew enough about Arlyne Brickman's freewheeling style to realize she would have to be strictly controlled. It was a federal prosecutor's nightmare to have an informant cum witness caught double-dealing on the government dole. Halle, therefore, admonished Arlyne that she was to have absolutely no unauthorized contact with Vinnie and Madeline. She was, furthermore, not to engage in any conversation that federal agents could not overhear. And she was not, under any circumstances, to tape the Quinella without the approval of the Justice Department. While not precisely deputized, Arlyne should consider herself an "arm of the prosecution," and as such, her conduct must be beyond reproach.

In exchange the government agreed not to prosecute her for any past crimes she might have committed—as long as she did not commit more. For the first time in her career, she was to receive a written contract and a salary of $500 a week. And if it became necessary to relocate her for her safety, she would be entitled to "moving expenses" up to $15,000. This was well below the $1,000-a-week stipend the government afforded witness Victor DiPenta. But for Arlyne, who lived from hand to mouth, it seemed like a "looot" of money.

Her employment was contingent upon getting Vinnie and Madeline back on the line. For all Arlyne knew, however, the loan was dead. She had not heard from the pair since the preceding fall when Manzo had declared her "off the hook." In listening once again to the tape, however, she realized that Vinnie had qualified her absolution, saying that she was off the hook "for now." This gave her a pretext to check in. Arlyne suspected that Vinnie might be happy to hear from her, since during Carmine's absence, and Jerry Lang's ascendance, his fortunes had continued to deteriorate. He might now welcome the chance to extract a few more dollars from a stale loan.

Arlyne called Manzo at the club and dangled the bait. She would like to take him and Madeline to dinner to share some "good news." Vinnie complained that Tommy's debt had still not been paid, so they made plans to meet a couple of days later at a West Village steakhouse called The Old Homestead.

Arlyne's mission was to convince Vinnie and Madeline that she had come into some money. Here the FBI allowed her imagination free rein and she invented a new boyfriend named "Howie," a wealthy rug merchant from Montreal. Howie was good to her, she said, and wanted to get her out of her "difficulties." To make it appear that she was back in the money, Arlyne convinced the FBI to get her diamond heart and a few bracelets out of hock. Then, decked out in her mélange of real and phony jewels, she set off in her white Lincoln for a curbside rendezvous with Oliver Halle. He activated her three-hour tape at shortly past five. Arlyne continued to the restaurant and, spotting Madeline outside, she beckoned her into the car. Almost immediately she could tell something was wrong. Vinnie, Madeline said, was "taking care of some business." He had given instructions for the two women to return to Arlyne's apartment, where he would meet them at 7:30 P.M.

Arlyne clutched. She could not turn off the Nagra, and if she left it running for two and a half hours until she met Vinnie, that would leave her only half an hour of taping time.

"I gotta work tonight," she protested. "I got somethin' so big you have no idea. We're gonna be all . . . out of our troubles." Arlyne hinted that she had "shit" that had to be dropped off in Chinatown later that evening.

"Why don't you see," she urged Madeline, "if you can get him at the club . . . and tell the motherfucker to meet us here."

Madeline jumped out to make the call only to return with the news that he wasn't there.

"He didn't wanna even hear my good news," Arlyne complained.

"He does. He does," Madeline assured her.

"If this goes through, I can help him . . . I mean, this is goin' on now how many years? Two years?" Arlyne probed.

"It's goin' on four years, Arlyne," Madeline replied sourly.

"I can't believe that Scappy would let anybody get away with ninety-six thousand dollars," Arlyne continued, "I mean, answer . . . me truthfully."

"I wouldn't put it past [him] that maybe there is some hanky shit goin' on and Vincent don't know about it," Madeline confided.

"In other words," Arlyne interjected incredulously, "you're tellin' me that Scappy's collectin' money without Vinnie knowin' it?"

"I'm not sayin' Scappy. It could be somebody else for all I fuckin' know. . . . As far as I'm concerned . . . the only friend Vincent's got right now is Scappy."

Arlyne excused herself and made a call to Oliver Halle. The agent had seen Madeline arrive but could not hear what was going on since Arlyne was working without a transmitter. She explained her predicament and he agreed it would be best for her to take Madeline home and try again another night.

On the drive back to Brooklyn, Arlyne complained about Vinnie. "He's an idiot," she goaded Madeline. "He's your boyfriend, but I [have] to say it."

"He's not an idiot," Madeline protested, her protective instincts aroused. "It's just that he tries to do too many fuckin' things at one time."

"I'm your friend," Arlyne pressed on. "That's why I say . . . you're never gonna get married. Never!"

"Don't put a jinx on me."

"I'm tellin' ya the truth. . . . If everything was good in this deal with Tommy . . . everything was gonna be beautiful, right?"

"Well, everything's not beautiful. . . . He can't offer me what he could offer me before. . . . Ya know how many fuckin' fights we had lately which never happened before?"

"All because of money?"

Madeline described plaintively how Vinnie couldn't even afford to take her out for dinner. He had to sell his mother's antique clock to buy a battery for his car.

"I was gonna treat him to some Dom Perignon tonight," Arlyne said as she dropped Madeline by her place. Then she shut off the Nagra at a quarter to eight, disgusted that her quarry had eluded her.

During a debriefing later that evening, it was decided that Arlyne would enjoy better control over these meetings if they took place in her apartment. So the following week, she invited Vinnie and Madeline over for dinner. Some hours before her guests were due to arrive, the FBI's Special Operations group examined the apartment, looking for the best location to place a video camera, and finally settled on the kitchen closet. The lens was trained on the kitchen table. Arlyne fretted that Vinnie or Madeline would find some reason to open the closet door, but Oliver assured her that it would be locked.

Shortly after the agents left, the Quinella knocked on her door. Arlyne greeted them with a dinner of veal and an open bottle of wine.

"Don't drink, Arlyne," Vinnie admonished her. "You fall asleep."

"I don't fall asleep," she protested. "I've been thinking about this for a year and a half . . . I think Scappy's been getting the money."

Vinnie had apparently entertained the same thought. "The thing is," he replied, "I can't prove it. . . . Could I go to Scappy and say, you took my fucking money?"

"Why can't ya?" Arlyne queried.

"He's got no backing," Madeline interjected. "What's he gonna prove it by?"

"What would you need for backing?" Arlyne asked theoretically. "You would need somebody with money . . . to put up as much as the other person's got. Supposing I come up with a lot of money. I'm meeting my end, half. I want them to meet their half, right there and then."

Arlyne had been authorized by the FBI to offer payments to match whatever Luca had paid. That way if Scappy was cheating Vinnie out of his cut by taking Luca's payments behind his back, he could be drawn into the open.

Vinnie was listening. "Yeah," he encouraged her.

"And that way, you would get your end . . . and we wouldn't have to worry and she'll get married to you and everything will be wonderful."

Vinnie waxed expansive at his improving prospects. "When I got money, we could make money with money . . . and I don't have to worry about a motherfuckin' thing."

"As long as he gives Scappy his end," Arlyne insinuated slyly to Madeline.

"Not him," Vinnie replied.

"Somebody else?" Arlyne pressed.

"Yeah . . . the main guy. The main guy."

"Carmine?" Arlyne pressed insistently.

"Ehhh," Vinnie answered obliquely, "as long as we give him his end."

"But . . . Carmine knows about this whole bordella here, right? With Tommy . . . with everything?"

"Yeah," Manzo replied.

Although Oliver Halle had urged a cautious tack, he was nonetheless excited to learn how Arlyne—through impertinent questioning—had gotten Vinnie to implicate Carmine Persico. It was an indiscretion for which Manzo could possibly pay with his life. There was still, however, no direct reference to Scappy. Two weeks later, Arlyne invited the Quinella over and gave Vinnie five hundred dollars to show her good intentions.

"Now, you're gonna do this little favor for me," she explained, "and you're going to take this to the 'little fella.' " (Vinnie had used this term in referring to Carmine Persico.)

"Yes, like you asked," Vinnie acquiesced. "That's what you got."

"Right," Arlyne said. "In other words, this will go to Carmine, not Scappy?"

"Yeah, this goes to Scappy," Vinnie replied heedlessly.

"Oh," Arlyne picked up the cue, "this goes to Scappy. But Carmine you're gonna go to and tell him the whole story."

"I'm gonna tell him the whole story," Vinnie assured her. "I'm gonna get ahold of his son [and say] 'tell your father . . . she's gonna match what he matches.' "

Running on recklessly before the camera's unblinking eye, Vinnie managed to draw Carmine's son, "Little Allie Boy," into the web of conspirators.

Agent Halle watched the tapes with Assistant U.S. Attorney Aaron Marcu, who marveled at Arlyne's audacity. He was troubled, however, by her street language. As the Colombo trial stood to run on for many months, the government would most likely find itself facing a jury of retired postmen and schoolteachers, good citizens who might be able to overlook rough language in a man, but who would find it reprehensible in a woman. Marcu asked Halle if he couldn't persuade Arlyne to watch her tongue. "But this is the way I talk," she replied. "It wouldn't be natural if I didn't."

Halle had observed that Arlyne was not a woman who took

criticism well. She needed to be petted and stroked. At the end of each surveillance she was in a fit of nervous excitement and needed to be told how wonderfully she had performed. The agent took pains to praise her on her work, which was clearly remarkable, and to compliment her appearance—though in fact she was forty pounds overweight. He got into the habit of calling her "Sweetie Pie." She called him "Ollie."

As Arlyne's case handler, it fell to Ollie to listen to her never-ending stream of complaints. Her teeth were bad. Her eyes were bothering her. She was worried about Leslie. Shadow was crazy. On Monday afternoons when Oliver brought his crew—which usually included Philly, Billy and a young agent named Paul Scudiere—to Arlyne's for strategy sessions, Shadow would snarl and lunge until he could be dragged into the bathroom. An animal lover, Halle arrived at a chilly rapprochement with the demented beast. Others were not so fortunate. Philly Buckles, driven to the top of a coffee table, once threatened to shoot the dog with his service revolver.

There were times when Arlyne's tirades against Tommy Luca wore on the detachment's collective nerves. During one of these harangues—triggered as always by some innocent, unrelated remark—Philly snapped, "Shut the fuck up about Tommy Luca. We don't wanna hear any more." Arlyne worried Ollie with her threats that she was going to take advantage of her day in court to finger Tommy as an informant. "Look," he told her, "I can't stop you from doin' it. But I'm tellin' you, you're gonna cause problems." Deep down Halle knew that when the moment arrived, she would go for Luca's throat.

Of particular worry, however, was the spectral Leslie Brickman, whose drug problem rendered her a threat to security. Living in her mother's home, she was privy to details of a highly confidential investigation. There was no assurance that she would not sell—or simply tell—this information on the streets. Arlyne tried to assure Ollie that she had this situation under control, but in fact she was not sure. Leslie hated cops. And she hated federal agents more. Whenever Halle and company showed up, she would drift from her bedroom to the kitchen and back without saying a word to the men gathered around her mother's table. One night when her mother had lured Vinnie and Madeline over for a videotaped meet, Leslie stood in front of the closet and stuck her backside into the camera.

Complicating matters was the fact that Leslie had always liked Vinnie. He had gone out of his way to be kind to her. One of his own sons had a drug problem and when Arlyne had once come to him for help with Leslie, he had gone out of his way to get the girl into a rehab program on Coney Island. Leslie Brickman would later insist that she didn't approve of Arlyne "ratting on friends." To that extent, her code of ethics was more conventional than her mother's. Her loyalties, however, were just as easily corrupted. Arlyne promised her daughter half of the money she received from the government, thereby buying her silence.

During her conversation with the Quinella, Arlyne had angled insistently for a meeting with Scappy and finally Vinnie told her, "If you're ready, I'll make an appointment." The meet was set for eight o'clock on August 23. She was to meet Vinnie at DiNotte's pizza house on Fifth Avenue and Carroll where Scarpati would join them.

Before Arlyne left that evening she met Ollie, who handed her twenty-five hundred dollars. "You don't give that money to anybody . . . but Scappy," he warned her. "Scappy's not there, you don't pay the money."

Arlyne arrived in Brooklyn about half an hour early. Vinnie was standing on the corner. He got into the passenger's side of the Lincoln and they drove up and down Fourth Avenue awhile. Things were "hot," he told her. A lot of cops around. As far as Arlyne could tell, he was referring to street cops. Unknown to Vinnie, or for that matter Arlyne, there were about six agents from the FBI's Special Operations group who were cruising the avenue in unmarked vehicles. Technicians in a parked van recorded their movements on film.

It was getting dark when they finally entered DiNotte's. Arlyne took a seat in the back while Vinnie excused himself to find Scappy. The door was wide open and she could see Vinnie cross the street and there join in conversation with a stocky man with a towel around his neck. It looked like Anthony Scarpati. A few minutes later, Vinnie returned— alone. Scappy would not meet with her, he said, because it was too hot. He then handed her a piece of paper on which Scarpati had purportedly provided a breakdown of all the payments Tommy had made since November 1983. It came to twenty-five thousand dollars.

Vinnie was waiting for his payment and Arlyne, remembering Oliver's admonition, had to stall in order to get further instructions.

"Forget it," she told Vinnie. "I'm going home." But he would not be shaken off so easily. "I'll meet you in front of your house," he said.

On her way home, Arlyne swung by the federal courthouse where Ollie was waiting for a progress report. Hearing the bad news, he thought for a moment. Then he told her to make the meet with Vinnie, instructing her to turn over the twenty-five hundred dollars only if she felt her life was in danger.

The meeting promised to be tense. Arlyne was furious at Scappy's snub. And she was taken aback by the sheet of paper showing that Tommy had ostensibly paid twenty-five thousand dollars. When the FBI offered to match Luca's payments, it was under the impression that he had paid nothing and that a few thousand dollars might be sufficient to lure Scappy into the open. Arlyne suspected strongly that the list of payments was a hoax contrived to wring the most out of her.

Vinnie and now Madeline also seemed primed for combat.

"Okay," Arlyne huffed, "did you know that there's been about [twenty-five thousand dollars] paid?"

"A thousand dollars a week," Vinnie replied.

"Then why didn't Scappy tell you that the [twenty-five thousand's] been paid already?"

"Why should he tell me?" Vinnie dodged.

Arlyne saw her opportunity to nail down the source of the loan.

"In other words, then you're telling me that this is Scappy's money?"

"Well, who . . ." Vinnie trailed off unintelligibly.

"Wait a minute." Arlyne was not going to let him slip away. "This is Scappy's money, right?"

"Yeah," Manzo acquiesced.

"How come he was ready to meet me tonight and all of a sudden, he changed his mind?"

" 'Cause it was hot," Vinnie replied.

"I didn't see it was hot."

"What was he supposed to do, go over and take you to see . . . if it was hot?" Vinnie shot back testily.

"Scappy doesn't get involved in the collections," Madeline interjected. He was worried about "entrapment," Vinnie said.

"Well, actually," Arlyne queried, "what does Scappy do?"

"It's his money, period," Madeline stated matter-of-factly. She had put the kiss of death on Anthony Scarpati. And then she asked slyly, "Why are you so interested in paying Scappy? I want to know."

Arlyne was getting the uneasy feeling that Madeline was wise. She and Vinnie were beginning to make not-so-subtle threats. At one point they indicated that Arlyne was "walking around alive" only because Vinnie had been making excuses for her. At another Vinnie told her outright that if Scappy wasn't taken care of, he would hang her "on a fucking meat hook."

Vinnie was clearly desperate to have that payment. Returning to the Avenue empty-handed, he told her, would make him look bad in Scappy's eyes. It was not a good idea, she concluded, to push him further. She handed over the twenty-five hundred dollars.

Agent Halle and his superiors were unhappy to hear that Arlyne had turned over the government's money to Manzo. They were cheered, however, to hear of Vinnie's death threats. Even more encouraging was Madeline's assertion that it was "his money—period"—fingering Scappy as the source of the loan. Arlyne had also managed to steer Manzo onto another discussion of the family hierarchy and he waxed so indiscreet as to refer to Carmine Persico as "the boss of bosses." In addition, Vinnie had promised to put her mind at ease about Scappy. In the future, he explained, she should come every Wednesday afternoon to a candy store on the Avenue. There she should hand her one thousand dollars to a clerk named Ronald, telling him, "This is for your friend." Scappy himself would be sitting at the counter. She should ask him, "Is everything okay?" And he would tell her, "Everything is being taken care of, thank you." Then he'd smile and that would be her cue to leave.

She must under no circumstances try to engage him in further conversation.

On the night Arlyne was to make her first drop, Oliver gave her the one thousand dollars, admonishing her to count it out to the clerk bill by bill. The Special Operations group would try to record as much of the transaction as possible. Around eight o'clock, Arlyne met Vinnie outside the Nestor Social Club and they walked toward the candy store. There was an open window through which customers could purchase items from the street. Peering through it, Arlyne saw a man sitting at the end of the counter. He wore tinted glasses and light blue shirt. He was dressed much as Scappy had been the night of the pizza parlor episode. But the man at the counter was emphatically not Anthony Scarpati. He was far younger, thinner and had more hair. Most telling, he did not have Scappy's distinctive scowl.

"That don't look like him," Arlyne hissed in an aside to Vinnie.

Vinnie turned to Ronald. "Who's that," he asked gesturing toward the man at the counter. "Tell her who that is."

"Scappy," Ronald replied without blinking.

"But Vinnie," Arlyne insisted, "that's not him."

"That is him," Vinnie assured her. "What's the matter with you? Are you gettin' delusions?"

"He certainly has changed an awful lot. . . . What did he do to his hair?"

"He cut it," Vinnie replied.

"This guy has changed so much," she persisted.

"We all get old, darling," Vinnie replied indulgently.

Arlyne handed the envelope to Ronald—she was so flustered that she forgot to count the bills—and after receiving a curt "okay" from the man at the counter, made her exit.

Arriving for her rendezvous with the agents, she sputtered furiously, "Oliver. This is not Scappy!"

This had happened once before during the Starquest investigation. A suspected union racketeer had sent an associate to impersonate him at a meeting with an undercover agent. So it did not surprise Oliver Halle that Scarpati had sent a ringer. The surveillance team had gotten photos of the man at the counter and since neither Halle nor any of his team could recognize him, they were sent to the U.S. Attorney's Office where a special investigator identified the mysterious figure as Robert Nigro, later described in a court brief as a member of Scarpati's crew. This deception stiffened Arlyne's resolve to beat Vinnie Manzo at his own game. She called Madeline and, conceding that she might have been mistaken about the man at the counter, confirmed that she would continue making her payments.

The following Wednesday, she showed up at the candy store. This time she counted the bills into Ronald's hand, under the pretext of wanting him to make a bet for her. Then she turned to Vinnie and asked, "Am I allowed to talk to him?"

Vinnie, who supposed she meant Ronald, replied, "Yeah, of course."

Arlyne walked over to "Scappy," sitting at his customary spot along the counter and gushed, "You look fabulous. What did you do to yourself?"

Nigro mumbled, "Got a haircut."

"You look younger," she persisted, "I swear. Oh, you know who I saw . . . Sunday . . . Joey Silvestri." Joey, she said, sent his regards.

Silvestri was a hood from Queens. If the man at the counter was Scappy, he would certainly know Joey.

"Yeah," Nigro replied. "How's he doin', all right?"

"Yeah," said Arlyne, "he's still in."

Nigro looked blank. "Where?"

"He's in Otisville," Arlyne snapped, secretly pleased with her performance on tape, which would later be played at trial.

That evening she called Vinnie and crowed, "I tested 'em today Vinnie. I tested 'em. He didn't know what the fuck I was talking about."

Vinnie was contemptuous. "He ain't gonna say nothing to you [about] who he knows."

"Vinnie," she reminded him, "you know, I know you a long time . . . you know, I'm not made with a finger. You understand? . . . I know what he looks like, that ain't him."

Vinnie hung up. Undaunted, Arlyne called right back and this time got Madeline. "I know what a person looks like," she continued her tirade, "because remember, I told you I had like a little crush on him. . . . So as a woman, I remember him. Okay?"

Madeline remembered, but she would not budge. The man at the candy counter was Anthony Scarpati.

Arlyne recounted Vinnie and Madeline's stubbornness to Oliver Halle, who discussed it with Assistant U.S. Attorney Marcu, and it was decided that she could not reasonably expect a face-to-face meeting with Scarpati. In light of that decision, she was brought several days later to the courthouse in Foley Square where she described the labyrinthine details of her dealings with Manzo to a federal grand jury.

Once again, Arlyne was offered Witness Protection. Once again she declined, electing instead to take the fifteen-thousand-dollar relocation money and move to an area of her own choosing. Oliver Halle and Aaron Marcu were uneasy when they learned that she had settled upon Florida. No locale outside New York had a higher concentration of Mafiosi. But Arlyne hastened to assure them that she would be quite safe in Miami, which, since the childhood visits under the indulgent wing of her father, had been like a second home to her. The government had one more task for her before she began the long hibernation awaiting trial: It wanted her to arrange one more meeting with Vinnie and Madeline, a meeting to bring the Quinella in contact with federal agents.

The government was not interested in indicting Manzo. Starquest was focused upon the family leadership and Vinnie was too small. If he could be turned, however, it would be a substantial coup. It was true that Vinnie was not a made man. Nonetheless, his ties to Allie Boy Persico and Anthony Scarpati put Vinnie in a position to reveal the ins and outs of the Colombo Family's street operations.

The plan was for Arlyne to propose a paydown subsidized by her absentee boyfriend, Howie. Arlyne had kept the Howie charade running throughout her discussions with Vinnie and Madeline, embellishing it with her own inventions. She gave him a last name, "Grossman." He was Jewish, of course, and she insisted he was a legitimate businessman. Howie, she suggested with the approval of her hovering federal prompters, might be willing to pay off her portion of the loan just to get her out of her troubles. Now, it was decided, was the time for Monsieur Grossman to make his move.

Arlyne made one more payment at the candy store, arriving in a Cadillac supplied by the FBI. Vinnie was there as usual and she made it a point to tell him that she had sold her car. When her identity as informant was revealed—as it surely would be—she did not want the Colombos cruising parking lots on the lookout for the great white Lincoln. She told Vinnie that she might not be around next week because it was a Jewish holiday and she was going to spend it with Howie in Montreal.

Two weeks passed before Arlyne again reached out to the Quinella. By this time she and Leslie had reached Miami where they had taken up temporary quarters near Billie Weiss. At the FBI's direction, Arlyne called Madeline at work: Oliver Halle patched the call from Florida through the FBI office in Manhattan. When Madeline heard Arlyne's voice, she was testy. "I've been trying to contact you for two weeks," she complained. Vinnie was getting nervous and Scappy was on his case. Arlyne reminded her that she had been spending time with Howie. The two of them would be coming into New York next week and Howie would like to sit down with Vinnie to work out a settlement.

Since Arlyne had talked to Madeline last, Allie Boy's mistress, Mary Bari, had been killed in what appeared to have been a contract hit. The agents instructed Arlyne to press Calvaruso on what she knew. Madeline, however, refused to discuss the matter except to say that people should not switch their loyalties.

Madeline and Arlyne arranged to meet for dinner at the St. Moritz, a spot designated by the FBI. Arlyne found the choice ironic since it was there she had had her first contact with Joe Colombo some twenty-five years earlier. Now it stood to be the site of her final farewell. Arlyne almost regretted that she could not make the scene in person. Oliver Halle and his superiors had agreed it was too dangerous to have her in the vicinity when Vinnie learned she was an informant. The double-date at the St. Moritz, therefore, would have to be staged without her.

It was conceived as a "light undercover" operation. In other words, the agents would not wear wires, but merely try to maneuver Vinnie and Madeline into a position where they could talk to them, play back their reckless statements about Scappy and the Persicos, and try to persuade them that they would be safer casting their lot with the government.

If Arlyne would not be available to greet Vinnie and Madeline at the St. Moritz, then it would be necessary for someone to play "Howie." Arlyne had limned her romantic invention in such detail that the FBI was obligated to find an undercover who was both old enough to be her lover and Jewish. One good prospect was Agent Mike Dennehy, brother of actor Brian Dennehy. Dennehy had posed as a sheik during the ABSCAM undercover. Agent Dennehy, unfortunately, was otherwise assigned. The role, therefore, fell to Squad Leader Damon Taylor. Though bearded and balding, Taylor did not look precisely Jewish. He was also rather young for Arlyne and considerably smaller than she was. (When Arlyne heard that Damon might pose as Howie, she snorted that if she got on top of him, she'd push him through the mattress.) He was, however, a skilled undercover operative who had played the wealthy buyer of stolen art in one of the earlier Starquest stings. It was decided that he could certainly play a lovesick rug merchant.

Several hours before Vinnie and Madeline were scheduled to arrive, Howie and his party checked into the St. Moritz, taking a pair of adjoining rooms with a door between them. Agent Taylor positioned himself in one; Agents Halle and Scudiere along with Philly Buckles in the next. When Vinnie and Madeline arrived at about 11:30 P.M., Howie opened the door and introduced himself. In the adjoining room, there was the sound of water running. Arlyne, he said, was taking a shower.

Vinnie and Howie passed a few awkward minutes in small talk about sports. On the other side of the door, Oliver listened, taking notes. The conversation, as he would later describe it in open court, went like this: Vinnie acknowledged that he was a "loanshark." Loaning money to Arlyne had damaged his reputation on the Avenue. When Howie proposed negotiating a settlement, Manzo said he didn't have the authority. He excused himself to make a call. About fifteen minutes later he returned to announce that he could accept a paydown of $25,000 plus an extra $5,000 sweetener for himself, for a total of $30,000.

At the moment Vinnie uttered that figure, the door to the next room opened, revealing, not the flamboyant figure of Arlyne Brickman, but two federal agents and a New York City cop. Vinnie was visibly shaken. Madeline muttered, "I knew it." Oliver Halle took a seat on the bed beside Vinnie and explained calmly, "Arlyne's been with us. She's going to be a witness for the government."

"I got nuthin' to say," Vinnie growled.

"Look, why don't we play a tape for you," Halle continued.

"I don't want to hear no fucking tape," Vinnie shot back.

But Madeline protested, "I want to hear the tape."

Oliver turned to Agent Scudiere, saying, "Paul, hit the button if you would." As Vinnie listened to his own words played back to him, notably the exchange where he referred to Carmine Persico as the boss of bosses, he looked as if he might weep. "I knew I shouldn't have crossed the bridge," he moaned, gesturing to his throat. "Now I'm up to my balls in cops."

When Agent Halle suggested they would be welcomed as government witnesses, Vinnie replied, "Look, can we talk for a few minutes? We need some time to think about it."

The decision to let Vinnie Manzo and Madeline Caruso walk out the door was one that would be debated at length by Monday morning quarterbacks at the Justice Department. Yet at the time, it seemed the thing to do. The pair were not under arrest. Furthermore, a show of confidence seemed likely to go a ways toward winning their trust. The Quinella had promised to return within the hour.

Agents Taylor, Halle and Scudiere and Detective Buckles all repaired to a bar in the neighborhood where they laid bets on whether Vinnie and Madeline would return. If they did so, it would most certainly be with the intent of turning. Philly Buckles, for his part, thought Manzo would fold. To a wiseguy, his neighborhood is his world. And should he suddenly find himself persona non grata, he has nowhere to run. Still, the agents concluded, there was the incalculable influence of Madeline. Throughout the encounter in the hotel room, she had sat tough and defiant. When told they could leave, she had quickly hustled Vinnie out the door. Madeline would doubtless have the final word.

It was nearly one when the agents returned to the hotel room. They waited for an hour, then two. Finally, they all left except Oliver Halle, who kept a vigil until dawn. Vinnie and Madeline did not show. The New York police issued a material witness warrant for their arrest. The only trace of the pair was Vinnie's car, which had been parked illegally and was towed. On foot, by cab or subway, the Quinella was on the lam, though on that October night in 1984, it was not clear whether they were fleeing the rod of justice or the wrath of Anthony Scarpati.

TEN

WITNESS

Letting Vinnie and Madeline stroll out of the St. Moritz was not, in the words of one assistant U.S. Attorney, "the greatest idea." The prospect of turning Manzo had promised a rich haul of intelligence. But it had, in fact, blinded government strategists to the difficulties that might arise should he decline. There was a chance that Vinnie, realizing his compromised situation, would flee the city and set up housekeeping in some safe haven. But where might that be? For Manzo it had been a major excursion "across the bridge." Montana would seem like the moon. Given their limited prospects, there was a good possibility that the Quinella might return to the Avenue and throw themselves on Scappy's mercy. If that happened, the security of Starquest stood threatened.

Although the agents had been careful not to divulge specifics at the St. Moritz rendezvous, a shrewd character like Scarpati would be likely to deduce that he was the subject of a grand jury investigation. Would he divine that the scope of the sweep extended to the boss of bosses? Scappy, whose impressive working knowledge of the RICO statute had been overheard by prying federal ears, was apparently engaging in counterintelligence of his own. Scarpati frequented the club of a labor racketeer named Jackie DeRoss. A bug in that establishment produced an extraordinary audio record of Scappy and DeRoss sitting around listening to FBI transmissions on their personal scanner.

Anxiety over what Scappy knew or stood to find out was suddenly rendered moot by a thunderclap from the New York *Post*. A little over a week after the St. Moritz affair, the paper published a story headlined "FBI Sting Hooks Mob Big," in which it reported that indictments of Carmine Persico and six unidentified "henchmen" were expected within two weeks. The disclosure threw prosecutors into an uproar and the Justice Department mobilized to investigate the leak. At that point,

however, there was nothing to do but to try to control the damage. The
government concluded its case before the grand jury and on October
24—a little over a week after the *Post*'s precipitous announcement—
eleven indictments came down.

The question now became, How many of those suspects remained
within reach? The FBI had tabs on at least one. Jerry Lang was
technically a fugitive on a perjury charge but FBI intelligence had
tracked him to a safe house in Brooklyn. Agents would have to attempt
to intercept the others at home or familiar haunts.

The arrests were to be accomplished in a single comprehensive
sweep emanating from the FBI command post in Lower Manhattan. The
night before, members of the Starquest team convened at Federal Plaza,
where they catnapped on the floor until close to dawn. Then they headed
out to predetermined locations, awaiting the signal to strike. It had been
the original plan for all of the arrests to take place at precisely six o'clock
to avoid spreading alarm through the Colombo ranks. Each car had,
furthermore, been equipped with secure radios so that neither media nor
mob could buy a crystal and monitor the frequency. Unforeseen events,
however, set the plan into tumult.

Oliver Halle and Billy Vormittag had drawn the watch on Scappy.
Shortly before dawn they had taken their position outside the loanshark's home in Bensonhurst, when a red Cadillac pulled up beside
them. The car was unfamiliar, but when Halle glanced at the passenger
side he caught the by now familiar profile of Anthony Scarpati. Halle
and Vormittag looked at each other in alarm, then shouted in unison,
"You're under arrest." Scappy stepped out of the Cadillac with his hands
up. Before Vormittag could nab the driver, however, he screeched off
into silent recesses of Bensonhurst.

Halle radioed headquarters to report that Scappy's unidentified
companion might alert the other suspects and after that the arrests came
quickly. Langella, DiBella and four others were picked up in the first
wave. The Colombo elite were hauled into Federal Plaza where they
were greeted by a mob of reporters who had been alerted to their
imminent arrival. Attorney General William French Smith himself flew
in for the occasion and announced exultantly that the government had
indicted "the entire leadership of the Colombo Family."

Only one cloud darkened this otherwise jubilant scene: Four of the
indicted were still missing—including Carmine Persico.

For the next four months the government marched toward trial
with bravura, playing down the fact that its chief target might be missing

from the prisoner's dock. Persico became the target of a massive manhunt predicated upon filaments of speculation that he had fled either to South America or to Southern Europe to join his fugitive brother, Allie Boy. The New Year came and went. Carmine became one of the FBI's "Ten Most Wanted."

Then during the first week of February an agent on the West Coast received a phone tip. Carmine Persico was holed up in a house on Long Island. Junior, it seemed, had learned about the indictments from a *Post* reporter even before the story made print. Thus alerted, he fled with his wife to a place called Gurneys Inn in Montauk Point on the eastern tip of Long Island. There he called a strategy meeting with Gennaro Langella and Anthony Scarpati. It was decided at this council that Carmine would surrender so as not to violate his parole, then he would try to beat the charges. Someone else would have to "stay out" and run the family. The nod went to Langella, since he was already on the lam and hidden securely—it was supposed—in Brooklyn.

These well-considered plans went awry on the morning of October 24 when the FBI picked up Langella in the general sweep. Left no alternative, Persico took upon himself the role of leader in hiding. Surprised and unnerved that someone had apparently given Jerry up, he decided he should find an unlikely hideout, one that was far away from his "old friends." He chose the home of Fred DeChristopher in Wantagh, Long Island.

Frederick DeChristopher was a fifty-eight-year-old insurance salesman who, to all appearances, enjoyed life in the mainstream. He was also Carmine Persico's cousin by marriage. DeChristopher had come into the family's orbit over two decades earlier, when he had prevailed upon Carmine's blood cousin, a soldier named Andrew Russo, to fix union problems for his corporate clients. A few years later, DeChristopher married Russo's sister Catherine and though continuing to sell insurance benefited from crumbs tossed his way by the family. When, in late October of 1984, Carmine showed up at his door seeking refuge, Fred was in no position to refuse.

The fugitive Persico settled into the attic of the DeChristopher house and into a more or less regular routine. Every afternoon at three o'clock he would wander downstairs for a light breakfast accompanied by espresso with anisette. For the rest of the day he read all the dailies and watched television for news of the arrests and indictments. At dinnertime, he would lend a hand in the kitchen. Carmine loved to cook.

At midnight, he would play cards with Fred, finally retiring at 3:00 A.M.

Over the weeks that followed, Carmine revealed to DeChristopher certain intimate details of family business. For instance, Carmine Galante, late boss of the Bonanno Family, had once proposed a contract of marriage between his own daughter, Nina, and Persico's son, Alphonse. He reportedly was imprudent on the subject of Mary Bari, who, he said, was killed because she had tried to locate Allie Boy on the lam. And he tried to implicate DeChristopher in a playful scheme to fool the FBI. If he died of natural causes, he told DeChristopher, he wanted to be buried under the fish pool in the back yard. Fred should then call the Bureau every couple of months to report that he had seen Persico here or there. That way, Carmine hoped to keep agents chasing their tails for the next ten years.

Persico also set up an "avenue" whereby information produced during discovery in the developing Colombo case could be forwarded to him through Andrew Russo. Now, instead of playing cards until the wee hours, Carmine and Fred would sit up reviewing audio- and videotapes. Among these was the one made in Arlyne Brickman's kitchen in which Vinnie Manzo likened Persico to the chairman of a corporation.

"That piece of shit," Carmine reportedly huffed. "I chased him off the farm. He used to hang out with my brother Allie. He used to drive my brother Allie around. That piece of shit is using my name."

Whenever Persico heard a tape that upset him, he would ponder his alternatives aloud. He had decided to "stay out" during the impending trial in order to get all the evidence into the open so that his attorney might evaluate it. If he felt he could beat it, he would surrender. If, however, the odds appeared to be running against him, he would join Allie Boy for life on the lam.

Throughout the weeks that he was forced to play host to his notorious in-law, Fred DeChristopher maintained a scrupulous facade of cordiality. But he was far from pleased. Although he had profited from his association with the Colombo Family over the years, he later professed to have no love for them. His marriage to Catherine was not altogether happy and he secretly hated her brother. Less than three months after the wedding, in fact, he had gone to the FBI and provided information on both Andrew Russo and Allie Boy Persico. His motives, he would later explain, were simply those of "Joe Citizen" doing his civic duty. He received no payment and after one year dropped off the Bureau's informant rolls.

In late 1984, he found his thoughts returning once again to the FBI.

Although Carmine had originally promised him he would be staying only two weeks, he remained in his attic haven until Christmas day. Then he left for what he said was a secret hideout in upstate New York. DeChristopher was never too clear about his reasons for turning on Carmine. Some of his later statements seemed to indicate that he was resentful at having spent so much time "under house arrest," as he put it, playing companion to Carmine. He was fearful for his life and wanted not to be implicated. In another statement made at trial, he appeared offended that Persico had left his home for another refuge. There was also the matter of a fifty-thousand-dollar bounty on the mobster's head, although DeChristopher claimed he was unaware of this until Persico was back in the hands of the law. Some speculated that Fred wanted to start a new life with another woman.

Whatever his reasons, DeChristopher stepped into a phone booth during the first week of February and dropped a dime on Junior.

It would be a week before Persico was picked up. Within days of his departure, he returned unexpectedly to Wantagh, with the explanation that the upstate New York hideaway was not as secure as he had thought. The FBI kept the DeChristopher house under constant surveillance. One afternoon in mid-February, Persico received a visit from a capo named Dominic "Donny Shacks" Montemarano and Andrew Russo's son, Jo Jo. As the three men conferred in the attic, the phone rang. Fred DeChristopher answered it and called out to his guests, "The FBI wants to speak to you." All four walked out backward with their hands up and were greeted on the lawn by more than twenty federal agents, New York cops and Nassau County police. DeChristopher was arrested and booked to preserve his cover, but the ruse apparently convinced no one. Over the next couple of days, the Colombos huddled in secret meetings to which DeChristopher was not invited. He would testify that he received a call from Jo Jo Russo inviting him to dinner to discuss the "problem of the arrest." DeChristopher asked if he should bring "Aunt Catherine," and Russo replied, "No. Leave her at home. You and I have to go somewhere."

Suspecting that his hours were numbered, DeChristopher fled home—without his bridgework and with only six dollars in his pocket—and placed a call to the FBI. With that, he was whisked off into federal protection.

Throughout this high drama, Arlyne Brickman sat fuming in isolation. She was settled—temporarily, she maintained—in a coastal town north of Miami. Her original plan had been to take an apartment in her mother's building on the seashore in Hollywood. The management, however, would not accept Shadow, so Arlyne settled into more modest accommodations nearby.

For the first few weeks of her exile, Arlyne had her hands full. Leslie agreed to enter a rehab program, but her recovery was cut short by the arrival in Miami of Willie. Arlyne pleaded with her daughter to turn him away, but Leslie refused and left to live with her lover in Coconut Grove. Soon she was back on drugs and behaving like a dangerous stranger. She and Willie found Arlyne's address book containing the telephone number of Anthony Scarpati and threatened to tell him where she was hiding. Arlyne gave them five thousand dollars to keep them quiet.

Under siege from her own flesh and blood, Arlyne was further distraught to learn that something was wrong with Shadow. His reliably vicious disposition was giving way to melancholia. She took him to a vet hoping to learn that this depression was a passing phase, but was taken by surprise to learn that her "little boy" had a brain tumor. For once in his life, Shadow seemed content to be held. Arlyne petted, doted and waited on him tenderly, intent that his end should come as peacefully as possible.

Throughout these difficult times, Arlyne's spirits were still buoyed by the rush of Starquest. During her six weeks' pursuit of Anthony Scarpati, she had enjoyed an unprecedented level of attention and prestige. And even after moving to Florida she had been drawn into the intrigue at the St. Moritz, rehashing the caper in long phone conversations with Ollie, Philly and Paul Scudiere.

Vinnie and Madeline fell for Damon's Howie routine! You let them walk out of the St. Moritz!

As the weeks passed, however, Arlyne was nettled by the uncomfortable realization that the real show was passing her by. The focus of the investigation had turned to the pursuit and capture of Carmine Persico. And on this matter, Arlyne could glean little intelligence. It became a daily ritual to call up members of the Starquest squad and hammer them for details. Through sheer, abrasive persistence, she was able to pick up details from the DeChristopher debriefing. It pleased her enormously to hear that while in hiding, Persico had viewed the videotape made in her apartment—the one where Vinnie referred to him as the chairman of a corporation—and had branded Vinnie a "piece of shit." But in the rush of superseding indictments that followed Carmine's arrest, and the backing and forthing over a date for the trial—which now looked as if it wouldn't start until fall—Arlyne Brickman felt neglected and, worse, dispensable.

Her isolation from New York threw her once again in constant contact with her mother. Billie, still recovering from Irving's death, seemed to welcome visits from her prodigal daughter and was remarkably understanding about Arlyne's current predicament. Despite the fights and screaming hysteria, Arlyne had to admit that her mother had remained a constant friend.

It was during one of her daily visits to Hollywood that Arlyne made a startling discovery. She was standing in her mother's building one morning when she spotted a young man on the telephone. Since the age of sixteen, Arlyne had enjoyed one infallible talent—spotting wiseguys. Now her radar flashed bogeys at twelve o'clock. Making discreet inquiries of her mother's friends, she learned that his name was Jo Jo Russo. He was there with his brother, visiting their mother, who had an apartment in the building.

Arlyne could hardly believe what she was hearing. Jo Jo was the son of Andrew Russo, confidant of Carmine Persico and brother-in-law of the government's star witness Fred DeChristopher. The prospect strained credulity. Arlyne passed the information along to Oliver Halle, who said, "Are you crazy?"

It would be dangerous for Arlyne to be seen by the Russos under any circumstances, but even more so now that Andrew Russo had been named in the new round of indictments, making him a codefendant of Carmine Persico and Anthony Scarpati. For her mother's sake as well as her own, Oliver warned, she must stay clear of Hollywood. In the absence of any other diversion, however, Arlyne had no intention of quitting the field. Not only did she continue her daily visits to her mother, she made a point of sitting directly next to the Russos by the swimming pool, even going so far as to make small talk. These brushes with danger made her more cheerful than she had been in a long time. The more she dared, the more invulnerable she felt. In the adrenaline-driven rush of a "surveillance," she felt she would live forever. It was only at night when she closed her eyes and tried to sleep that her nerve deserted her.

A *meat hook*, Vinnie had said. What did little Vinnie know about meat hooks? Had he actually seen anyone strung up? Arlyne doubted that very much. Someone had told him to say it. But who? Scappy? Arlyne struggled to recover her bravado by imagining herself taking the witness stand, the cynosure of all eyes. She was going on a diet and by then—what was it, seven, eight months away?—she would be as slender as she had been in her twenties. Well, maybe her thirties. And her complexion would be smooth. She would have the old skin burned away with chemicals. She would have her broken teeth capped. And she would buy a fashionable suit. Some classic with padded shoulders to take the emphasis away from her bottom. When she took the stand, she would be as haughty and unassailable as Virginia Hill deflecting the barbs of the Kefauver Committee beneath the brim of her picture-frame hat.

In the high flood of fantasy, she would drift off to sleep only to be awakened by a recurrent nightmare. It was about Abie Reles, the poor little snitch who had crossed Uncle Meyer. In this version, however, Abie did not lie waxen and peaceful in his coffin at the Blum and Oxman Funeral Home. He was falling, falling, screaming as he fell, until he hit the ground like a broken starling.

Far from being forgotten, however, Arlyne was very much on the minds of federal prosecutors. She had become the object of a tug-of-war between the Southern and Eastern districts, between which existed a long-standing rivalry extending to the control of witnesses. When Assistant U.S. Attorney Diane Giacalone, who was still planning to use Arlyne in the Gotti prosecution, learned that her witness had been appropriated by the Starquest investigation, she called Aaron Marcu to complain. That conversation resulted in a shouting match during which Marcu declared that the witness was in seclusion and unavailable.

In the interests of Arlyne's credibility it was important to keep her off the federal witness circuit, to avoid reinforcing the impression that she was a snitch for hire. As far as Marcu was concerned, Arlyne was a victim. This stood to be a difficult proposition to sell in light of the fact that she had never met, much less been threatened by, Anthony Scarpati.

As commendably as Arlyne had performed during her six weeks with the Starquest team, one awkward fact remained: She had not gotten a meeting with the suspect. Furthermore, the FBI crime lab in Washington had been unable to find the loanshark's prints on the sheet bearing the vig figures. Aaron Marcu remained convinced he could get a conviction. His optimism was heightened by a chance remark overheard by a member of the Special Operations group the night Arlyne was stood up at the pizza parlor. It had come to the prosecutor's attention after that surveillance that a special agent named Ron Andachter had seen Vinnie and Scappy in conversation and had gotten close enough to pick up fragments of their conversation. He claimed to have heard Scarpati say, "What's the fucking problem? She owes us the fucking money."

While Arlyne's integrity might be called into question, Andachter was a clean-cut young federal agent whose testimony could not be so easily assailed. Marcu's strategy would be to direct the jury's attention to the overheard comment as well as other "non-Arlyne testimony," such as the photographs, tapes and documents—in short, materials not subject to cross-examination.

In the back of the prosecutors' minds was concern about how Arlyne would stand up to the rough treatment she would surely receive at the hands of defense attorneys. When recounting her story to friendly agents and sympathetic prosecutors, she was confident enough. But her bravado collapsed under the slightest criticism. Her excitable nature would not serve her well on the witness stand. If she was to go through with this, she must be carefully prepped. To this potentially arduous detail, Marcu assigned a young assistant named Frank Sherman.

Sherman was a late-comer to the Colombo prosecution, having transferred from the U.S. Attorney's Office in Philadelphia in the spring of 1985. He, nonetheless, seemed the perfect complement to the erratic Arlyne Brickman. Calm and soft-spoken, he was not the sort to be derailed by hysteria. His extensive experience as a trial attorney left him eminently attuned to a witness's vulnerable spots. In short, he was an effective trouble-shooter.

His first reading of the Brickman file left him with one major concern. To begin with, she had been employed by a number of agencies. He counted sixteen. While the government would do its best to style Arlyne as a victim, the defense could easily sell her to the jury as a cold-blooded mercenary. One could argue that Arlyne's long employment history reflected well upon her credibility as an informant, but she was emphatically not a victim.

During the summer of 1985, Sherman flew to Florida for a meeting with the witness. His concerns multiplied. Not only was she excitable, but she had a terrible memory for dates. She had told the grand jury that she had met Vinnie in 1979, but a careful review of the facts seemed to suggest that was much too early. Arlyne was emphatic that Tommy had introduced her to Manzo the day she bet on the horse Summing who was running in the Belmont. Summing, it turned out, had taken the triumphant stretch not in 1979, but in 1981.

The prosecutor was also shocked and initially dismayed to learn that as early as 1981, Arlyne had made a surreptitious tape with Manzo under the supervision of FBI agents in Queens. The Manhattan office later took over the Colombo investigation and had no record of Arlyne's earlier work. In all of her conversations with Oliver Halle, Philly Buckles and Aaron Marcu, she had simply forgotten to mention it.

Even as he issued an order to locate the missing tape, Sherman was apprehensive. There was a chance, of course, that it would contradict Arlyne's story, in which case the indictment would have to be thrown out. When the recording finally arrived at his office, he was relieved to hear Arlyne insisting to Vinnie that they should get their act together so that "the people can have respect for me on the Avenue like they had before." Not only did the tape support her version of events, but it established that as early as 1981 she was aware and even fearful of Scappy, whose name she invoked several times.

Arlyne's inadvertent discrepancies could be easily remedied. Of more pressing concern to Sherman and the prosecution team was her criminal past. Compared to government witnesses like Jimmy Fratianno and Joseph Cantalupo, she was relatively clean. She had no federal rap sheet—only a local one from Fort Lee. That showed a minor bookmaking conviction for which she had served no time. What troubled Sherman was not so much the recorded crimes as any that may have gone unreported. It would be necessary to make a conscientious reconstruction of Arlyne's history with the underworld. One reason for this was that the government was obligated to make available to defense counsel not only records of actual arrests and convictions but even casual intelligence about any "bad acts" that a government witness might have committed. Judge John Keenan seemed intent upon enforcing this provision vigorously.

A second reason was that the government did not wish to be blindsided by some goblin in a witness's past. Arlyne Brickman's coziness with organized crime went back thirty years—at least. Unearthing every conceivable misdeed she might have committed during that time would try the skills of an archaeologist. Indeed, Arlyne had seen so much action that it was possible that not even she could remember certain criminal capers. Unfortunately, others might. The defense team presumably had contacts in Brooklyn, Queens, Jersey and the Lower East Side who could turn up more dirt in a single afternoon than Arlyne was willing, or able, to supply over a period of months. It was possible that Vinnie and Madeline had thrown themselves on Scarpati's mercy and were being held in the wings to impeach her testimony. But what, after all, could they say? That she made it all up, in which case the tapes remained as incontrovertible proof to the contrary. A more likely scenario was that Vinnie would fall on his sword, claiming that the money was his, not Scarpati's, and that he had invoked the capo's name as an intimidation tactic. In that case, the government would have to hope that a jury would believe Agent Andachter, who insisted he had overheard Scarpati tell Vinnie, "She owes us the fucking money."

Scarpati's attorney would not have to look very far to discover Arlyne's long-running liaison with Tommy Luca. In doing so, he might well turn up a connection to drugs. Had Arlyne been a man, this might not have loomed as such a devastating possibility. Juries seemed to take evidence of depravity in the government's male witnesses in stride. But if a loud-mouthed mob girl could be linked, however tenuously, to the distribution of drugs, she might be viewed as a monster.

The government enjoyed one tactical advantage in such instances. First at bat, a federal prosecutor could introduce potentially damaging information so matter-of-factly as to neutralize it. By the time the defense got around to needling a witness for alleged deficiencies of character, a jury would find it old news. It was known as "drawing the sting." In order to diminish the impact of Arlyne's involvement, however, the government had to know its scope.

The resulting inquiry required all the tact and delicacy that Frank Sherman could muster. While Arlyne did not flinch when he raised the subject of drugs, neither did she respond with her characteristic flood of candor. Every time he reached for her, she darted into a vague yet impenetrable semantic refuge. Yes, she and Tommy had supplied pot to smoke shops, but that didn't mean she was a *dealer*. They weren't her drugs. She wasn't buying or selling. She didn't make a living at it. Tommy was the brains. She was only a bystander; she only drove the car. Of cocaine, she admitted to having known about a small sale that Tommy made in 1981—but she didn't participate. That same year, he discussed a heroin transaction, but nothing came of it. During the latter episode, she claimed, she was funneling information to the government.

Arlyne had a tendency to portray all of her excursions into drugs as incidental to her work as an informant. In some instances, there was a record to support this, in others, not. From the little he knew of Arlyne's fitful personal life, Sherman surmised that during certain halcyon interludes, she and Luca had done things that she had not confided to agents. At one point she had slipped. In her eagerness to nail Luca, Arlyne had described to Eastern District prosecutors Tommy's $300,000 heroin purchase. That incident occurred in late 1982, but she did not tell the DEA until 1983. Certainly some member of the defense team would seize upon this evidence of double-dealing and raise questions about whether Arlyne had also been committing crimes under the nose of the Starquest team.

Sherman, like Grady O'Malley, did not believe that Arlyne had ever been a major player. She had become even less potent a force on the streets when Luca walked out on her. The split with Tommy, he was sure, had signaled the end of Arlyne's career in the drug business. At that critical juncture, it could be argued, she had repented of her crimes— including double-dealing—and crossed over finally and unequivocally to the side of justice.

As the trial date drew closer, a stream of federal emissaries was dispatched to Florida to attend to the needs of Arlyne Brickman. Sherman, who made the trip every few weeks, would meet her at the FBI offices in Fort Lauderdale where they continued their laborious debriefing. Arlyne liked Sherman, largely because she did not feel threatened by him and remained confident in her ability to deflect his queries. But he was a straight-arrow who made no pretense of being her friend. He was also too close-lipped to suit Arlyne, who loved nothing better than gossip. To satisfy her hunger for camaraderie, Arlyne had to wait for the arrival of Philly Buckles, Billy Vormittag and Paul Scudiere, whose chief mission was to keep her happy. When that crew rolled into town it was party time. Scudiere took them all to restaurants of the sort that served little ices between courses. Arlyne was very impressed with his ability to order from a French menu and select fine wines. Since the Sunday afternoons of her childhood when Irving Weiss had squired his family to the Grotta Azzurra, Arlyne had gotten a reliable flush of pleasure dining in the company of a man who seemed to know his way around. On these evenings, Arlyne was at the height of her glory, feeling adored and important.

At times like these the longing to return to New York was so strong it nearly overwhelmed her. As much as she dreaded testifying, her year in hiding had left her feeling left out. New York was now in the throes of mob frenzy as U.S. Attorney Rudolph Giuliani was waging war on several fronts at once. The Southern District was set to try twenty-two defendants who had allegedly used pizza parlors as distribution points for heroin. In addition to this so-called "Pizza Connection Case," the government was bringing RICO cases against two "mob bigs," as the press was fond of calling them, Gambino boss Paul Castellano, whose car theft ring reputedly doubled as a hit team, and Matthew "the Horse"

Ianniello, whose racketeering practices had allegedly left him in control
of major restaurants and clubs. The putative pièce de résistance of
Giuliani's campaign was the Commission Case, wherein leaders of all
five Mafia families would be brought to the dock and tried for crimes
ranging from labor racketeering to drug trafficking. The Commission
Case would be a legal extravaganza of a magnitude rarely seen, even in
New York. The U.S. Attorney himself would step in to try it. Yet
momentous as it promised to be, the Commission Case owed its life and
possibly its outcome to the Colombo Case, which was set to come to
trial five months earlier. Much of the evidence against the commission
derived from the Colombo prosecution, and if the government failed to
bring a successful case against one family, that certainly did not bode
well for bringing down the ruling council. The importance of the
Colombo Case was not lost on Arlyne Brickman, who was coming to see
her impending trial date not so much as an ordeal as her ticket back to
New York. And she would return, she was sure, trailing glory.

On November 4, 1985, the government brought to trial Carmine Persico
and ten codefendants on charges of racketeering. It was not an
auspicious beginning. The case had been consigned to one of the smaller
courtrooms, leaving the defendants and their attorneys and the federal
prosecutors jammed shoulder to shoulder. The overcrowding created an
atmosphere of tension, which was further exacerbated by a tendency of
the defendants to burst into loud, apparently orchestrated laughter
whenever prosecutors introduced evidence detrimental to their interest.

The trial began slowly, derailed by concerns about the defendants'
health. Thomas DiBella suffered from heart trouble and had been
severed earlier. Likewise Dominic Montemarano, who was awaiting
cancer surgery. A little over a week after the trial began, one of the
defendants, Ralph Scopo, suffered a seizure during which he gripped the
railing of the jury box and had to be raced to the hospital, where he was
diagnosed as suffering from angina and hypertension. During the first six
weeks there were only four days of actual testimony. An IRS agent was
the first to take the stand and there he remained for about four weeks
recounting the details of Carmine Persico's attempts at bribery to obtain
preferential treatment in the federal prison system. The following month
a succession of contractors took the stand to tell how the Colombo
Family elicited payoffs to buy labor peace. The trial dragged on through
November, December and January. From her distant vantage, Arlyne
Brickman fretted over the delays. The labyrinthine details of bribes and

payoffs bored her. Her spirits remained depressed until the beginning of February when the trial entered a markedly more glamorous phase. The government called Jimmy "the Weasel" Fratianno.

The seventy-two-year-old Fratianno no longer cut the formidable figure he once had. For nine years the government's star witness and a veteran of over a dozen mob trials, the Weasel's prestige was on the wane. When he was first introduced to the circuit in 1977, he possessed intimate and current intelligence on the structure of the mob, and it was a commodity for which the government was willing to pay handsomely. But such information has a shelf life, and once a witness has turned, he has effectively forfeited the avenues and associates that might keep him abreast of gossip. He is obliged, at some point, to cede the crown to a younger or more recent turncoat like the government's current favorite, Joseph Cantalupo. Still, Jimmy the Weasel's name carried cachet and over protests of defense counsel that an appearance by Fratianno was simply "prosecutorial overkill," the government put Jimmy through his hoops to identify Jerry Lang and Andrew Russo as Colombo capos, hence players in a criminal enterprise.

The appearance of Jimmy the Weasel raised conflicting emotions in Arlyne Brickman. Were one to ask if she admired him, she would respond in expletives. (It is common for one informant to assail the probity and expertise of another as a means of increasing his own stock.) But secretly, she envied him. Arlyne followed Jimmy's Colombo gig as a Vegas lounge singer might sneak backstage to catch a glimpse of Sinatra.

Jimmy, she knew, was being held under tight security at a safe house on Governor's Island, the same spot for which she was destined. Word had gotten back to her that he was being given the celebrity treatment. Officials from the FBI and the Justice Department would ferry out to the island to dine with him. Often Jimmy would do the cooking, turning out an impressive array of pasta and sauces on his hot plate.

It was possible, Arlyne thought, that they might meet. But then what would she say to him? Would he give her the time of day? Jimmy, after all, had killed five men and she was just a mob girl with a bush-league conviction for bookmaking. As time for the journey north drew close, one prospect continued to nettle her: that her time in the sun might be spent in the shadow of Jimmy Fratianno.

On the morning of her scheduled departure, Arlyne sat waiting in her apartment with only one bag. In her salad days, she could never have set out on such a trip with fewer than two, preferably three, valises. That she was traveling light indicated a sort of despair. The hopes she had for losing weight had been thwarted by anxiety. Eating calmed her nerves and she had gorged herself to an all-time high of 180 pounds. Under the circumstances, there seemed no point in having expensive suits made. Instead, she sorted through her existing wardrobe for items that were "slimming" and came up with an ensemble of fluffy sweaters and tight pants. For footwear she chose backless, high-heeled springolators.

Billie Weiss came by to say good-bye. She was in tears. A very polite agent named Hughes showed up to escort Arlyne to the airport. As he carried Arlyne's bag down the stairs Billie called after him, "Don't let anything happen to her!"

At Miami International, Hughes handed her a ticket for a commercial flight. The agent inspected the empty aircraft. Arlyne was allowed to board before the other passengers. She noticed that the name on the ticket was not her own. The FBI had decided that it was safer to avoid bringing Arlyne into New York and had routed her into Newark, New Jersey. She was met at the airport by a small armed escort headed by Paul Scudiere, who explained that she would not be going to the safe house as Fratianno was still in residence.

Arlyne's first response to the news was irritation, as it seemed a confirmation of her suspicion that she was destined to play second fiddle to the Weasel. Her pique subsided, however, when her escort deposited her at the Meadowlands Hilton. While not as absurdly luxurious as the Seacoast Towers or other apartments where she had plied her trade as a kept woman, it was certainly posh enough to flatter her vanity. Paul Scudiere fluttered around her attentively. So too, did Oliver Halle and the obligatory female agent, a plain, decent woman named Colleen. Ever since the Fischetti case, when she had been forced to undergo the intimate drug searches and wiring at the hands of Dewanna Stratton, Arlyne had had an aversion to female agents. Colleen, however, was unobtrusive and aroused Arlyne's maternal instincts. Before long she was haranguing the girl to perk up her appearance. "Colleen," she would implore, "how the hell could you walk around the way you're walking around? No makeup! Your hair needs a touch up. Lemme get my hands on you!"

Colleen was a sport. She allowed Arlyne to do her toenails—though she wouldn't go for the hair dye. And for the week that Arlyne was to remain holed up in the Meadowlands Hilton, the two of them had fun. Colleen allowed Arlyne free run of room service, and the latter, who had given up on dieting altogether, ordered chocolate layer cake and mousse and double orders of roast beef. Colleen left on the pay channel so Arlyne could watch movies around the clock. Her favorite was *Prizzi's Honor,* which she saw ten times. Not uncritically. Kathleen Turner, she opined, must have been modeled on Tilly Palladino, but, in fact, was a cream puff. She was far more taken with Anjelica Huston, particularly the scene where she kissed the godfather's ring. Now that was "strictly the mob."

Paul Scudiere got the bill, and dispensing with his characteristic courtliness, inquired, "What the fuck is going on here?"

By that time, however, Jimmy Fratianno had wrapped up his testimony and vacated his digs on Governor's Island, and it was time for Arlyne to move in.

In the space of an afternoon, Arlyne was whisked from the Hilton to the safe house—the site where mythic government witnesses held court—and it seemed like a demotion. The safe house, Arlyne thought, was a "hellhole." There were two adjoining apartments, one for her and the other for her federal escort. Both were foul from the stench of Fratianno's cigar. She cast one dubious look at the bathroom and proceeded to scrub it down with a can of Lysol, which she kept in her purse for such occasions. Every time one of her attending agents used the john, she would give it another furtive cleaning. While luxuriating in her little nest at the Hilton, Arlyne had not been aware of the extreme cold that gripped the metropolitan area. On Governor's Island it was painfully apparent. The heat in her compartments was weak and erratic. Agent Scudiere took pity on her clopping around in her springolators and accompanied her to the PX where she bought socks and sneakers. These measures did not prevent her from coming down with a head cold.

Further delays increased Arlyne's misery. She had been told that she would be taking the stand within a couple of days after her arrival, but that was now going on two weeks. She had too much time on her hands. To fill it she began knitting a little yellow sweater for one of the female agents who was several months pregnant. She kibitzed with Paul and Oliver and began actually to look forward to the sessions with Frank Sherman, who visited her every evening to continue their marathon debriefing. Arlyne was acutely aware, however, that she was receiving visits from none of the higher-ups who, she had heard, came to pay their respects to Jimmy Fratianno. She was galled by the slight. Every night she went to extraordinary lengths to get to a phone just to talk to someone in the outside world. Usually this was Billie, though one evening she was overwhelmed with such despair and longing for intimacy that she entertained the notion of calling Tommy Luca. She felt like a condemned prisoner, dreading the walk to the chair but unable to face one more day of anxious waiting on death row. When at last Oliver Halle gave her the word that tomorrow was a go, she was relieved and terrified.

On the appointed morning, February 24, Oliver called for her at six o'clock. They took the car ferry to Manhattan where Arlyne was bundled into a van. One car carrying heavily armed FBI men rode in front, another behind, as the van made its way unimpeded from the ferry dock to Foley Square, where it slipped quickly into the basement of the Federal Courthouse. From there she was hustled as quickly as her bulk would allow up a back staircase to a spare room that was used for rifle practice. For a long time, it seemed, she sat there quivering.

Frank Sherman dropped by to reassure her. He was disheartened to see the figure she cut. Although he realized it was unrealistic to expect her to show up in Laura Ashley prints, he was nonetheless taken aback to find her wearing slacks and a pair of spiked heels. She was, moreover, visibly nervous, a condition that might either cause the jury to dismiss her as unreliable or make her appear softer, more sympathetic, than her tough exterior would suggest. There was no way of knowing how twelve average citizens might view Arlyne Brickman until she actually took the stand.

As Arlyne entered the courtroom, it seemed to her that she was moving in slow motion. She mounted the stand and from below she heard sniggering. Carmine and his friends were laughing at her. She lifted her chin and pretended not to notice. A shot of adrenaline awakened her street instincts, which reminded her that it was imprudent to show fear. Settling into the witness seat, she drew herself erect, staring past the attorneys directly into the eyes of Anthony Scarpati.

"Ms. Brickman," Sherman opened, "can you tell us where you were raised?"

"In New York," she responded without emotion.

"Do you know an individual named Tommy Luca?" Sherman queried.

"Yes," she replied. "I do."

Arlyne proceeded to explain how she had lived with Luca "on and off" for fifteen years, during which time he had incurred serious gambling debts.

How, Sherman asked, had Luca generated income to pay these

debts? He had, Arlyne responded, borrowed heavily from shylocks, including Vincent Manzo.

"During any period of time," Sherman proceeded carefully, "were you involved . . . in any gambling business?"

"Yes," Arlyne replied, then faltered. "Well, toward the middle of 1975, we started a single-action business."

"Who is 'we'?" Sherman asked.

"Tommy Luca and I," she replied.

Arlyne went on to explain how she and Luca ran the numbers business, which led to their arrest in 1975. She told how she had pleaded guilty and gotten a year's probation and a fine.

"After that . . . did you and Mr. Luca continue in the numbers business?" Sherman persisted.

"Yes," she replied. "We went right back into it. We had to make a living."

"During that period," Sherman pressed on, "did Mr. Luca, to your knowledge, engage in any other illegal activity?"

"We went into another business . . ." Arlyne replied.

"Did you go into that business with him?"

"Well," Arlyne demurred, "let's say I helped along."

"What was that business?"

"That was the smoke business . . . marijuana."

That began in 1978 or 1979, Arlyne explained, and continued through 1983.

"During that period from '78 to '83," Sherman pressed, "were there any drugs other than marijuana that you and Mr. Luca were involved in?"

"We went into the cocaine business and heroin," Arlyne replied blankly.

"The nature of the business was you were selling it?"

"Yes."

Sherman then asked pointedly, "When is the last time that you saw Mr. Luca?"

"In 1983."

"And from that time on, did you have anything to do with the drug business?"

"No," came the emphatic reply.

Arlyne had come through a difficult passage very well. For the rest of the day, Sherman led her methodically over the terrain they had traveled so many times before. She explained how she had been introduced to Vinnie on the day of the Belmont Stakes. How Tommy had set her up to borrow from him and how Luca had later told her the money belonged to Scarpati. How they tried to pay off their mounting debts with the phony sports business and when that failed, how she turned to the FBI. Arlyne was frustrated that the judge would not let her tell the story of how Tommy instructed her to rat out Vinnie to the Feds.

The government played portions of the first tape Arlyne had made with Vinnie on Canal Street, in which she told him she wanted to clear out her debts so that "people can have respect for me on the Avenue" again. Thereafter, Jack Evseroff, Anthony Scarpati's attorney, rose to question her about whether she had enjoyed control over her own Nagra. Instinctively, Arlyne knew she was on dangerous ground. Ever since her Nagra had slipped during the dinner with Billy David, she had insisted on carrying the recorder in her purse, which threatened to give rise to the suspicion that she could turn off the machine during exchanges that stood to incriminate her. She shot a quizzical look at Frank Sherman, who returned an inscrutable prosecutorial stare. With nothing to guide her, she explained that while she could theoretically turn the Nagra on and off at will, her supervising agents had, in fact, manned the switches. To her surprise and relief, Evseroff seemed content with this explanation and dropped the line of questioning.

Toward the end of the day, Sherman introduced the tape that Arlyne had made surreptitiously with Vinnie and Madeline, in which Vinnie assured her that Tommy's new sponsors had cut a deal and that she was "off the hook." Arlyne explained how she had continued to see Vinnie and Madeline "all the time" right up to the point when she entered into the agreement with the FBI. Left vague was the exact nature of her relationship with the Quinella, and what motives might have impelled her to go after them.

When court recessed shortly thereafter, Arlyne was giddy with relief and eager for her reviews. Oliver Halle, who escorted her back to Governor's Island, told her she had been terrific. In fact, Frank Sherman had been quite happy with the way his witness had acquitted herself. Bathed in approbation, Arlyne acquired fresh confidence, which enveloped her when she came to court the following morning.

Arlyne enjoyed another easy day, fielding prosecutor Sherman's queries with carefully rehearsed replies. Only one seemingly lighthearted episode hinted at what might be in store. During a discussion of the secret tape recordings made at her apartment she inadvertently referred to the asterisks marking deletions as "asteroids." Jerry Langella's attorney, David Breitbart, seized upon this slip with glee, referring to ellipses thereafter as "asteroids." The defendants laughed, the jury laughed, leaving Arlyne with the uncomfortable realization that she was being mocked.

The uneasiness created by this quipping turned into humiliation during the third day of testimony, as the government concluded its questioning and turned its witness over to Evseroff. Based on their earlier exchange over the Nagra, Arlyne felt Evseroff could be managed. And, indeed, the questioning began on a deceptively innocuous tack with questions about her age and how long she had been divorced.

"In 1981," Evseroff continued, "what were you doing for a living?"

"In 1981 what was I doing," she faltered. "Could you repeat that?"

The judge intervened, hoping to clarify. "How did you work, if you worked, in 1981?"

"I was a housewife," Arlyne replied.

The courtroom resonated with laughter.

Evseroff turned his inquisitorial skill to ascertaining when Arlyne had made her first surreptitious recording for the government. But he could not pin her down. At first she thought it was 1975. Then 1967. Then 1970. (It was actually 1977.) Apparently despairing of pinning down that particular date, the attorney ticked off a partial list of agencies she had worked for and asked her which was the first. The New York State Police, she replied. In 1970. (It was, in fact, 1972.)

"You and Tommy Luca were involved in something in 1970 that had to do with the state police?" Evseroff pressed.

"We were furnishing information," she responded.

"Both of you?" The questioner was incredulous.

"Correct," came the emphatic reply.

Evseroff, it seemed, could not believe his ears.

"You were informers for the state police, is that correct?"

"Through me."

"Through you?"

"That is right."

Arlyne's determination to finger Tommy as an informant—a resolve that had deepened during the three years since their split—was realized. Although she had envisioned this scene unfolding more dramatically—as an angry denunciation—it came tumbling out almost as an afterthought. The revelation and its possible consequences, however, did not slide by federal prosecutors, who hastily dispatched a messenger to warn Luca, through his attorney, that he had been fingered by Arlyne Brickman.

Seemingly oblivious to the havoc she had wrought, Arlyne continued to confound her examiner as he turned to the question of drugs.

"Is it a fact," he queried, "that you, along with Mr. Luca, participated, in that you acted in concert, aided and abetted in the distribution and the sale of marijuana with [Billy] Ricchiutti in 1980?"

"No," she replied.

"Were you involved in it?"

"To a certain extent."

"Did you make money out of it?"

"Yes."

"How much money?"

"House money," she replied.

Again, there was laughter in the court.

"Some people live in slums, others live in Trump Tower," Evseroff persisted. "What does 'house money' mean?"

Arlyne explained that she had used the money to pay bills and vigorish.

Advancing to heroin, Evseroff got her to admit holding the three hundred thousand dollars, but she insisted she had never seen the drugs, nor had she been present during the transaction.

"What was your end?" Evseroff pursued. "I don't mean house money. I mean dollar sums."

"I received a Christmas present," Arlyne replied innocently. "I received a dining-room set for my house." The set, she explained, cost eleven hundred dollars.

The prosecutors shifted uncomfortably, since Arlyne had never mentioned having received any consideration for her role in the heroin caper.

"You are aware, are you not," Evseroff continued, "that in the state of New York, the sale and possession of a large sum of heroin, a controlled substance, is what is characterized as an A felony punishable by twenty-five years to life imprisonment if convicted? Are you aware of that?"

Arlyne shot an imploring glance toward the prosecutors.

"Don't look at Mr. Sherman, please, when I ask you questions," Evseroff commanded.

"Yes," she replied equivocally. It was not clear whether it was a question or an answer.

"Were you aware of that?"

"No, I wasn't aware of that," she demurred.

Evseroff got Arlyne to assert that she had had nothing more to do with cocaine after starting to work for the FBI in 1984. No sooner was this entered into the record, however, than he pointed to a comment she had made to Madeline during their abortive dinner engagement at the Homestead. "I've got four ounces of this shit on me."

"Do you really think I had that on me?" Arlyne responded contemptuously.

"You have never been involved in selling cocaine, have you?" Evseroff continued cunningly.

"No."

Evseroff called her attention to her testimony of the day before when the prosecutor had asked her if she had sold heroin and cocaine and she had answered "yes."

"Is it your testimony that [what] you said on direct examination was untrue, that you really weren't selling heroin and cocaine, or was the answer true that you gave to Mr. Sherman on direct examination? Which was it, Mrs. Brickman?"

"It was true to a certain extent," she conceded. "In other words, I told you that Mr. Luca was conducting business, and I received whatever from it. So . . . we are a 'we.' "

Evseroff reminded her that Sherman had asked her if "the nature of the business was you were selling it," and that she had replied "yes." "Mrs. Brickman," he pressed. "If . . . 'we were a "we," ' who is 'you'?"

"I can't answer the question," she replied.

By day's end, Arlyne was frantic. Having come into court that morning flush with confidence, she now felt she had lost all control, a condition that filled her with anxiety. All the way back to Governor's Island she kept repeating, "I'm not going back tomorrow. I'm not going through that." Oliver tried to soothe her. "Sweetie Pie, c'mon," he cajoled. "Let's just go and have a nice dinner tonight. Relax and forget about it." But Arlyne stewed endlessly over the indignities inflicted on her by Jack Evseroff.

Frank Sherman, for his part, was happy—or perhaps relieved—over the way Arlyne had handled her first day of cross. Although Evseroff had managed to turn up the fact that Arlyne had received a dining-room table in exchange for her services in the heroin deal, he had not scored any real hits. It was Evseroff's style to try to outreason a witness, which was not one hundred percent successful against Arlyne's infuriating vagueness. What worried the assistant U.S. attorney was how she would fare against the next batter up: David Breitbart, attorney for Gennaro

Langella. To date, attorney Breitbart had had a field day with government witnesses, particularly Jimmy Fratianno, whose manhood he had
assailed by asking if, when he was made, he had worn a dress. Where
Evseroff wheedled, Breitbart's questions fell like hammer blows, accel-
erating to a crescendo of abuse. It was not the sort of onslaught Arlyne
was likely to bear with tranquillity.

Arlyne had been warned of Breitbart's tactics, but nothing could
prepare her for the ordeal to come. When on the following day, Jack
Evseroff ceded the floor to his colleague, Breitbart began his slow but
rhythmic assault.

"Mrs. Brickman," he asked, "do you know what scales are used for
in the drug business?"

"Yes," she replied.

"What about spoons," he queried, "do you know what a spoon is?"

"Yes."

"Do you know what snorting cocaine is?"

"Yes."

"Do you know what mainlining heroin is?"

"Yes."

"Do you have any personal involvement in the utilization of
drugs?"

Frank Sherman objected, but the judge allowed the question,
proceeding to clarify, "Personal means you yourself."

"No," Arlyne replied.

"Have you personally seen the results of the use of heroin and
cocaine in your own family?"

Sherman objected and this time the judge sustained the objection.

"Yes," Arlyne replied nevertheless.

"At the period of time when you were sitting in that car with the
three hundred thousand dollars in the two shopping bags, waiting for
the three kilos of heroin, did you know what heroin does to people?"

Objection. Sustained.

"Do you know how many deaths can be attributed to tens of
thousands of dosages of heroin in the street?"

"Yes," Arlyne replied numbly.

"Did you consider that when you sat in the car with the three
hundred thousand dollars in cash?"

"No."

"Did you care?"

"Yes."

"So it was after caring and consideration that you got involved in the heroin transaction?"

"I don't know."

"When you were sitting with those shopping bags full of money to buy the three kilos of heroin, did the DEA know you were sitting there?"

"I don't remember."

"Weren't you asked that yesterday afternoon?"

"Yes."

"And isn't it a fact you indicated that you didn't become an informant with regard to that drug deal until after the transaction?"

"Yes."

Arlyne was feeling dizzy and unwell. Breitbart continued his relentless pounding.

"You were in the dope business for many years, is that right?"

"Not many—no," she parried ineffectively.

"Did you indicate to us on direct that between 1978 and '83 you and Tommy Luca were in the grass business?"

"Yes."

"Is that drugs?"

"Yes," she conceded.

"You knew that you were violating the narcotics laws at that time?"

This time Arlyne replied "yes."

"Did you do that knowingly and intentionally?"

"I don't know."

"You don't [know] if you did it knowingly?" Breitbart mused. "Did someone force you to do it?"

"Yes," she replied.

"Tommy Luca forced you to do it?"

"I don't know," Arlyne countered weakly.

"Did Tommy Luca force you to do drugs?"

"Yes," she replied.

"Did you love Tommy Luca?"

"Yes."

"Were you willing to do anything that he asked you to do?"

"Yes."

For the rest of the day, Breitbart found and fired on Arlyne's weaknesses. Divining her pretensions to being a mob girl, he insinuated that she was a common "gangster buff." He lured her into describing the single-action business, whereupon she became mired in her own explanation.

"No wonder you lost money in the numbers game," he mocked her.
"Now you know why . . . Mr. Luca needed money," she reparteed.
The courtroom rocked with laughter.

Breitbart got his dizzied prey to concede that Manzo might have come to suspect that she was an informant. He went further to suggest that Vinnie might also have been working for the FBI, giving rise to the suspicion that the two of them had worked in concert to implicate Scarpati.

Here he hit a nerve.

The specter of "entrapment" continued to prick Arlyne's conscience. When she had first confided her qualms to Oliver, and later to Frank Sherman, they had taken pains to assure her that everything she had done was perfectly within the bounds of law. She had not been recruited to entice Scappy into making an illegal loan. Rather, her services had been sought because she already had a loan outstanding. Arlyne knew this was true. And she was positive that the money belonged to Scarpati. Still, she wondered if this was all fair. She had, after all, never spoken to Anthony Scarpati.

Throughout her years as informant, fairness had concerned Arlyne very little. Fairness, friendship, loyalty were all casualties of an overriding compulsion to bag another trophy and bask in the approbation of the agents. Even her betrayal of Paulie Messina, which might rightly have aroused some shame or at least pity, had been at the time just another cause for a victory celebration. Perhaps it was vengeance carried out on such a subterranean level of consciousness Arlyne never had been able to acknowledge it. Perhaps she had considered her cold-blooded campaigns against former uncles and lovers and uncles cum lovers to be vigilante justice. What was certain was this: Arlyne had never had to look a man in the eye as she sent him to jail. Now for the first time in almost fifteen years, she was required to tell her incriminating stories in full view of the defendants.

Throughout Arlyne's days on the stand, Scarpati sat directly in front of, and slightly below, her. In contrast to Carmine, who looked as if he had just come from his haberdasher, Scappy looked down-at-the-heels and avuncular, clad usually in a sweater and smacking a worn piece of gum. He was a far cry from the Scappy Tommy had pointed out to her on the Avenue. Perhaps his inaccessibility then had caused him to appear more imposing. Held captive in the cramped confines of court, the lord of Third Avenue appeared ludicrously ineffectual. It was a sight that would ordinarily have inspired Arlyne Brickman to nothing but contempt. Now, she found herself curiously aroused. A warm feeling rose like a phosphorescent wave from her pelvis up the muscles of her torso.

She sat breathless, dreamy, seeming to feel Scappy's hands grasp the back of her head, lift her hair and lay kisses down the length of her neck. She felt herself sinking through space and after a long fall landing on a floor. Then the slow, suffocating press of a body on top of hers. In this dark chasm that had opened up in her imagination, she was a young woman with silky auburn hair and long legs. Through some peculiar sleight of mind she watched herself writhing in the embrace of a dark, featureless man. Scarpati? Tony Mirra? Tommy Luca? She desperately wanted to be possessed by—to belong to—the phantom. At the same time they were locked in a battle to the death.

Somewhere above this phantasmagoric reverie, she heard the voice of David Breitbart asking, "Did Mr. Halle or another agent assigned to you indicate that he was interested in making a case against someone in the Colombo family?"

"I don't remember."

"Well," he continued, "is it an accident that you would bring Mr. Scarpati's name into the tape? Was it an accident or intentional?"

"I can't answer that."

"But the intentional insertion of Mr. Scarpati's name was at the direction of the FBI?" Breitbart pressed.

"I can't remember."

The harder Breitbart hammered, the worse her memory became.

That afternoon Arlyne Brickman's ordeal came to a close, but not before a couple of disquieting encounters with two more members of the defense team. Carmine Persico's attorney, Frank Lopez, asked her if she knew someone by the name of "John Gannon." She replied that she didn't.

"Didn't you tell Manzo," Lopez asked her, "that in your opinion John Gannon . . . was the most dangerous person in the whole world?"

"I don't remember," she replied.

Arlyne figured that Lopez was referring to John Gotti and that, in doing so, he was trying to frighten her. She could not figure out why he would mispronounce the name. Frank Sherman, who was listening carefully to this exchange, thought he detected another agenda. Gotti was set to go on trial in the Eastern District in coming months and it was still possible that Arlyne would be called to testify against him. If she was on the record saying that she did not know him, then it would damage her credibility. The prosecutor guessed, though he could not be sure, that Lopez was doing this as a favor for Gotti's attorney. At recess, Sherman advised the court reporter that the name had been mispronounced.

After Lopez came Michael Coiro, counsel for Dominic Cataldo. Coiro was brief. After taunting her for her imperfect memory—she had answered "I don't remember" 150 times by his count—he accused her of participating in an FBI "plot" to go after the defendants.

"And now there is just one thing left for you to do," he queried darkly. "Isn't there one thing left for you to do?"

There was a pause, then he continued.

"Explain to this jury how you are going to fade away."

Sherman objected hurriedly, removing the necessity for reply, but the threat hung in the air even as Arlyne descended for the final time from the witness stand. How indeed to "fade away"? Repeatedly throughout the course of the Starquest investigation Oliver Halle, Frank Sherman and Aaron Marcu had urged her to enter Witness Protection, but each time, she had declined. In the back of her mind was the hope that she could lie low until the dust settled, then return to Queens. She had confided this once to Frank Sherman, who had told her she was living in a dream world. Her work for the government was at an end.

No sooner had she descended from the stand than she was escorted briskly to the office of the U.S. Attorney. It was not a victory lap. She had screwed up on the stand. She was sure of it. By virtue of that performance she had not only made mortal enemies of the mob, but fallen from grace with the government. Arlyne Brickman felt totally wretched. When she arrived at Aaron Marcu's office he and Frank Sherman took pains to tell her what a good job she had done. But the praise rang hollow. She could see that they were eager to be rid of her. That was the way it was with the government. When they needed you, you were the Queen of May. Otherwise, they were on to something else. Another case. Another bust. Another informant. She would never be important again.

Arlyne would have liked to linger and rehash the caper as in the old days. But a couple of agents she didn't recognize were waiting to take her to the airport. Her bags were already packed and in the car. They would have to rush to catch a four o'clock plane. As before, the agents escorted her onto the aircraft before other passengers and then they said good-bye.

The plane filled and she waited. And waited. Arlyne could never recall for sure how much time passed. Probably less than an hour, though it seemed much longer. Finally, one of the flight crew got on the intercom to announce that there were mechanical difficulties and passengers were asked to disembark. Arlyne entered the stream of jostling bodies and was carried back into the waiting room. There was no sign of the agents.

Arlyne felt suddenly vulnerable. Someone bumped her and she flinched. The passerby disappeared down the corridor without looking at her. Indeed, as Arlyne studied the crowd, she came to the realization that no one was looking at her. She felt a rush of relief. She was free. She would hail a cab to Queens. She would go back to her apartment, which still waited unoccupied for her to return. She would pick up her life where she had left off. But the euphoria subsided as soon as it peaked. Queens and the apartment with its antiques and carpets reflecting the exquisite taste of Irving Weiss was now, for all practical purposes, a mirage. Arlyne was suddenly very tired. She took a seat in the waiting room. And waited. Alone and invisible in the fluorescent twilight.

FADE AWAY

During that solitary interlude in the airport waiting room, Arlyne resigned herself to exile. She caught a late evening flight to Miami. But she did not go gently into retirement.

No sooner had the plane touched the runway than the enormity of what she had done dawned on her. For several days she would not leave her apartment. Boredom finally drove her outdoors, but each time she turned the key in the ignition of the white Lincoln, she would hesitate, not daring to draw a breath until she heard the engine idling safely beneath her.

In March Oliver Halle telephoned her with the news that Carmine, Scappy and the whole crew had been convicted. Scarpati would later receive a sentence of thirty-five years. The jury had believed her—or at least her tapes. Or perhaps they had believed Agent Andachter. At any rate, Arlyne was vindicated. She could also breathe easier knowing that the Colombos' back was broken and that coming after her now might be the least of the family's concerns. Yes, it was a relief. Still, as she thought of Scappy, she began to cry.

At the back of her thoughts remained always the intention of returning to New York. This was just a temporary exile, she told herself. When things cooled down, she would motor back to the city and pick up her old life. It took one final stroke of fate to convince her that her banishment was irrevocable: a subpoena to testify against John Gotti.

Undaunted by the obstacles thrown up by the Southern District, Assistant U.S. Attorney Diane Giacalone still had every intention of using Arlyne Brickman as a witness to the Gambinos' alleged loansharking activities. The trial was in progress in the Eastern District when the prosecutor summoned Arlyne for another interview. The two women did not like each other any better now than they had on their first meeting two years earlier. Giacalone displayed increasing irritation with

Arlyne's vagueness about the circumstances of her purported payments to the Gottis. At length, she questioned whether Arlyne had ever, indeed, known or had *any* contact with the defendants. Under those circumstances, she certainly could not be brought to the stand. Arlyne was dispatched back to Florida.

On one hand, she was relieved to be spared the ordeal of testifying. On the other, her situation had clearly deteriorated. Even if she didn't take the stand, there was a chance that the Gottis would somehow find out about her grand jury testimony. And now with Giacalone on the warpath, Arlyne had few friends among the Feds. She could not risk an unauthorized return to New York.

In the weeks to come, Arlyne was increasingly lonely. Shadow's brain tumor had rendered him helpless. He lay quietly in her arms until she was forced to put him to sleep. To ease the loss, she bought a Shih Tzu puppy whom she named Lucky in honor of Uncle Meyer's associate, Lucky Luciano. Lucky was an affable, though not intelligent, beast who allowed himself to be coddled like a baby and fed with a spoon. But he did not fill the need for human companionship. What Arlyne missed most was someone with whom she could discuss her glory days. As Leslie always considered her mother a snitch, she certainly did not want to hear old stories. Though less judgmental, Billie was never sure her daughter had done right by turning on friends.

Arlyne's thoughts turned sometimes to Tommy Luca, who, as far as she knew, was still living with Gina in Brooklyn. Naming him as an informant had had no apparent consequences. She guessed that the Italians preferred to believe one of their own rather than a Jew broad. Tommy, she heard, had cancer and she knew she'd never see him again. Virtually everyone for whom Arlyne had felt any affection was dead, in jail, on the lam, estranged like Leslie or suspicious like her mother. She stood on the brink of her twilight years, friendless.

She did not have time to dwell upon loneliness, however, for, up north, events were unfolding that would draw her back into the loop of intrigue. Ever since she had left New York, Arlyne had wondered what had become of Vinnie and Madeline. Her conscience had been raw of late over what she had done to Scappy, and he was not even a friend. Despite the fact that they had threatened her, Vinnie and Madeline had been her occasional chums. When she reflected, she remembered Vinnie's kindness to Leslie. And she remembered little Madeline strutting around in her short shorts and talking like a moll. No one had heard from the pair since they had walked out of the St. Moritz. (Scappy had clearly not produced them at trial to refute Arlyne's testimony.) There was a possibility that they were dead. The thought gave Arlyne a dull ache behind the eyes.

Then, one year after the Colombo convictions, Vinnie and Madeline suddenly resurfaced, on paper at least. In April 1987, Anthony Scarpati filed a motion for a new trial on grounds of "newly discovered evidence." To this document he appended an affidavit from Manzo and Calvaruso to the effect that the money loaned to Arlyne Brickman belonged to them, not to "Anthony Scapatti" *[sic]*. It was dated March 1987.

Had Vinnie and Madeline waited only a few more months to come forward, they would have been safe from prosecution, as the statute of limitations on their loansharking offenses would have expired. Now, however, they were fair game. The U.S. Attorney had them indicted for attempting to collect loans through extortion and the FBI put out a warrant for their arrest. But Vinnie and Madeline dropped once again from sight. In the fall of 1989, the case agent, Kenneth Brown, received word from an informant that the fugitives were being sheltered by a man he knew only by his street name, "Mysterious Jim." This Jim was apparently a familiar of Scarpati's and visited him regularly in prison. Brown checked the visitors' list and found a "James" from Staten Island who, it was discovered, owned a horse farm in Reeders, Pennsylvania, a sleepy little town in the Poconos. Ken Brown and Oliver Halle promptly paid a visit to Reeders where they showed photos of the Quinella to the local postmistress. She identified the pair, saying that they came into the post office almost every day. Brown, Halle and a detachment of agents and state police staged a stakeout in downtown Reeders. As predicted, Vinnie arrived in a little red car, and when he entered the post office, a female agent tapped him on the shoulder and said, "Mr. Manzo." After a flutter of protest, Vinnie allowed himself to be handcuffed and taken docilely to the horse farm where the agents found and arrested a very glum Madeline Calvaruso.

Vinnie and Madeline were extradited to New York where—in light of their habit of disappearing—they were held without bail while awaiting trial.

When Arlyne learned that they were alive, she was at first relieved, then uneasy. As she saw it, her enemies were assembling beyond some distant frontier. What this alliance stood to mean to her, she could not fully comprehend, but it very soon became clear that she would be called back to New York to testify, this time as a star witness. As usual, she was ambivalent. Arlyne had never quite gotten over the feeling that she had never received her share of the Starquest glory. (The Colombo trial had been knocked off the pages of New York dailies by a city corruption scandal during the period that Arlyne took the stand. Her name never appeared in print.) At the same time, however, she quavered before the prospect of returning to the scene of an earlier drubbing. Her past was what it was; whatever could be dredged up to impeach her in 1986, could be easily resurrected and amplified in subsequent prosecutions. Her fears were increased when she learned that Vinnie would be represented by none other than Carmine Persico's personal attorney, Frank Lopez. This time she stood to be worked over by a heavy hitter. Arlyne was not sure that she cared to subject herself to that.

This matter, it turned out, was entirely beyond her control. The government players had changed. Aaron Marcu and Frank Sherman had left the U.S. Attorney's Office to go into private practice, leaving the Manzo prosecution in the hands of a young assistant named Jon Liebman. While Sherman and Marcu had been inclined to humor Arlyne during periods of mania, Liebman was not similarly disposed. He informed her that if she would not appear of her own free will, he would have her subpoenaed. In April 1989, a sullen Arlyne Brickman once flew north to testify. Her transit to the stand, however, was cut short.

The trial was to begin on a Monday morning. The preceding Saturday night, Arlyne—in the company of Oliver Halle and the rest of her FBI entourage—had gone out to dinner. The mood progressed from tense, to lighthearted, to raucous, reminiscent of the good times Arlyne had enjoyed with the agents in times past. She arrived back at the safe house feeling happier than she had in months. It was then that she received a call from her sister, Barbara. Their mother was dead. Billie had flown to New York shortly after Arlyne to consult her tax attorney. During dinner with Barbara's family, she had complained of stomach pains and was rushed to the hospital. Her condition deteriorated rapidly and finally her heart failed.

In happier times—and even not so happy times—Arlyne would quip that if her mother should die, she would have to stuff and mount her. Billie had always been there, and her daughter could not imagine life without her. Now, faced with this loss, Arlyne was plunged into a fit of such wild distraction that even prosecutor Liebman could see that she was unfit to take the stand. Faced with the choice of dropping charges against Manzo and Calvaruso or attempting to try the case without his star witness, Liebman chose the latter and infinitely riskier route.

During the resulting four-day trial, Madeline took the stand and insisted she had just made Arlyne a loan among friends, that the money had come from her own savings and that she and Vinnie had simply introduced Scarpati's name to impress Arlyne. (This was considered by government observers to be an attempt orchestrated by Scarpati, whose 1987 motion had been denied, to provide a basis for a new trial.) The judge, in her instructions to the jury, however, advised them to disregard testimony about the source of the money, since the only question before them was whether Vinnie and Madeline had used threats to collect the loans. Prosecutor Liebman had introduced Arlyne's tapes, methodically dissecting them and isolating the meat hook comment and other ominous utterances. Vinnie and Madeline were convicted. He was sentenced to five years in prison, and she to four.

Whatever joy or regret Arlyne may have felt at hearing this news was blotted out by her personal grief. When she returned to Florida after burying Billie, she was dazed. Since she had left New York, Arlyne and her mother had been on the phone with each other at least once a day. Their respective bills ran in the vicinity of six hundred dollars a month. Arlyne felt impelled now to make peace with her daughter. She longed to establish with Leslie the link she had always felt to Billie, and the link that Billie, in turn, had felt with her own mother.

In the past year there had been some developments that raised Arlyne's hope for a reconciliation. Leslie had left Willie and, freed from his influence, managed successfully to complete a detox program. She had also found another boyfriend, Jim. Although he ran with a group of bikers, Jim had steady work as a carpenter. He also had custody of a three-year-old daughter by a previous marriage. When Leslie moved in with Jim, she took charge not only of running the house but of caring for the child. Arlyne had always said there was a lot of the Little Mother in Leslie. In the past, these maternal impulses had been perversely misdirected toward her junkie boyfriends, but now she seemed reborn, boasting to old friends, "I have a little girl now." Arlyne found that for once in their lives, she and Leslie could enjoy a calm conversation.

Whenever Arlyne thought about friends she had hurt, she was beset by guilt. But it was her treatment of Leslie that now aroused the keenest regret. She thought of how she had taken baby Leslie on the errands she had run for Tony Mirra. At the time the only thought was that no one would harm a woman with a child in her arms. And the time she had told the five-year-old Leslie that she was going shopping and then ran away to Florida for six months. There were the lies about Norman

Brickman. And, of course, the drugs. Arlyne still refused to admit that she had contributed to her daughter's drug problem. The business she did with Tommy was—well, business. Leslie's addiction to pills and heroin was the result of her own weakness. Now and then she heard the strident tones of David Breitbart.

Have you personally seen the results of the use of heroin and cocaine in your own family, Mrs. Brickman?

Did you know what heroin does to people, Mrs. Brickman?

Mrs. Brickman, did you care?

She shut her ears and resisted a moral reckoning.

In the spring of 1988, Leslie Brickman developed a cough. It lingered for weeks before turning into bronchitis. She took antibiotics but they seemed to have no effect. Finally, she was admitted to a hospital for a full battery of tests. She was found to be HIV positive.

At first, Arlyne was uncomprehending. She knew little about AIDS. She had a vague impression that it was shameful. It was a homosexual's disease, and her daughter was not one of those people. Her infection had most likely come through a contaminated needle. In her heart Arlyne raged against Willie and raged against Tommy. Still, she would not point the finger toward herself.

There was a time during Leslie's junkie days when her own life meant so little to her that she would not have lifted a finger to save herself. Now with Jim and his little daughter to live for, she was desperate to be well. She rested, she ate fresh fruits and vegetables, she sat in the sun tanning her pale skin to simulate the glow of health. Her white blood cell count continued to drop.

Arlyne took her to one doctor after another. Leslie couldn't tolerate AZT. A drug called pentamidine seemed to halt the progress of the disease, but only for a time. Leslie became so weak she slept most of the afternoon. She could no longer take care of the child. The little girl's mother reappeared and took her away. Leslie became listless and unresponsive. Finally, Jim could not—or would not—continue to care for her. Arlyne brought her to her own apartment. Although she hired a nurse, she insisted on tending to her daughter as intimately and lovingly as Billie had cared for Irving in his final days.

A year after Leslie learned of her illness, she was taken to the hospital with a virus of the brain. Arlyne stalled for time. She screamed at doctors. Fired them. Hired new ones. She moved Leslie to a Catholic hospital with a reputation for aggressive and compassionate treatment of AIDS patients. It was not enough. All of her life Arlyne had been able to go to someone for a favor, a fixer who could get her out of a jam. But she knew no one powerful enough to save her child. For the first time in her life Arlyne experienced a perfectly selfless emotion: a desire to give her life if it would save her daughter's.

Leslie Brickman lapsed into a coma. At first she was sustained by IVs and a respirator. Arlyne came every day at noon and remained well into the night. There were times she thought Leslie knew when she entered the room, for she seemed to breathe more deeply. But she decided that was an illusion born of false hope. Sometimes she talked to her daughter. Other times she just watched her lying there like a little doll in a big bed. And for no particular reason she would remember the expensive stroller Irving had bought for Leslie, the one that reminded her of a Cadillac.

Arlyne was not completely alone. A kind neighbor from the building often came to sit with her. Barbara flew down to be with her sister. She was, as usual, beautiful and serene. For once Arlyne did not resent those attributes. The sisters did not talk much about the past. Instead they occupied themselves with matters of death: disposing of Billie's estate and determining where Leslie would be buried. Arlyne found her sister's presence comforting and was glad that in a moment of playful malice so long ago she had not persuaded her three-year-old sibling to leap off the roof of Knickerbocker Village. But the strain of watching Leslie wasting to the bone began to wear upon Barbara and she returned to her own healthy, orderly family.

Every morning and evening the nurses washed Leslie's face, so as she lay there wasting away she appeared clean. Almost wholesome.

The death vigil stretched on. And in the night she heard the voices in her conscience.

Have you personally seen the results of the use of heroin and cocaine in your own family, Mrs. Brickman? Did you care?

The doctors decreed that Leslie Brickman had no hope of recovery. After much agony, Arlyne decided to have her daughter removed from life support. The girl was consigned to the hospital's hospice wing and placed on a morphine drip. But her heart was strong and she continued breathing. "It's only a matter of time," Arlyne told herself, and she forced herself to make the trip each day. She thought what it must have been like for Billie to watch Irving die. And she began to cry because she wanted her mother.

Did you know what heroin does to people, Mrs. Brickman? Did you care?

It was usually in the late-night hours that she was most successful in conjuring up memories of Ida Blum. They triggered a brief release from sadness. In her mind's eye, Arlyne saw The Grandmother, bejeweled and dusted in matzo flour, holding court in her noisy kitchen. And she tried to remember the smell of the old woman's perfume and the texture of her silk blouses. Arlyne found it hard to imagine Ida grieving, though she knew it had been so. She had buried two children of her own. (It is unnatural, Ida had said, for the parent to outlive the child.) And then she had gone off to the Concord to recover her joy. Arlyne could not imagine a life beyond Leslie's bedside.

The death watch continued. Leslie's vital signs became so faint, it seemed her frail system could not hold out for one more hour. Arlyne resigned herself to grief. Then the corpse would rally, and the death watch would be jolted out of its natural rhythms. Only once did Leslie regain consciousness. She looked at her mother and whispered, "Help me." Finally, her heart gave out.

Leslie Brickman was buried one mild Sunday in December. Loved ones were invited to gather that morning at the Forest Hills Funeral Home, where seven years earlier Irving Weiss had been laid to rest among a throng of lifelong friends and admirers. There was no one to mourn Leslie but her mother and aunt. The casket was closed. (Under the circumstances, the undertaker thought it best.) It was opened only briefly so Arlyne could pay her last respects. When the heavy lid was lifted, she gasped and cried, "Her face!"

The person she saw lying on clouds of satin was not the child whose face the nurses scrubbed each morning. It was not the Leslie whose repudiation of her mother's ideal of beauty had caused her to live her own life bare-faced. In the hope of making her "look a little better," Leslie's features had been covered with what appeared to be thick theatrical makeup. Ethel Becher had once observed darkly that the sins of the parent are visited upon the child. And if that was so, every sin that Arlyne had committed—greed, venality, betrayal, a lifetime of wanton selfishness—was now reflected back to her in those still features. As the casket was closed and Leslie consigned to her grave, Arlyne Brickman was condemned to live on, haunted by the vision of her daughter, the only good thing in her life, made up in a grotesque parody of a mob girl.

Arlyne Brickman lives alone in an undisclosed location with her lapdog, Lucky.

BIBLIOGRAPHY

Books

Bonanno, Joseph, with Sergio Lalli. *A Man of Honor: The Autobiography of Joseph Bonanno.* New York: Simon and Schuster, 1983.

Cantalupo, Joseph, and Thomas C. Renner. *Body Mike: An Unsparing Exposé by the Mafia Insider Who Turned on the Mob.* New York: Villard Books, 1990.

Cummings, John, and Ernest Volkman. *Goombata: The Improbable Rise and Fall of John Gotti and His Gang.* Boston: Little, Brown and Company, 1990.

Demaris, Ovid. *The Last Mafioso: The Treacherous World of Jimmy Fratianno.* New York: Times Books, 1981.

Drake, St. Clair, and Horace Cayton. " 'Policy': Poor Man's Roulette," in *Gambling.* Edited by Robert D. Herman. New York: Harper & Row, 1967.

Eisenberg, Dennis, Uri Dan, and Eli Landau. *Meyer Lansky: Mogul of the Mob.* New York: Paddington Press, 1979.

Gosch, Martin A., and Richard Hammer. *The Last Testament of Lucky Luciano.* Boston: Little, Brown and Company, 1974.

Joselit, Jenna W. *Our Gang: Jewish Crime and the New York Jewish Community 1900–1940.* Bloomington: Indiana University Press, First Midland Book Edition, 1983.

Meskil, Paul. *The Luparelli Tapes.* New York: Playboy Press, 1977.

Messick, Hank. *Lansky.* New York: G. P. Putnam's Sons, 1971.

Mustain, Gene, and Jerry Capeci. *Mob Star: The Story of John Gotti, the Most Powerful Criminal in America.* New York: Franklin Watts, 1988.

O'Brien, Joseph F., and Andris Kurins. *Boss of Bosses: The Fall of the Godfather: The FBI and Paul Castellano.* New York: Simon & Schuster, 1991.

Pileggi, Nicholas. *Wiseguy: Life in a Mafia Family.* New York: Simon & Schuster, 1985.

Pistone, Joseph D., with Richard Woodley. *Donnie Brasco: My Undercover Life in the Mafia.* New York: New American Library, 1987.

Turkus, Burton B., and Sid Feder. *Murder Inc.: The Inside Story of the Mob.* New York: Farrar, Straus & Giroux, 1951.

Wolf, George, with Joseph DiMona. *Frank Costello: Prime Minister of the Underworld.* New York: William Morrow and Company, Inc., 1974.

Periodicals

American Lawyer: "Surprise! They're Winning the War on the Mafia," Steven Brill, Dec. 1985; "Rudolph Giuliani," Connie Bruck, March 1989.

American Mercury: "Underworld Confidential: Virginia Hill's Success Secrets," Lee Mortimer, June 1951; "The Auction Party for Virginia Hill," Feb. 1952.

Bergen Record: "Seven Arrested in Gambling Ring in N.J. and N.Y.," Dec. 20, 1974.

Harper's: "Secret Agent on Skis," Struthers Burt, Feb. 1952.

The New Republic: "No, Virginia, There Is No Santa Claus," Bruce Bliven, April 2, 1951.

New York Daily News: "Sally Burns Got Ambitious—and He Got Dead," William Federici, Oct. 8, 1970; "Three Found Guilty of Racketeering," Natalie P. Byfield and Don Gentile, July 31, 1989.

New York magazine: "After Gotti: Though Cornered in Court, the Mob's Still in Business on the Street," Nicholas Pileggi, Oct. 27, 1986.

New York Post: "Informant: Persicos Now Head Colombos," Dan Hays and Don Gentile, June 21, 1980; "Mafia Boss Suffers a Fate Worse Than Death," Jerry Capeci, Nov. 10, 1981; "Woman, 25, Rescued in Bizarre Coke Kidnap," Cy Egan and Leslie Gevirtz, April 13, 1983; "FBI Sting Hooks Mob Big," Jerry Capeci, Oct. 17, 1984; "From Profaci to Persico," Oct. 25, 1984; "Colombo Gang's Rise and Fall," Mary Ann Giordano and Stuart Marques, Oct. 25, 1984; "FBI Yacht Landed Them," Frank Faso and Paul Meskil, Oct. 25, 1984; " 'Love Boat,' Trap Snares Mob Family's Top Brass," Marvin Smidon and Jerry Capeci, Oct. 25, 1984; " 'The Snake' Took His First Prey on B'klyn Mean Streets," David Ng, Feb. 16, 1985; "Mafia Boss Boasted of 1957 Rubout," Jerry Capeci, June 3, 1986; "Mafia Turncoat Reveals Mob Blood Rite," Marvin Smidon, May 20, 1989; "Three Mobsters Guilty in Cop Slaying," Michael Shain, July 31, 1989.

New York Times: "East Side 'Village' Under Way May 1," April 1, 1933; "New Dewey Drive Begins on Racket in Electrical Jobs," Jan. 14, 1937; "Two Seized in Drive on Truck Racket," March 20, 1937; "Two Go on Trial in Truck Racket," June 3, 1937; "Racket Shooting Challenges City, Dewey Declares," Oct. 4, 1937; "Gurrah and Lepke Slip Hands of Law," Nov. 21, 1937; "Dewey to Tell How Thugs Went Scot-Free for Years," Dec. 8, 1937; "Reputed Chief Aide of Lepke Gives Up," Feb. 11, 1938; "Gurrah Convicted Gets 3-year Term as Fur Racketeer," June 18, 1938; "Lepke Surrenders to FBI; Racketeer Never Left City," Aug. 25, 1939; "Roseland Ballroom 25 Years Old," Jan. 14, 1944; "City Apartments and Hotels Keep Full Occupancy," March 12, 1944; "Capone Dead at 48: Dry Era Gang Chief," June 26, 1947; "Tampering Trial Opens: Futterman is Accused of Bribing Witness in Macri Case," Dec. 10, 1952; "Jury Here Convicts Macri Case Figure: Futterman is Found Guilty of Subornation of Perjury and of Bribing a Witness," Dec. 20, 1952; "Little Augie Pisano is Slain with Woman in Auto Here," Sept. 26, 1959; "Police Pressing Gangland Leads in Killing of Pisano and Woman," Sept. 27, 1959; "Phone Clue Found in Pisano Murder," Emanuel Perlmutter, Sept. 29, 1959; "Little Augie Linked to Raceway Project," Emanuel Perlmutter, Sept. 29, 1959; "Little Augie Faced Questioning by Senate Rackets Committee," Emanuel Perlmutter, Sept. 30, 1959; "New Lead on Pisano Slaying Provided by Racketeer Friend," Emanuel Perlmutter, Oct. 1, 1959; "Pisano Hurried to His Death After Mysterious Phone Call," Oct. 2, 1959; "Governor Studies Little Augie Case," Oct. 3, 1959; "Big-Time Gangs Still Function: Technique is Shown in Pisano Murder," Emanuel Perlmutter, Oct. 4, 1959; "Little Augie Buried," Oct. 7, 1959; "Agent at Racketeering Trial Denies Accusation of Theft," Arnold H. Lubasch, Aug. 10, 1982; "Eleven Indicted by U.S. as the Leadership of a Crime Family," Arnold H. Lubasch, Oct. 25, 1984; "F.B.I. Hunting 4 Indicted as Colombo Mob Chiefs," Arnold H. Lubasch, Oct. 28, 1984; "Reputed Leader of Colombo Crime Group is Arrested as a Fugitive on L.I.," Arnold H. Lubasch, Feb. 16, 1985; "Tapes Said to Reveal a 'Commission' of Mobsters," Selwyn Raab, Feb. 18, 1985; "U.S. Indictment Says 9 Governed New York Mafia," Arnold H. Lubasch, Feb. 27, 1985; "Reputed Crime Bosses Arraigned," Arnold Lubasch, March 4, 1985; " 'The Snake,' 'a.k.a.' 'Junior,' " March 6, 1985; "Persico Relative Is Found Dead," June 14, 1985; "Eleven Plead Not Guilty to Ruling Organized Crime in New York," July 2, 1985; "More Trials Are Due on Organized Crime," Oct. 1, 1985; "Reporter's Notebook: Picking Racketeering Trial Jury," M.A. Farber, Nov. 4, 1985; "Trial Jury Picked for Colombo Case," Nov. 2, 1985; "Opening Statements Made in Racketeering Trial of 11," M.A. Farber, Nov. 5, 1985; "Defense Lawyers are Split at Colombo Rackets Trial," M.A. Farber, Nov. 6, 1985; "Tax Agent Tells of Bribe for a Persico Visit Here," M.A. Farber, Nov. 7, 1985; "Jury in Persico Trial Hears Bribe Tapes and Testimony," M.A. Farber, Nov. 8, 1985; "Tape Says Persico Refused to Inform," M.A. Farber, Nov. 9, 1985; "Illness Interrupts Racketeering Trial," Nov. 14, 1985; "Defense Bid Fails in Colombo Trial," Nov. 22, 1985; "Tapes at Colombo Trial Offer Glimpse into the Undercover World," M.A. Farber, Nov. 25, 1985; "Colombo Witness Tells of $3,000 Bribe," M.A. Farber, Nov. 27, 1985; "Colombo Witness Testifies About Bribe Attempt," M.A. Farber, Dec. 4, 1985; "Defense Says Key U.S. Witness Terrorized Persico," M.A. Farber, Dec. 8, 1985; "Colombo Trial Defense Complains About Pressure," M.A. Farber, Dec. 10, 1985; "F.B.I. Varied Tactics in Colombo Case," M.A. Farber, Dec. 15, 1985; "Five Organized-Crime Factions Operating in New York Area," Glenn Fowler, Dec. 7, 1985; "Concrete Contractors Tell of Payoffs to a Union Leader for Labor Peace," M.A. Farber, Dec. 18, 1985; "Federal Jury Hears Tapes on Labor Payoffs," M.A. Farber, Dec. 19, 1985; "Contractor Says Head of Union Made Threat," M.A. Farber, Dec. 20, 1985; "Court Orders Lawyer to Tell of Fees from Crime Figure," Arnold H. Lubasch, Jan. 10, 1986; "Jury is Told Crime Families Control Concrete Business," Ronald Smothers, Jan. 15, 1986; "Persico Trial Witness Reports Project Payoffs," Jan. 16, 1986; "Tapes Played at Mob Trial Focus on Money and Power," Ronald Smothers, Jan. 26, 1986; "Informer in Persico Trial Testifies on Restaurant Extortion," Ronald Smothers, Feb. 2, 1986; "Evidence of a Murder Excluded from 'Pizza' Trial," Arnold H. Lubasch, Feb. 6, 1986; "Mobster Tells Jury 3 Defendants Were Members of Colombo Group," Ronald Smothers, Feb. 9, 1986; "Persico Informer Says He Got $50,000 Bonus," April 24, 1986; "Persico Convicted in Colombo Trial," Arnold H. Lubasch, June 14, 1986; "Peter Marino Strikes Again," Charlotte Curtis, May 13, 1986; "Gotti's Courtroom Foe: Diane Frances Giacalone," George James, Sept. 25, 1986; "Informer Calls Persico Colombo Boss," Arnold H. Lubasch, Sept. 30, 1986; "Persico Opposed 1979 Slaying of Mafia Boss, An Informer Testifies," Arnold H. Lubasch, Oct. 3, 1986; "Persico, His Son, and 6 Others Get Long Terms as Colombo Gangsters," Arnold H. Lubasch, Nov. 18, 1986; "What's Ahead in '87: Family Quarrels," Selwyn Raab, Dec. 29, 1986; "Jury Convicts 3 Mob Figures in Rackets Case," Glenn Fowler, July 31, 1989; "About New York: A Union Head Forever Rooted to Delancey St.," Douglas Martin, Jan. 20, 1990.

People magazine: "On Trial in New York, Mafia Chieftain Carmine Persico Takes The Law into his Own Hands," Ken Gross, Nov. 3, 1986; "Cold-Blooded King of A Hill Under Siege," Ken Gross, March 27, 1989.

Associated Press: March 12, 1987

United Press International: Jan. 18, 1982; August 5, 1982; Aug. 9, 1982; June 17, 1985; Nov. 14, 1985; Dec. 13, 1985; August 24, 1987.

INDEX

(Asterisks denote pseudonyms.)